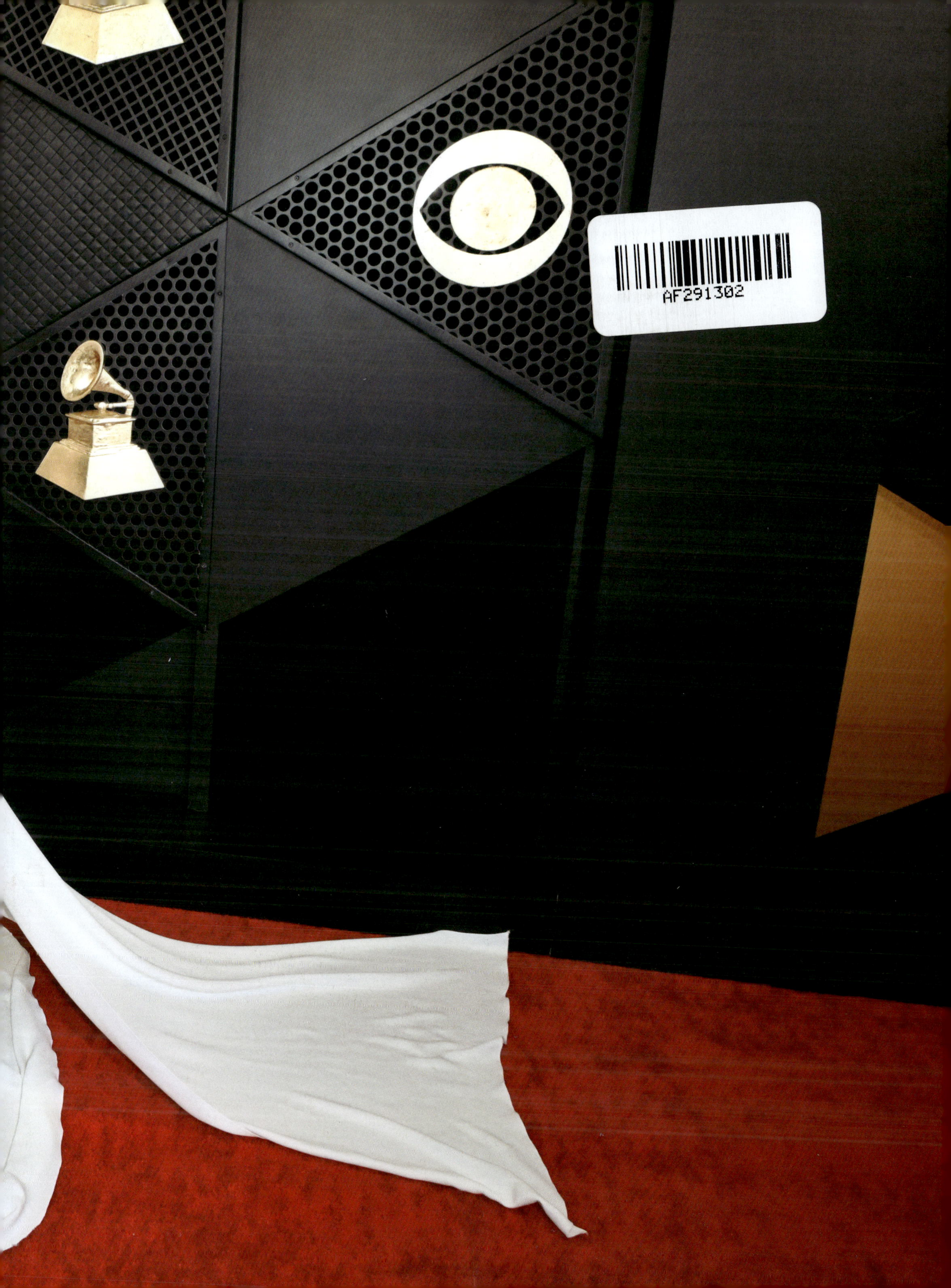

AF291302

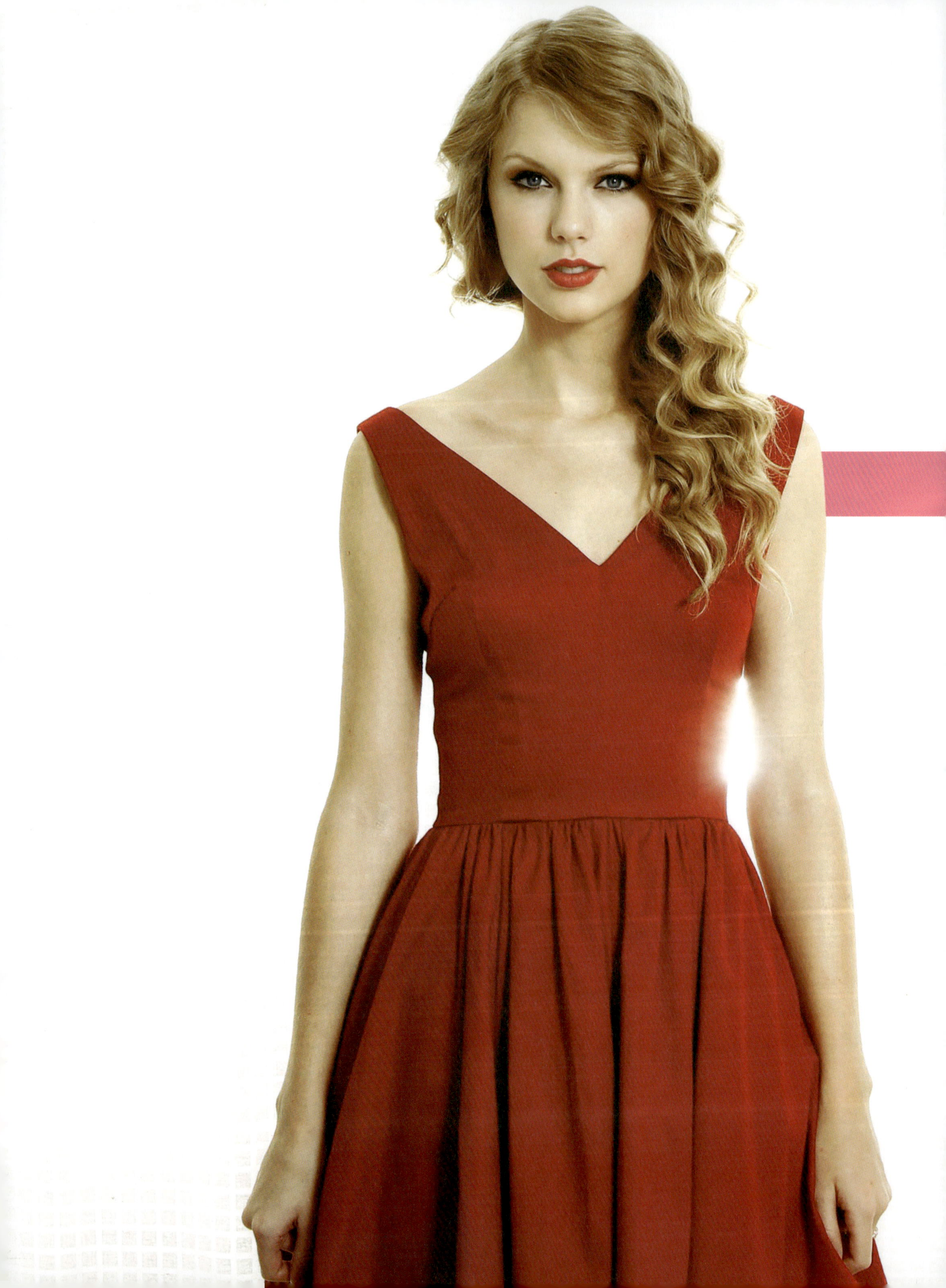

TAYLOR

MADE

Alison James

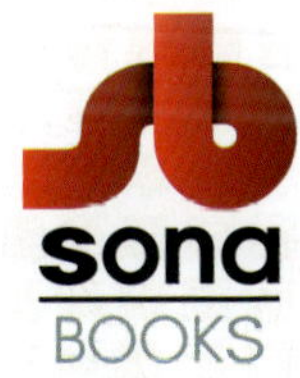

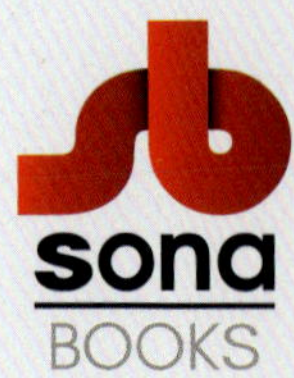

sona
BOOKS

© Danann Publishing Limited 2025

First published in the UK 2025 by Sona Books an imprint of Danann Publishing Ltd.

WARNING: For private domestic use only, any unauthorised copying, hiring,
lending or public performance of this book is illegal.

CAT NO: SON0628

Photography courtesy of

Getty images:

Ethan Miller	Christopher Polk/TAS	Alishia Abodunde	Kevin Winter/TAS23	John Shearer/TAS23
Gareth Cattermole	Kevin Kane	David Benito	Ashok Kumar/TAS24	Axelle/Bauer-Griffin
Rick Diamond	Stringer	Asanka Ratnayake	Gareth Cattermole/TAS24	Robyn Beck
Denise Truscello	Jude Edginton	Attitude Magazine	Taylor Hill/TAS23	Amy Sussman
John Shearer	Ignat/Bauer-Griffin	Alliance for Women in	Bob Levey/TAS23	Michael Buckner
Tony R. Phipps	David Livingston	Media Foundation	Andreas Rentz/TAS24	Emma McIntyre/AMA2018
Lester Cohen	Steve Granitz	Angela Weiss	Jamie McCarthy	Tas Rights Management
George Napolitano	Don Arnold/TAS18	Terry Wyatt	JMEnternational	Jason Squires
Fred Duval	Jun Sato	Sascha Schuermann	Dimitrios Kambouris	Dimitrios Kambouris/LP5
Jon Kopaloff	Bruce Glikas	Amy Sussman	AFP / Stringer	Noam Galai
Marcel Thomas	Taylor Hill	Gotham	Jeff Kravitz	D Dipasupil
Neil Mockford	Daniel Torok	Neilson Barnard	Dave Hogan	Alessio Botticelli
Stephen Lovekin	NBC	Lisa O'Connor	Robert Gauthier	Ignat/Bauer-Griffin
Robert Kamau	Toni Anne Barson	CBS Photo Archive	Charley Gallay / Stringer	Mike Marsland
Kevin Mazur	VCG	Kevin Mazur/TAS23	Neilson Barnard	Jeff Kravitz/BBMA2019

Alamy images:

WENN Rights Ltd	Australian Associated Press	Sipa US
Everett Collection Inc	Sam Kovak	Associated Press
ZUMA Press, Inc.	AFF	UPI

Other images Wiki Commons

Book cover design Darren Grice at Ctrl-d
Layout design Alex Young at Cre81ve
Copy Editor Sofia Della Valle

Made in EU.
ISBN: 978-1-915343-91-8

CONTENTS

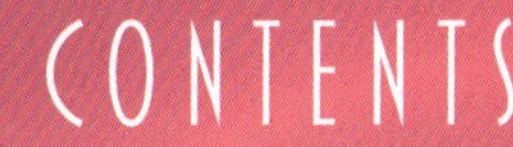

INTRODUCTION 8

CHAPTER ONE: COUNTRY CHIC (2006/7) 10

CHAPTER TWO: FEARLESS FASHION (2008/9) 26

CHAPTER THREE: SPEAK NOW STYLE (2010/11) 38

TAYLOR'S SHOES 48

CHAPTER FOUR: IN THE RED (2012/13) 52

CHAPTER FIVE: IT'S 1989 (2014/15) 62

BAG LADY 72

CHAPTER SIX: REPUTATION ROCKS (2017/18) 76

CHAPTER SEVEN: LOVER LOOKS (2019/20) 86

SWIFTIE FASHION 96

CHAPTER EIGHT: FOLKLORE & EVERMORE 102

CHAPTER NINE: SPARKLY MIDNIGHTS 112

SWIFT'S SARTORIAL SIGNALS! 120

CHAPTER TEN: ERAS 124

TOP RED CARPET 130

BY DESIGN 138

INTRODUCTION

Music and fashion have long been intertwined, each reflecting and influencing the other, and shaping cultural and style trends worldwide. Iconic musicians have become fashion icons, with their personal style influencing the wardrobes of millions. Taylor Swift is one such icon. Over the years, she has made a significant impact on the fashion world as her sartorial sense has evolved from country-chic looks in her early years, to more sophisticated and bold styles – purposely reflecting the different stages of her life, music and album era. Her 1989 era (2014), for instance, featured many 1980s inspired looks while her *Folklore* and *Evermore* periods, born out of the 2020/21 pandemic, brought muted, cottage-core-inspired styles.

Taylor is known for effortlessly blending classic elegance with contemporary trends – and, speaking of trends, her influence is infinite. Whether it's popularizing red lipstick, sequins, vintage-inspired dresses or more edgy looks, her style choices often lead to spikes in demand for similar items. When it comes to high fashion, Swift consistently makes best-dressed lists at major events like the Grammys, Met Gala, and various other award shows. Her Red Carpet choices are glamour personified. Ditto her dazzling collections of stage outfits over the years. She works with top designers and fashion houses, bringing unique creations and visionary designs to life on the world's biggest stages! But beyond the Red Carpets and performances, Taylor's trendy yet accessible street style serves as another source of inspiration for many.

Taylor Swift wearing a classic, cascading ivory dress as she attends the "American Woman: Fashioning a National Identity" at the 2010 Met Gala

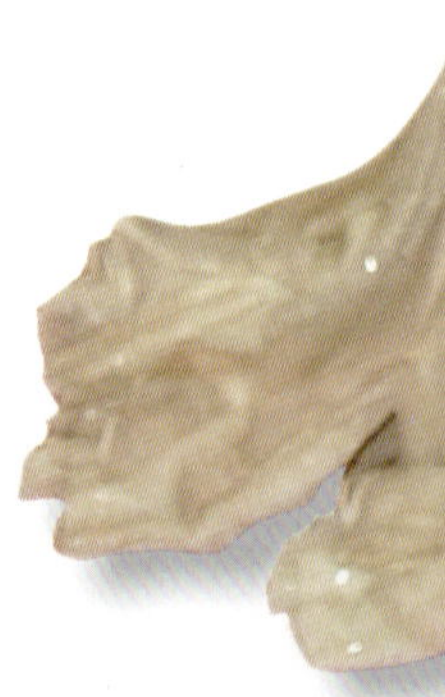

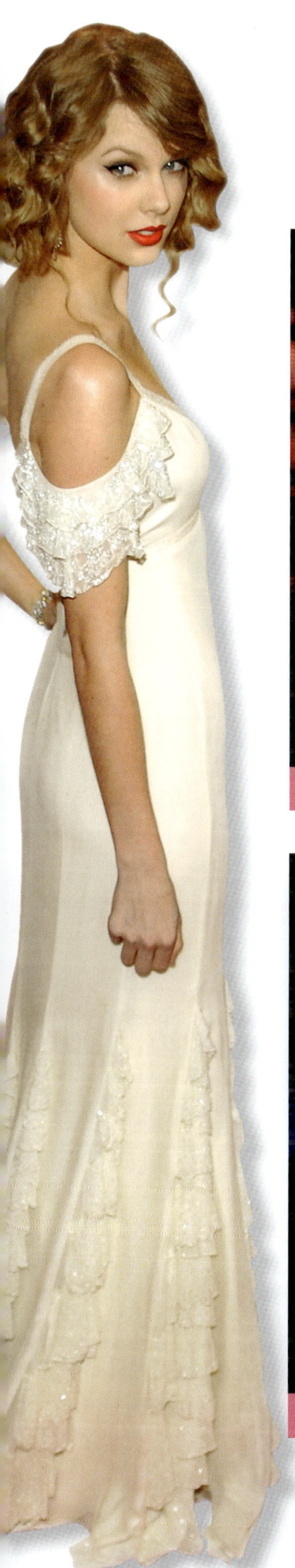

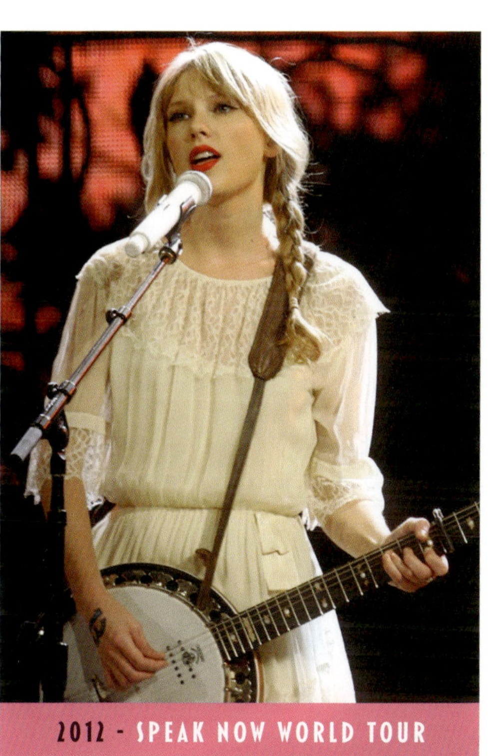

2012 - SPEAK NOW WORLD TOUR

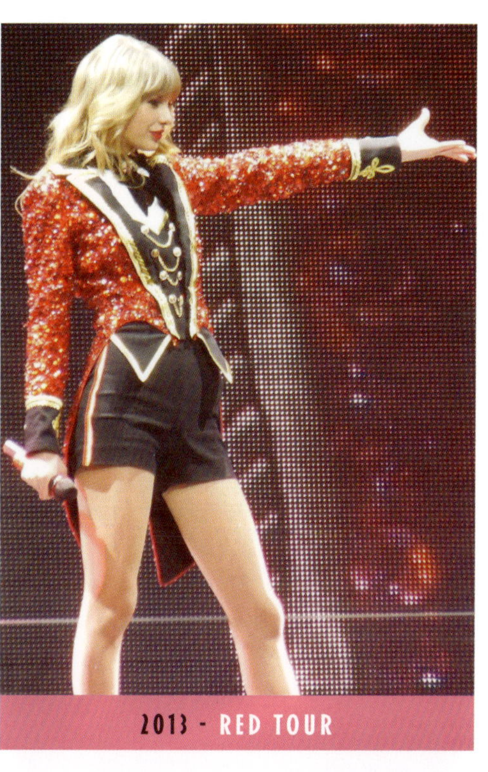

2013 - RED TOUR

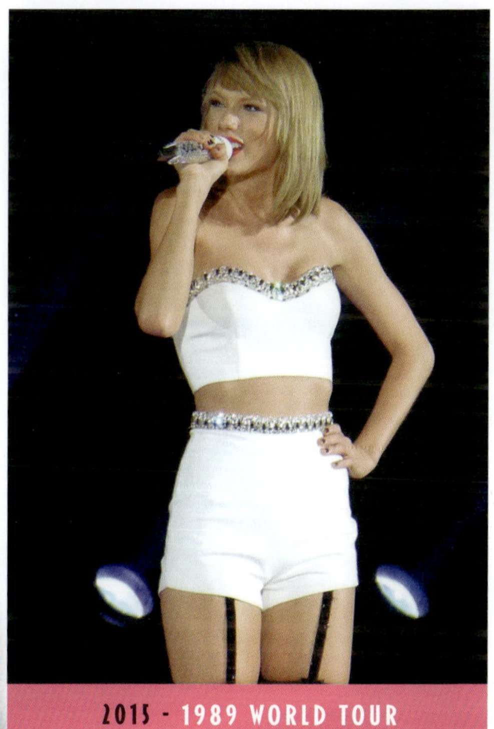

2015 - 1989 WORLD TOUR

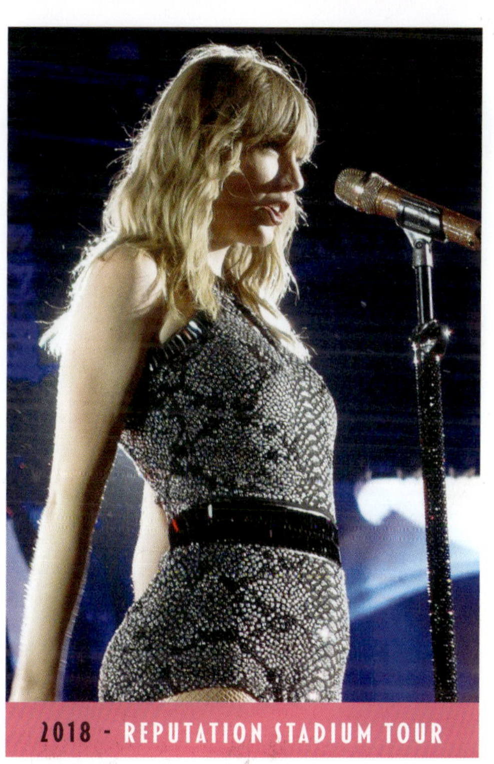

2018 - REPUTATION STADIUM TOUR

COUNTRY

CHAPTER ONE

CHIC

2006/7

I t was country music that brought Taylor Swift to prominence, so it follows that her early sartorial savvy was also heavily Nashville nuanced, coupled with Taylor's youthful, feminine charm.** We're talking her 'debut era', circa 2006, when she released her first album, entitled, quite simply, *Taylor Swift*. Here's what she wore...

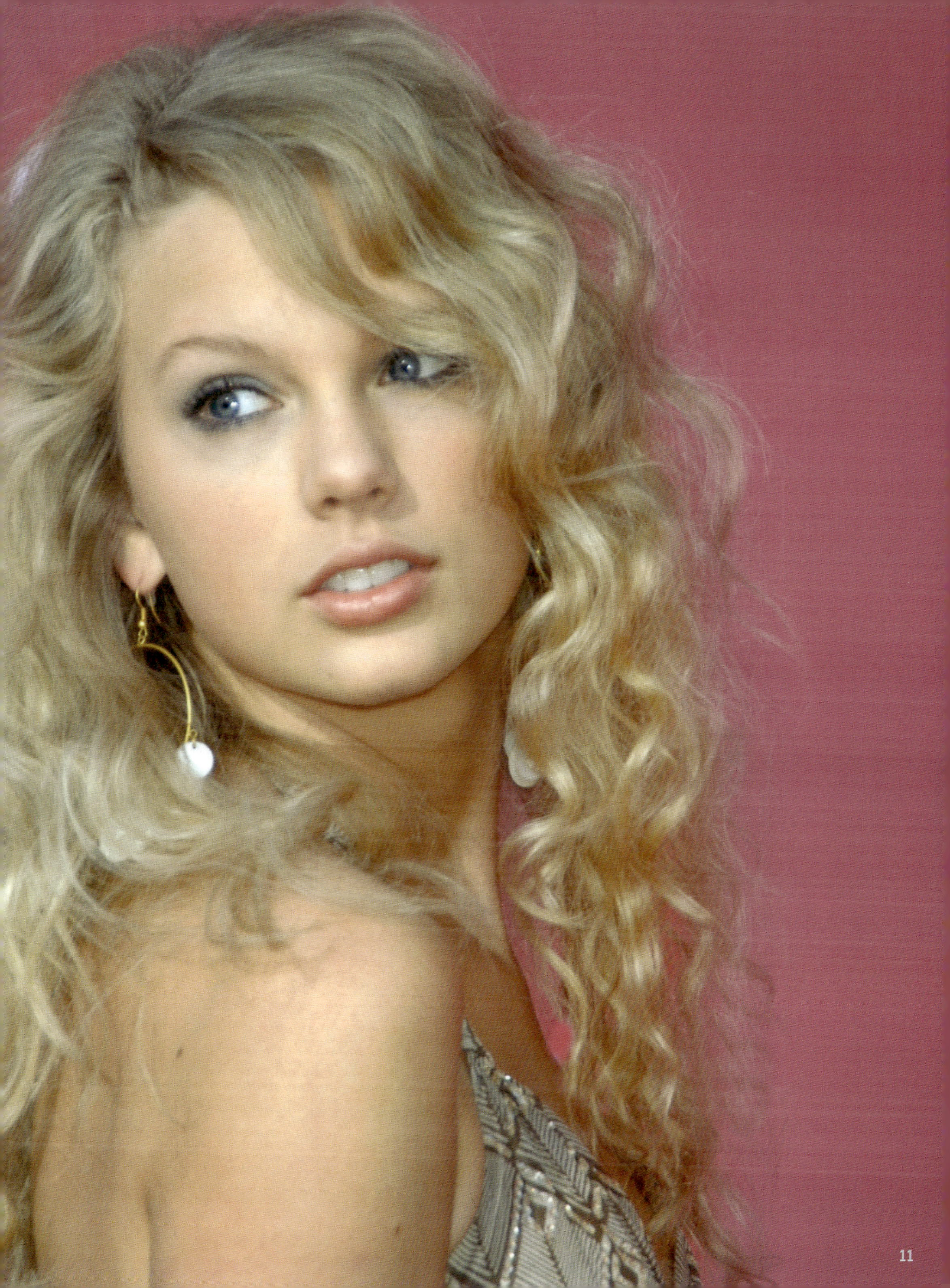

CLASSIC COWBOY BOOTS

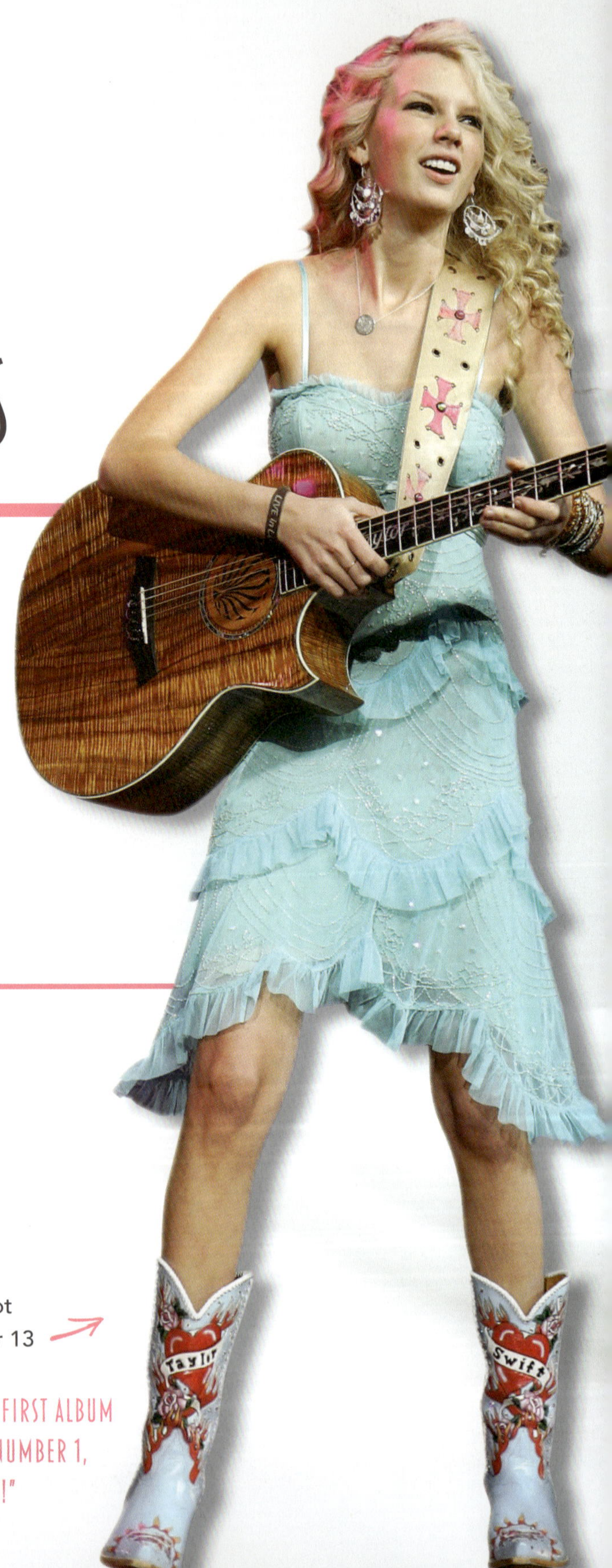

One of the most iconic elements of Taylor's country chic look was her love for cowboy boots. She often paired them with a variety of outfits, from dresses to jeans, making them a staple of her early style. These boots added an authentic country vibe to her overall appearance, reflecting her Nashville roots.

Taylor's famous cowboy boots designed by Liberty Boot Co. featuring Taylor Swift's name and her lucky number 13

"I WAS BORN ON THE 13TH, I TURNED 13 ON FRIDAY THE 13TH, MY FIRST ALBUM WENT GOLD IN 13 WEEKS. ALSO, MY FIRST SONG THAT EVER WENT NUMBER 1, IT HAD A 13 SECOND INTRO, I DIDN'T EVEN DO THAT ON PURPOSE!"

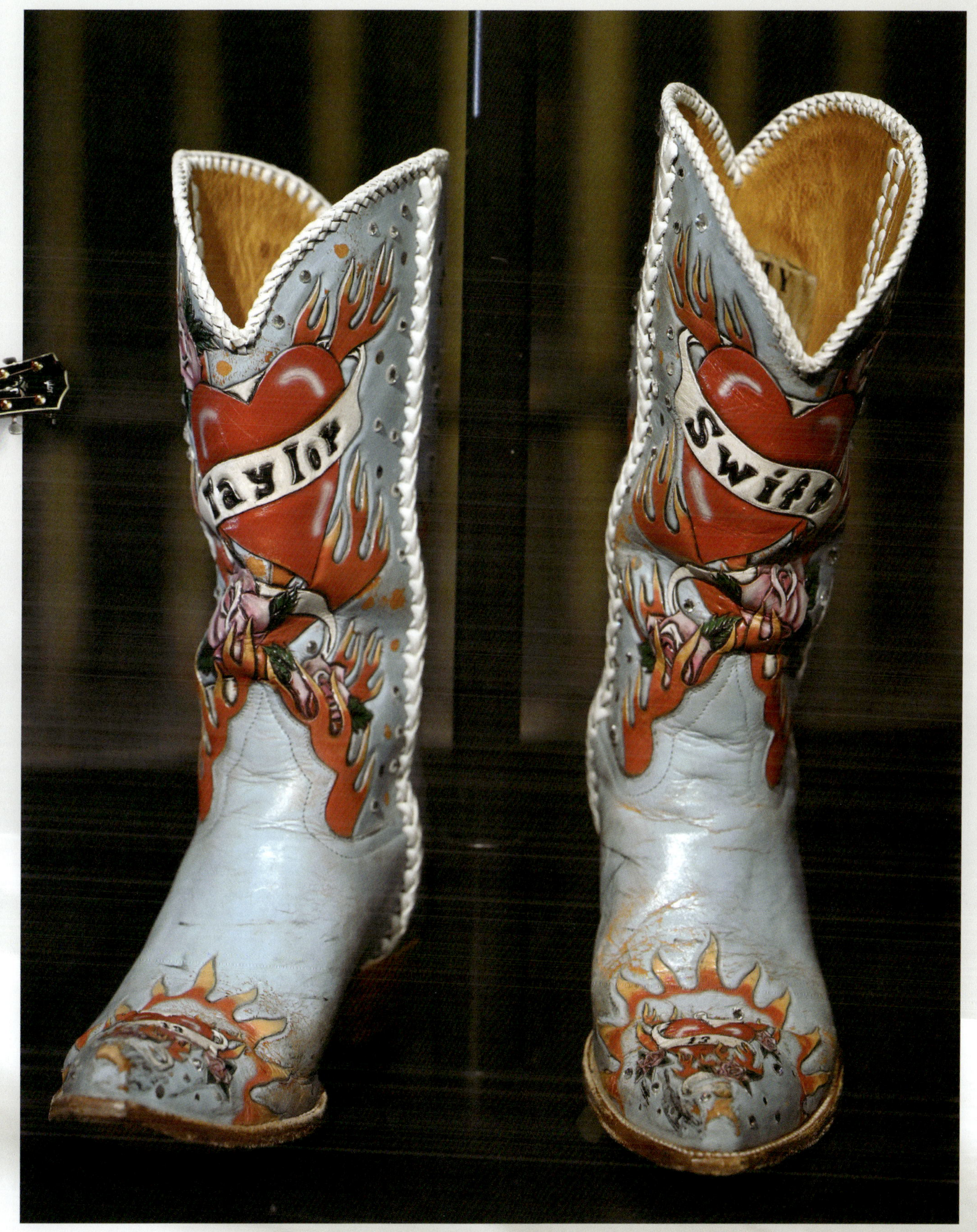

Taylor
Swift

FLOATY FLORALS AND FRINGES

Taylor frequently wore sundresses with floral prints or simple patterns during this period, which added a soft, romantic touch to her look. These non-designer dresses were often knee-length or slightly above – occasionally with a handkerchief hem - and with feminine details like ruffles, lace, and cinched waists. These pieces embodied the 'girl-next-door' image that resonated with her young fans.

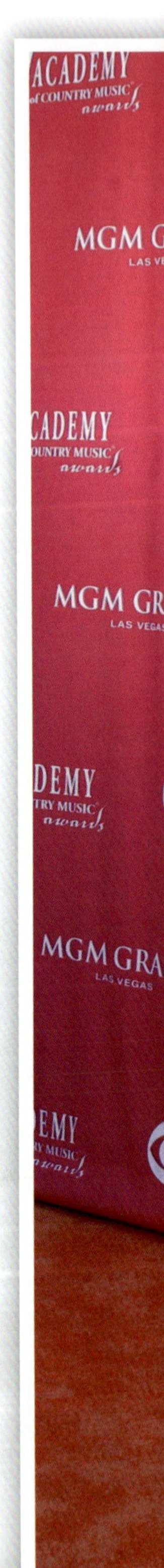

Taylor in floaty, floral halter neck sundresses at the 2006 Annual Academy of Country Music Awards (left) and arriving at the London studios to appear on GMTV London (right)

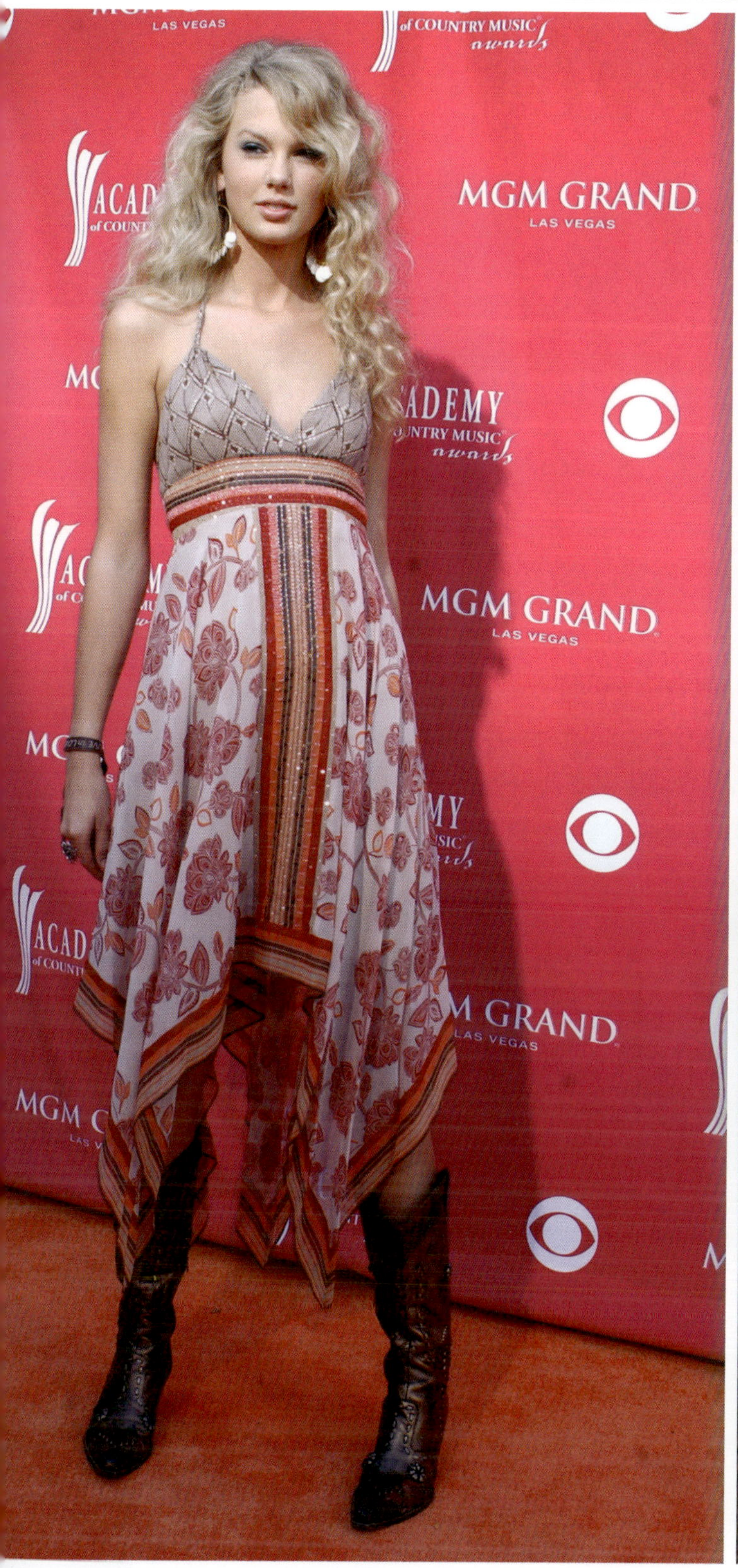

of COUNTRY MUSIC
awards
ACADEMY
of COUNTRY
MGM GRAND
LAS VEGAS
ACADEMY
COUNTRY MUSIC
awards
MGM GRAND
LAS VEGAS
ACADEMY
of COUNT
MGM GRAND
LAS VEGAS

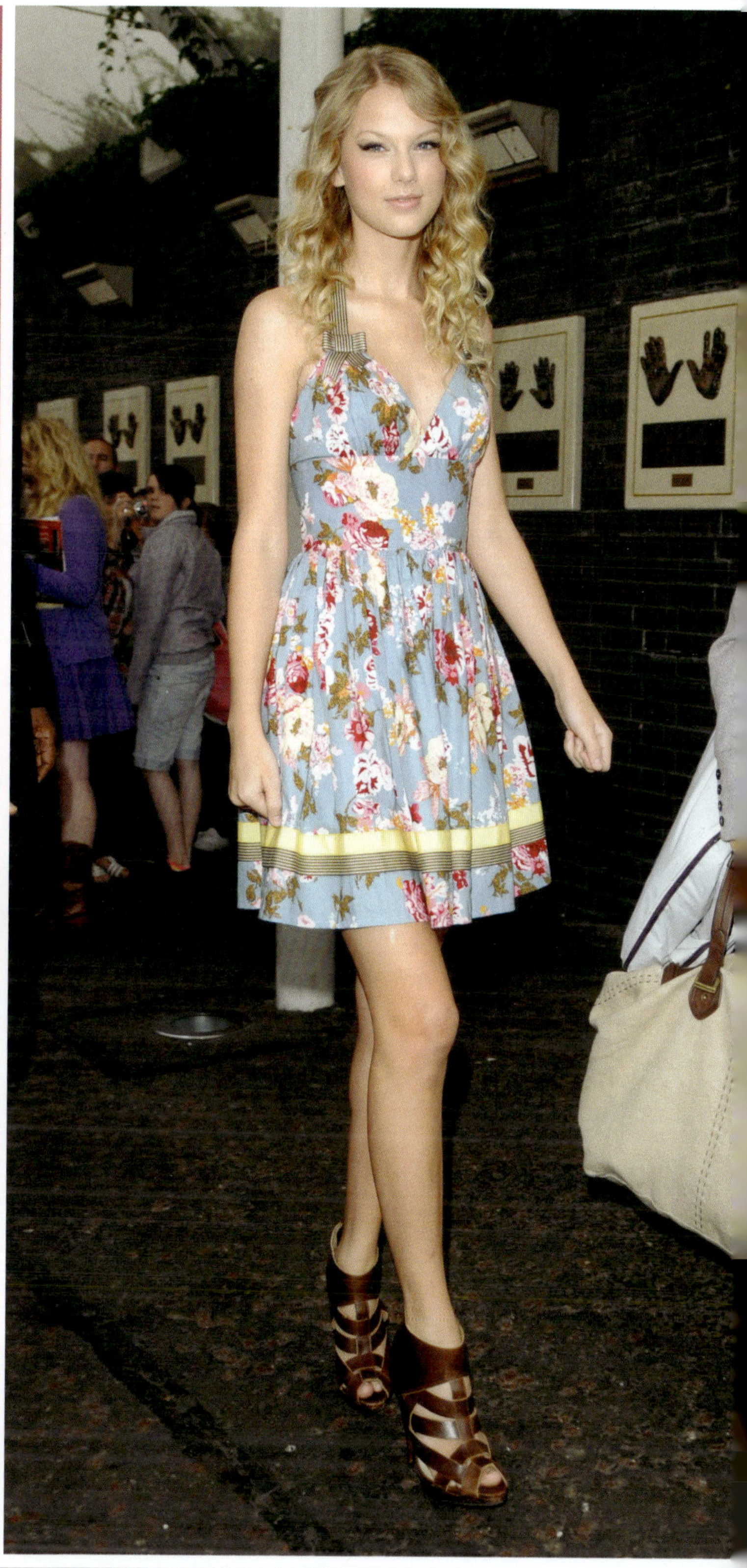

DENIM 'N' PLAID

Denim jackets, skirts, and jeans were another essential part of Taylor's country chic wardrobe. She often combined denim with plaid shirts, either tied at the waist or layered over a tank top. This casual yet stylish approach was a nod to traditional country fashion, made fresh and youthful by her own individual styling.

Taylor in youthful, casual country fashion

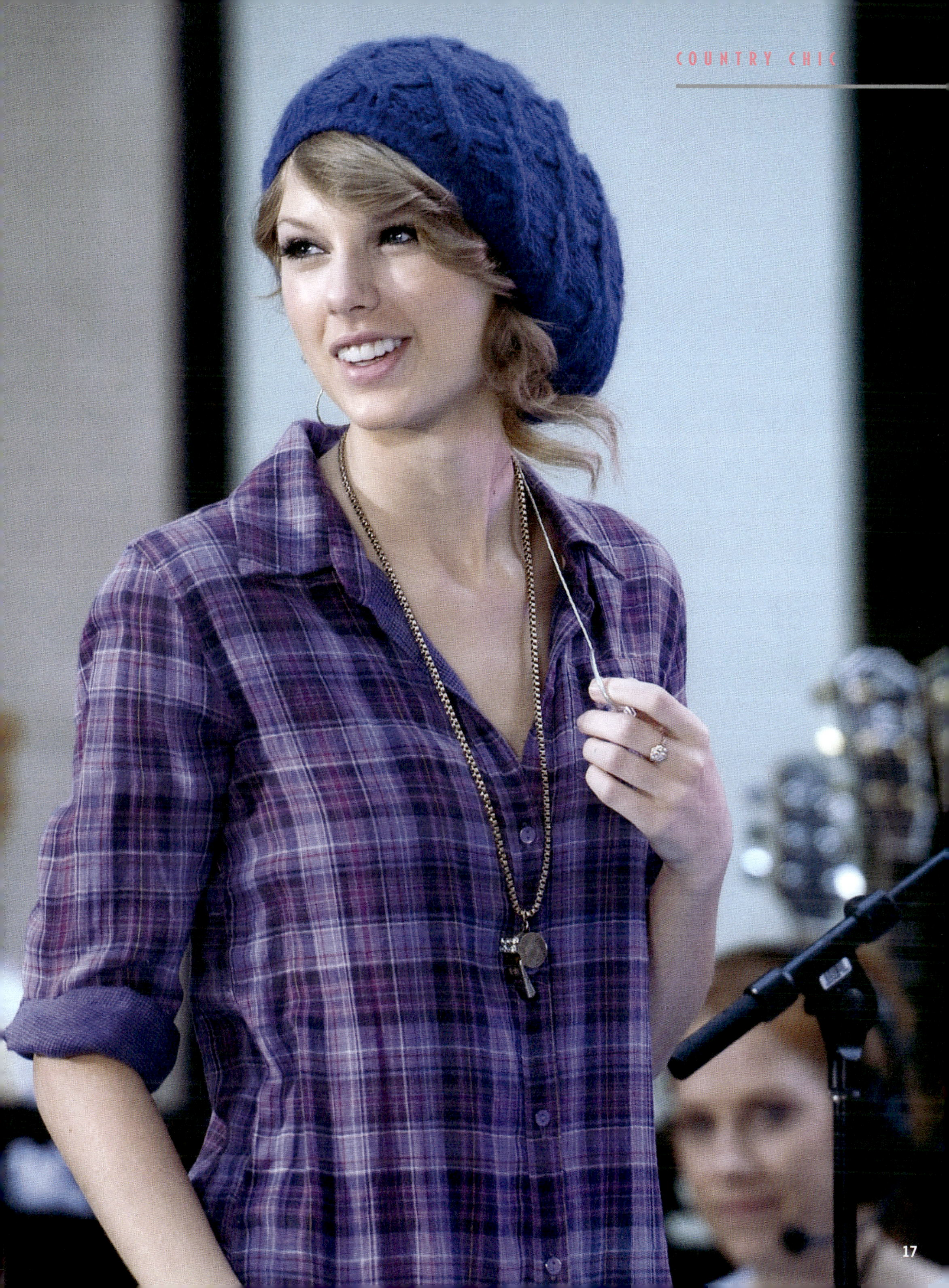

LIKE A RHINESTONE COWGIRL

Rhinestones and Sequins! Her stage outfits included sparkly dresses and tops, often paired with cowboy hats, reflecting the glitzy side of country music.

Sparkling dress and guitar as Taylor performs on stage at the 41st Annual CMA Awards, 2007

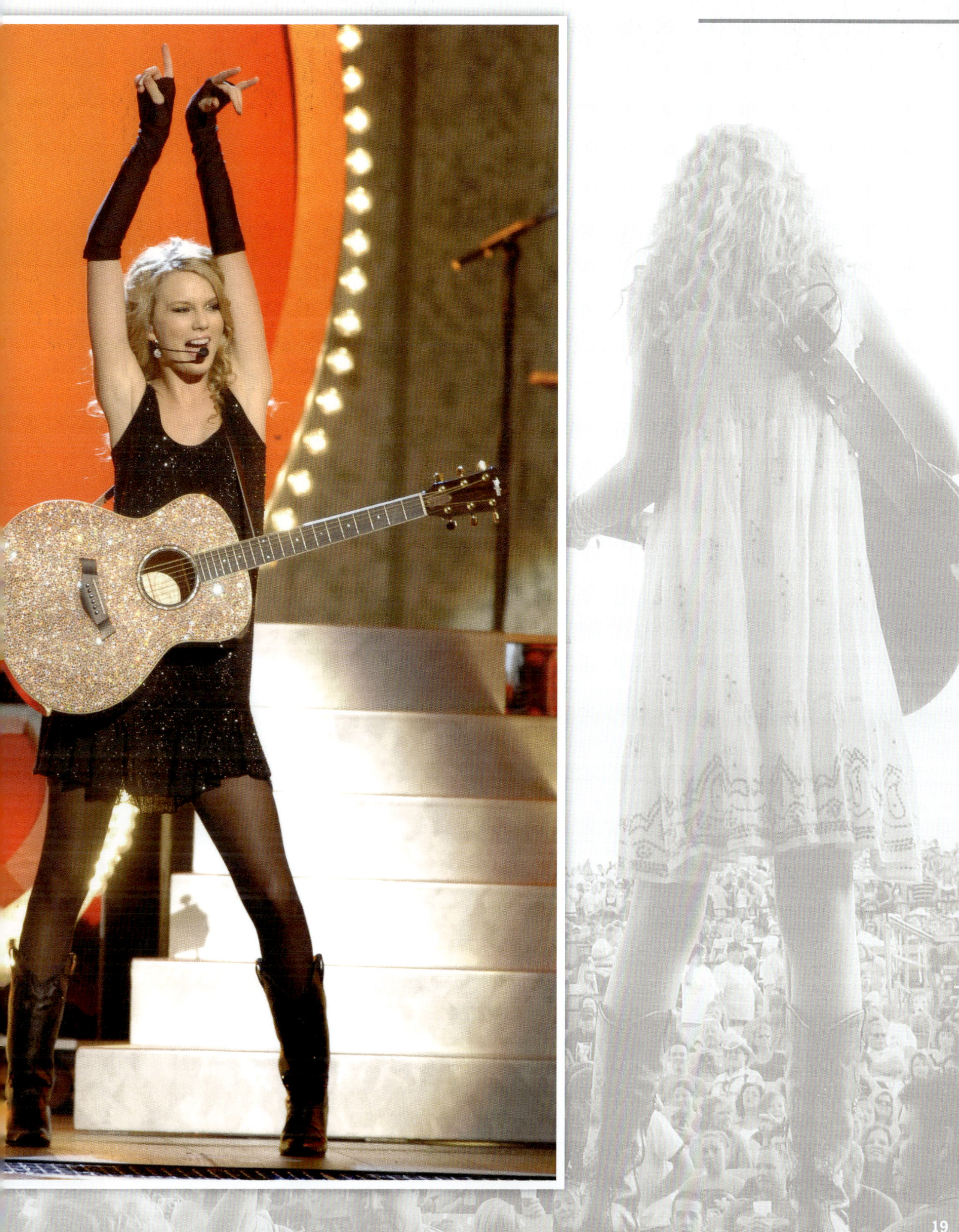

CURLY LOCKS AND NATURAL MAKEUP

During this era, Taylor's signature blonde curls were a key part of her look. She often wore her hair down in loose, natural waves, which complemented her fresh image. Her makeup was typically minimal, with a focus on a natural complexion and occasionally a pop of colour on her lips.

Taylor looking fresh with her iconic blonde curls as she arrives at the 2006 CMT Music Awards

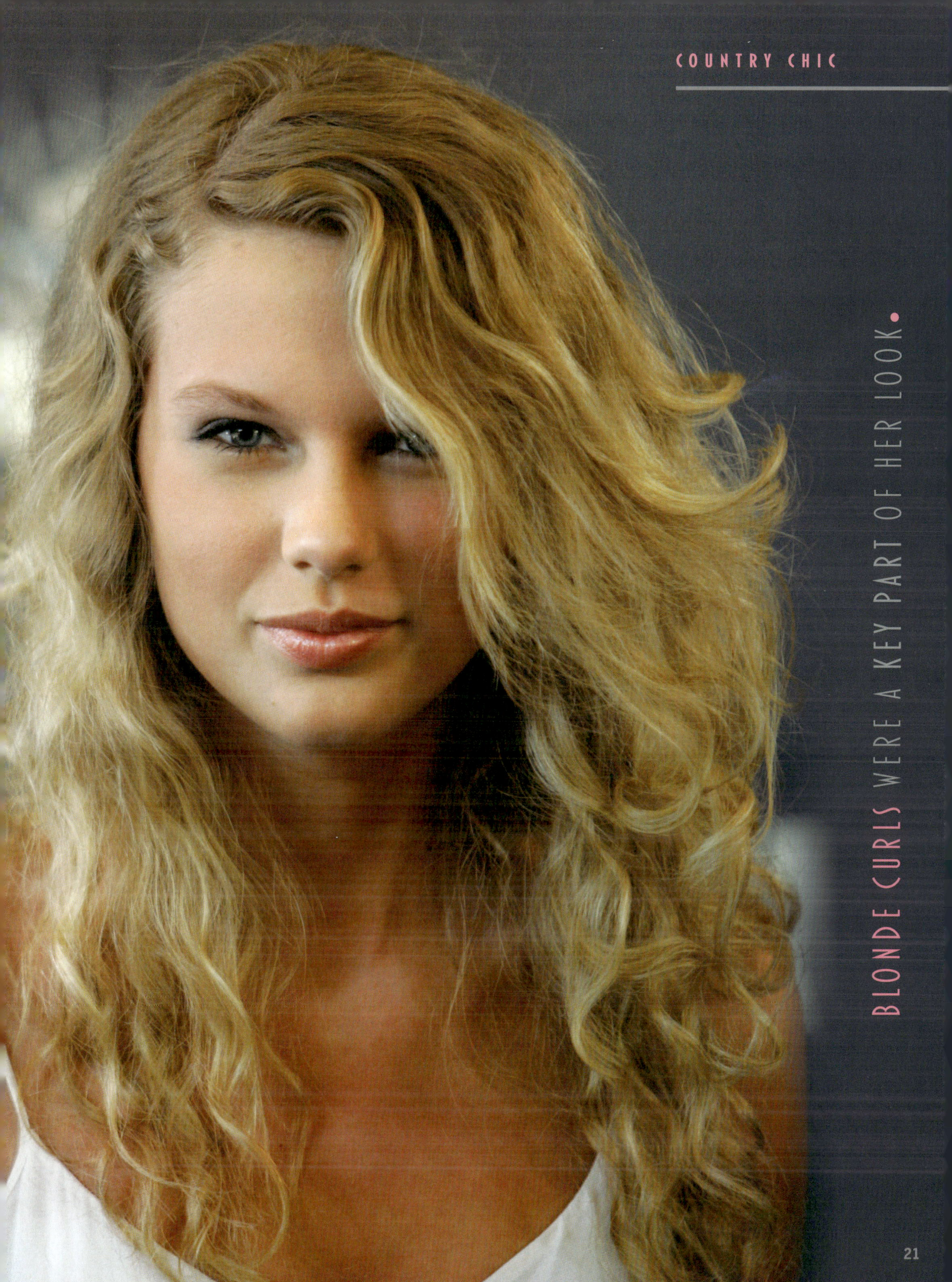

BLONDE CURLS WERE A KEY PART OF HER LOOK.

ACCESSORIZE

Taylor's accessories during her country chic phase were simple yet effective. She often wore delicate necklaces, charm bracelets, statement earrings and, occasionally, beanies that added a touch of bohemian whimsy to her outfits.

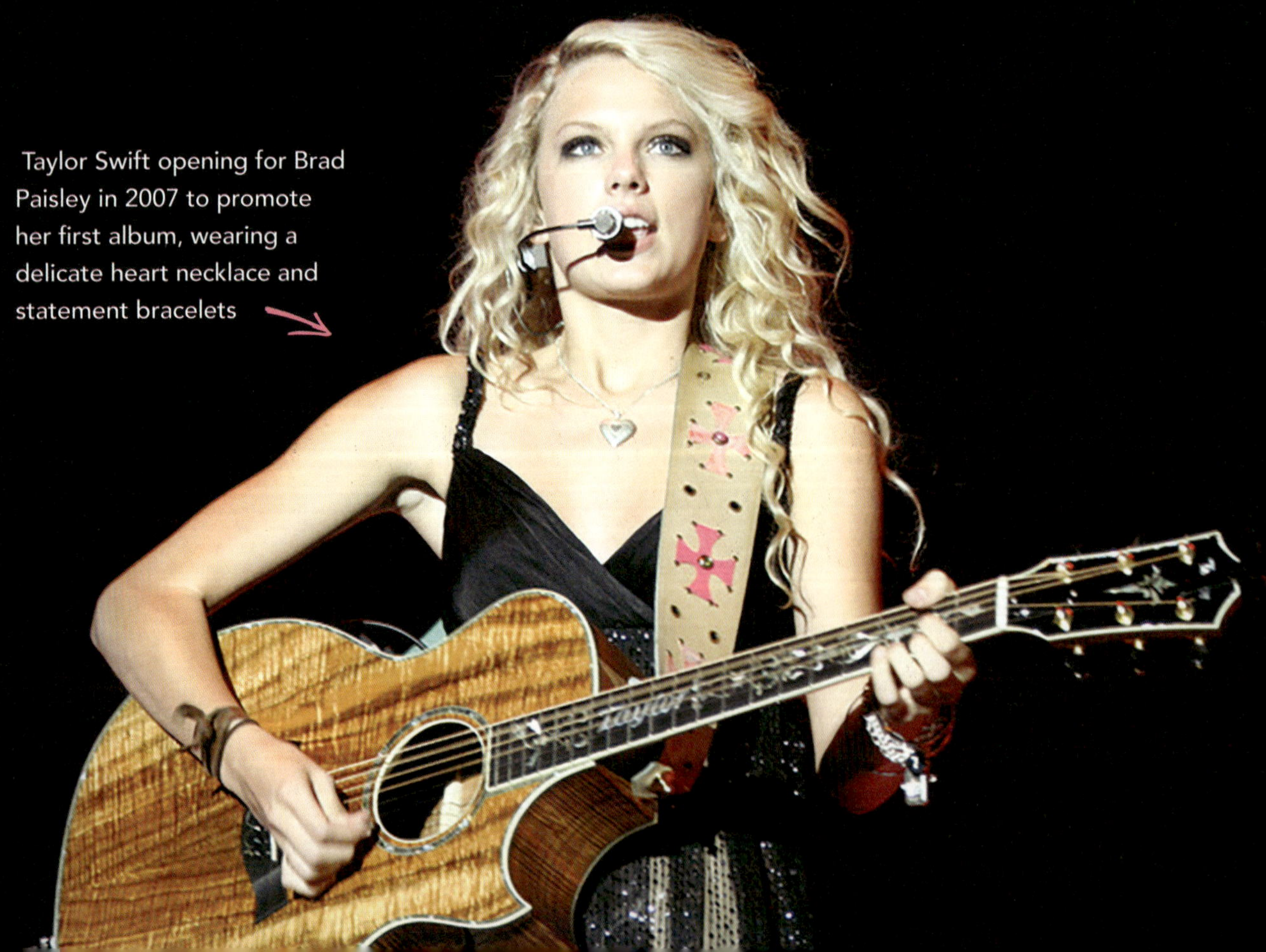

Taylor Swift opening for Brad Paisley in 2007 to promote her first album, wearing a delicate heart necklace and statement bracelets

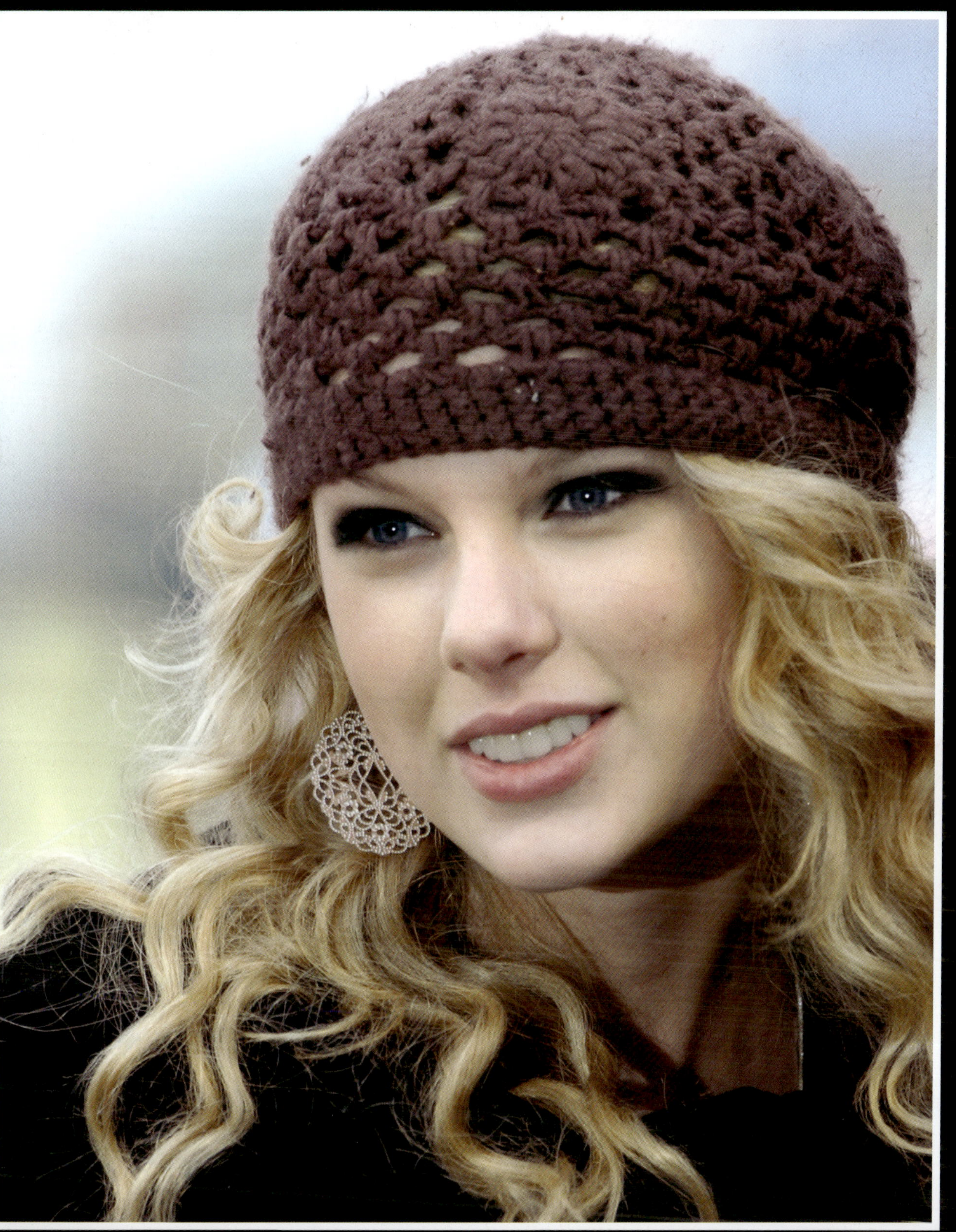

Country chic with a cozy touch, Taylor wore a hand-knit brown beanie, and a set of intricate, lacy metal earrings whilst performing the national anthem before the Reading Phillies opening game in April 2007

GLAMOUR GIRL

As Taylor's star began to soar, she went full-on glam on the Red Carpet. At the 2006 CMA Awards, Taylor went vamp with a black velvet gown and gloves, paired with perfectly curled ringlets.

At the 2006 CMA Awards, Taylor went for a vampy, all-black look, stunning in a floor-length satin dress with matching gloves

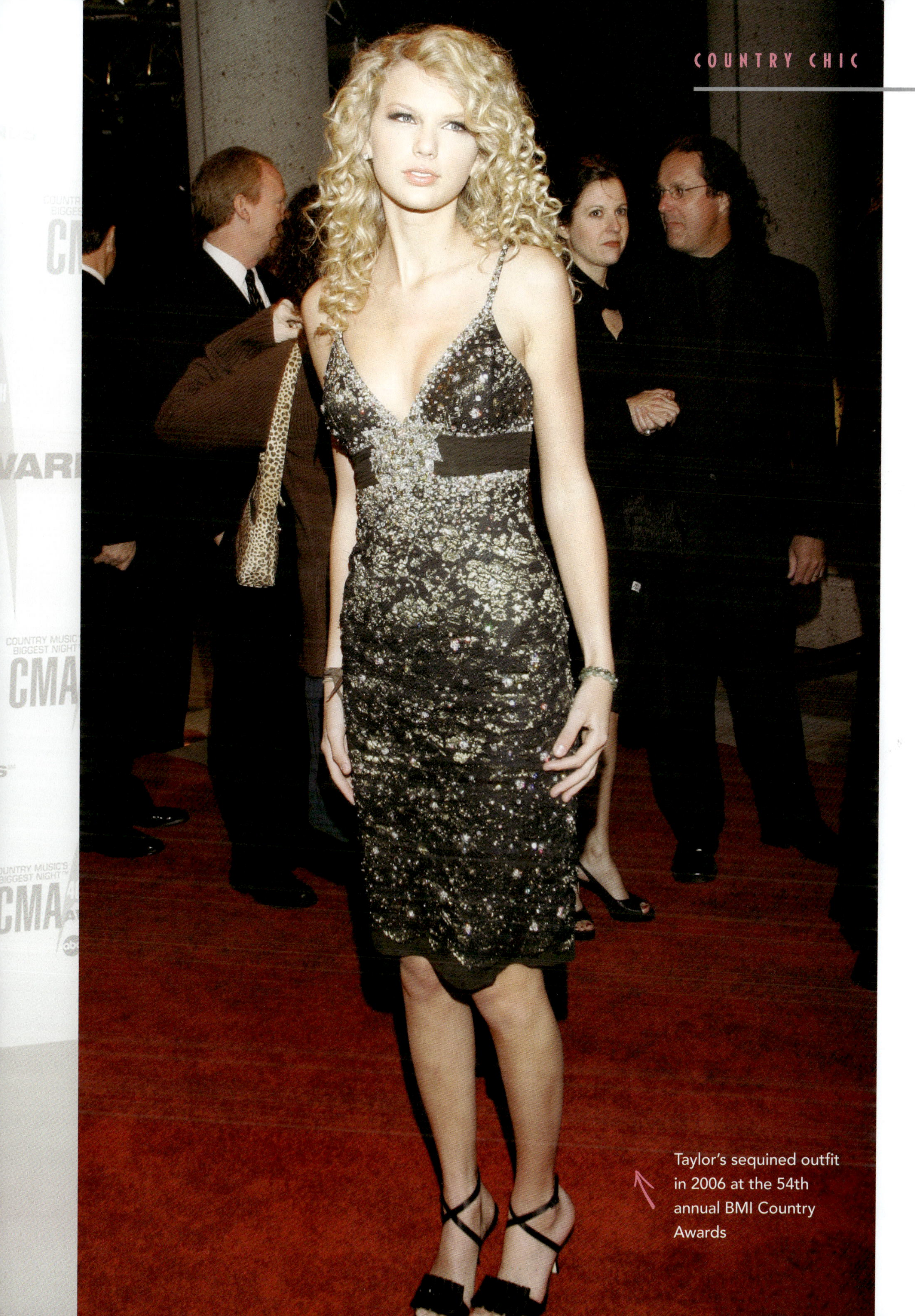

Taylor's sequined outfit in 2006 at the 54th annual BMI Country Awards

FEARLESS

CHAPTER TWO

FASHION

2008/9

During Taylor's *Fearless* era (2008-2009), her fashion was a blend of romantic and classic styles, reflecting the fairy-tale themes of her music at that time. This era was defined by her embrace of vintage-inspired fashion – her outfits memorable for their elegant, whimsy, and classic appeal, making them a defining aspect of her early career.

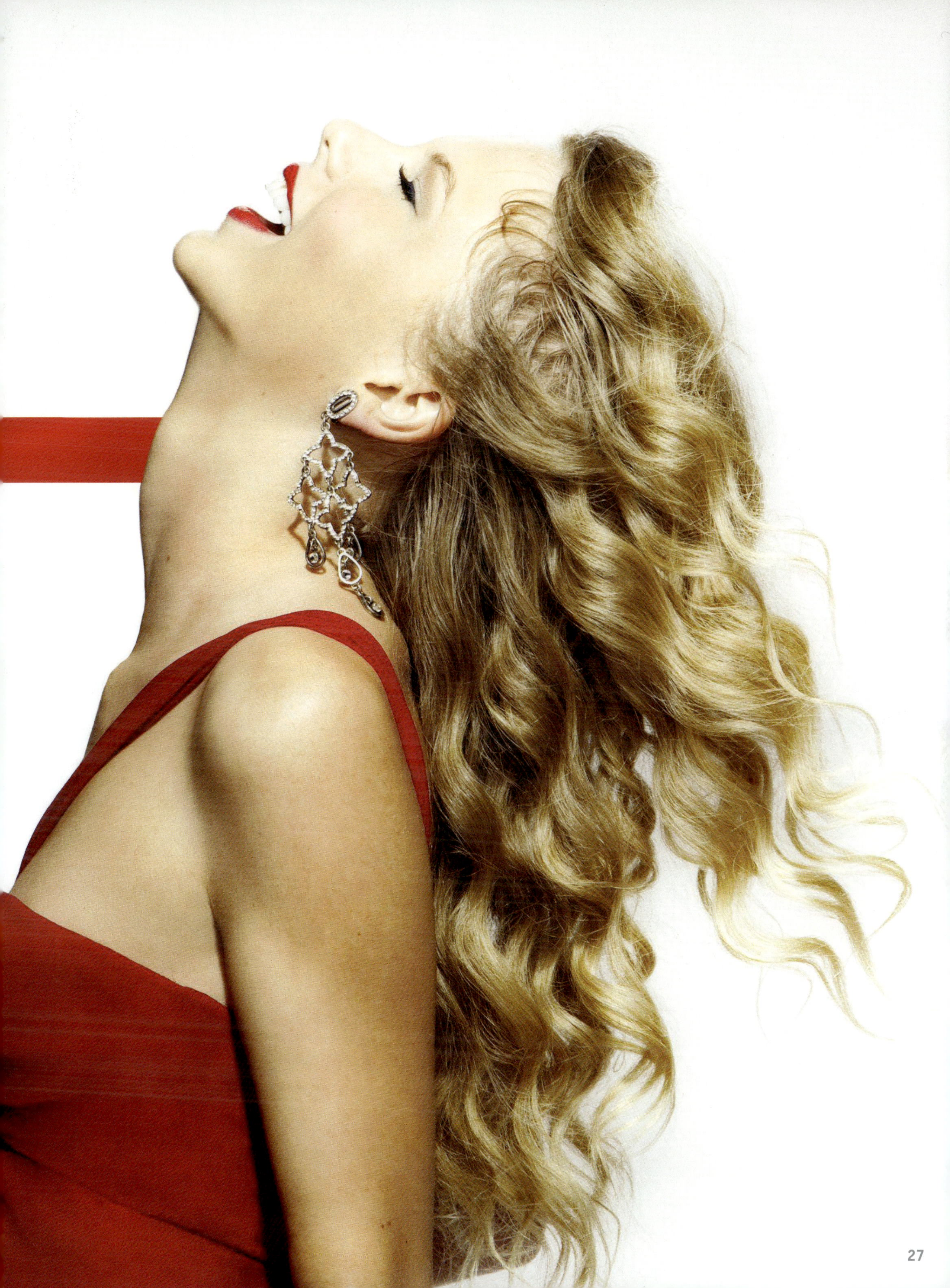

ROMANTIC DRESSES AND GOWNS

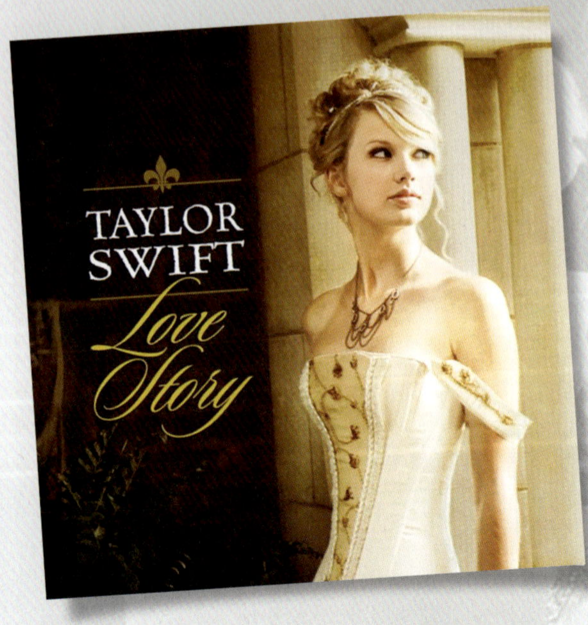

During this time Taylor often wore elegant ball gowns with intricate beading and sequins, which suited the dreamy, fairy-tale vibe of the era. These dresses were often in gold, silver, or pastel colours. Feminine styles with floral prints and ruffled details were also favoured, enhancing the romantic and whimsical feel of her fashion. For performances, Taylor wore elegant stage costumes, again often of a pastel hue and enhanced with sequins. These outfits were designed to stand out and reflect the grandeur of her live shows. On the Red Carpet, Taylor started to model couture gowns or designer pieces that featured intricate detailing and classic silhouettes, reflecting her dreamlike persona.

Taylor on the cover of Love Story in 2008 wearing a stunning ball gown with a fitted bodice and a full skirt, perfectly capturing the song's fairy-tale theme

In a lilac, floor-length strapless gown adorned with embroidered leaves, the singer attends her first-ever Grammys in 2008, where she was nominated for Best New Artist

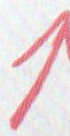

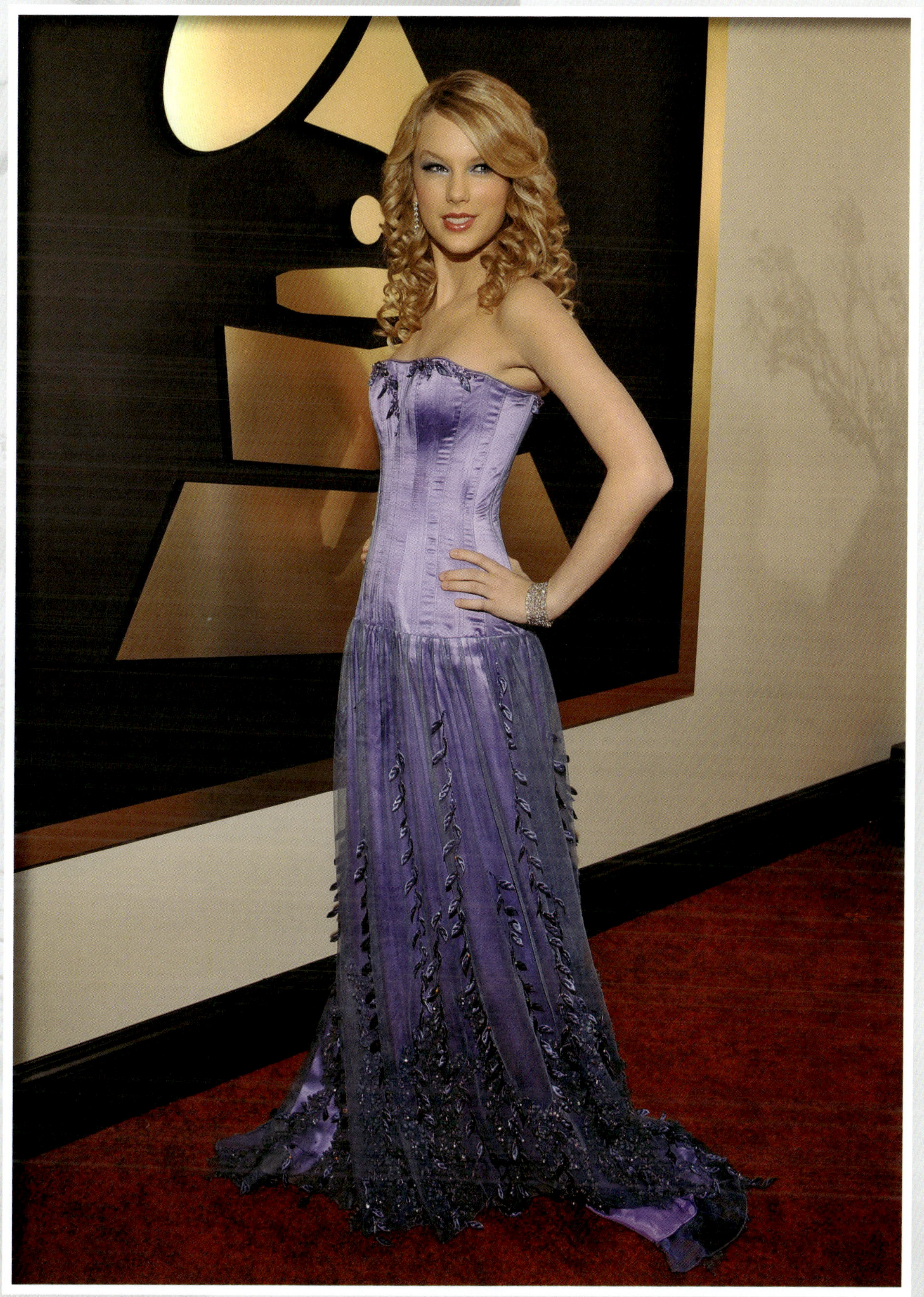

CLASSIC AND VINTAGE-INSPIRED PIECES

Taylor was frequently seen in knee-length dresses, which were both vintage-inspired and yet youthfully fresh at the same time. These dresses often featured cinched waists and full skirts. She incorporated classic cardigans and sweaters into her wardrobe, adding a cosy and casual element to her outfits. These were often worn over dresses or paired with skirts.

Taylor Swift wearing a vintage inspired dress at the V Festival in Hyland's Park in Chelmsford on August 22, 2009

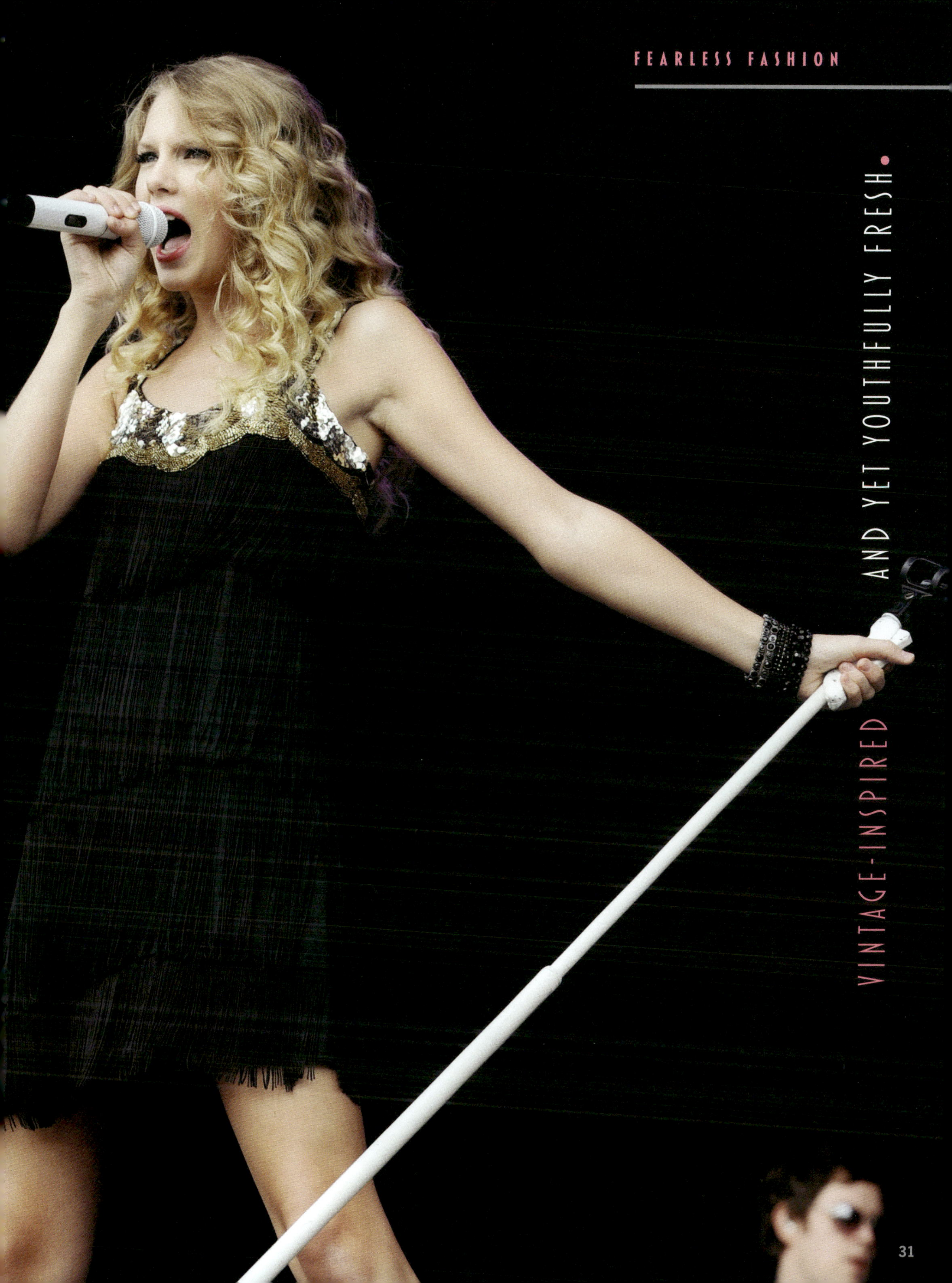
FEARLESS FASHION

VINTAGE-INSPIRED AND YET YOUTHFULLY FRESH.

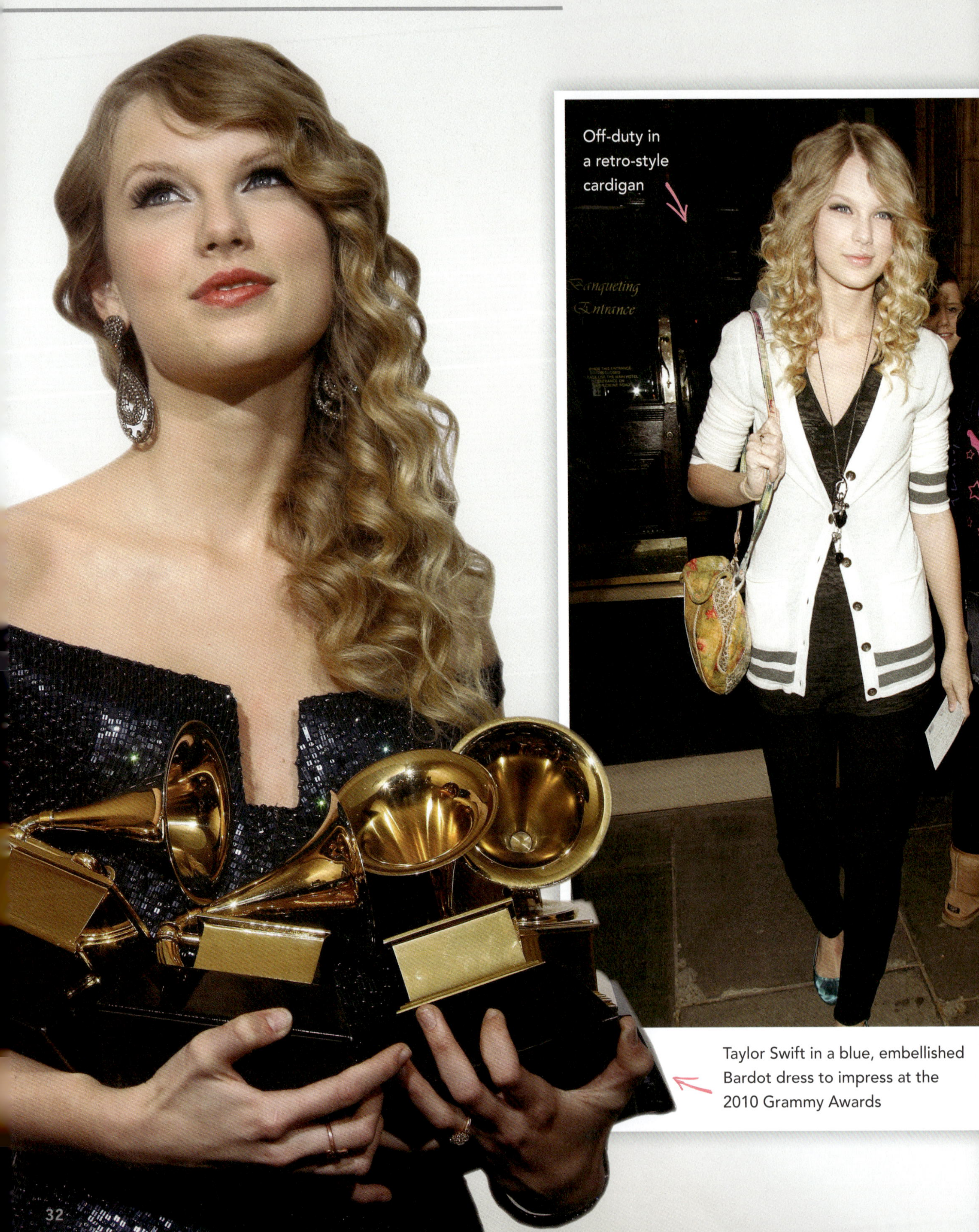

Taylor Swift in a blue, embellished Bardot dress to impress at the 2010 Grammy Awards

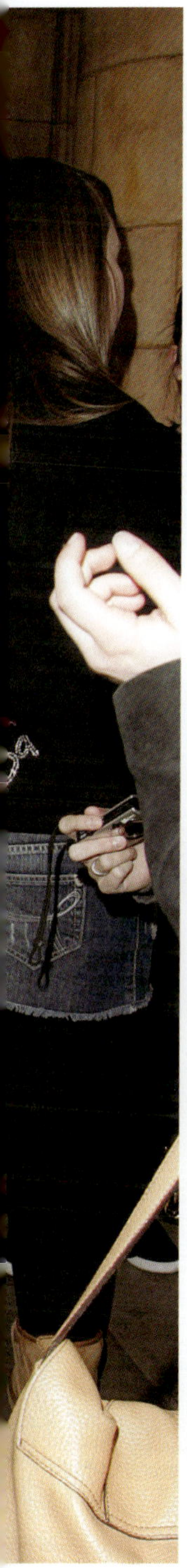

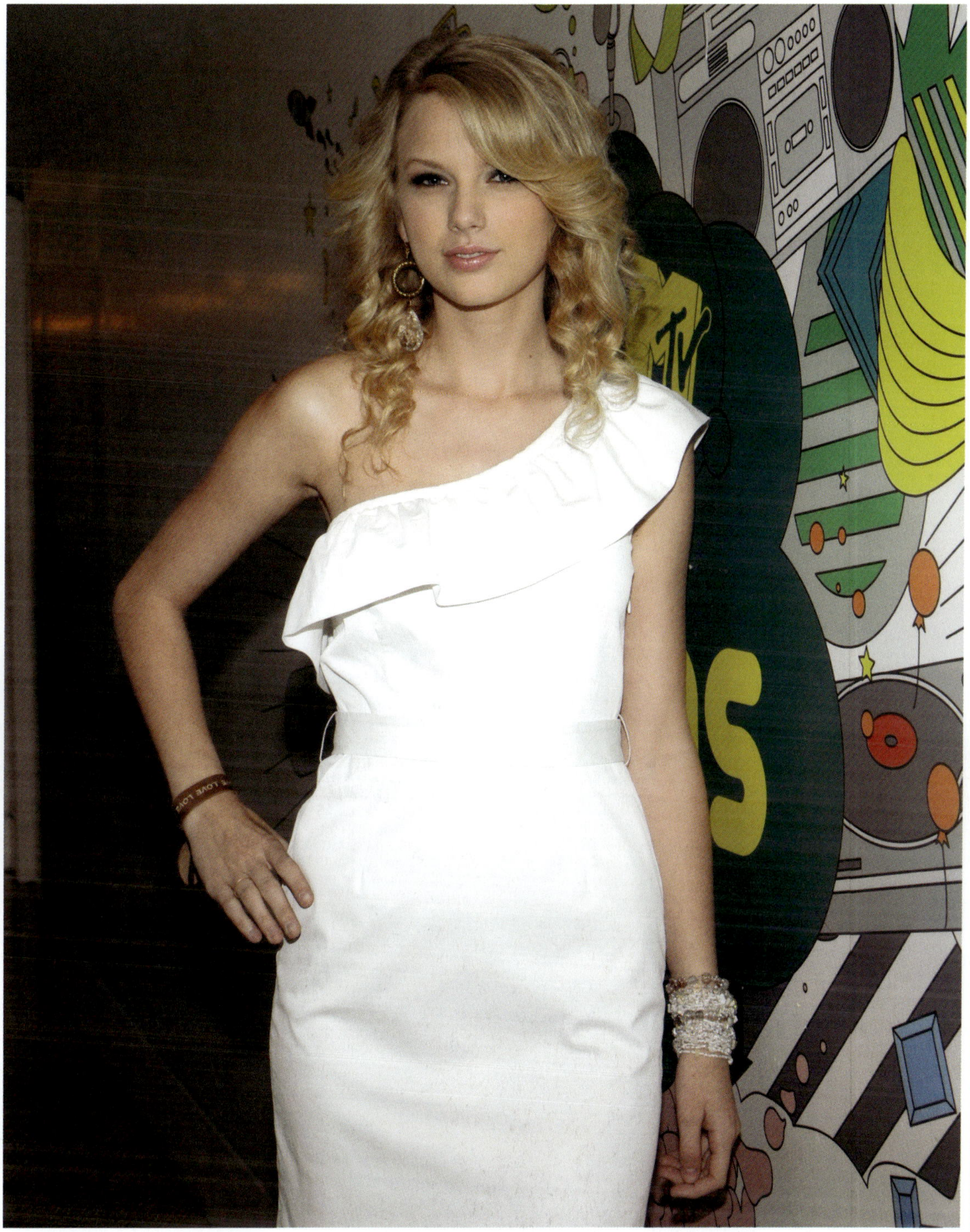

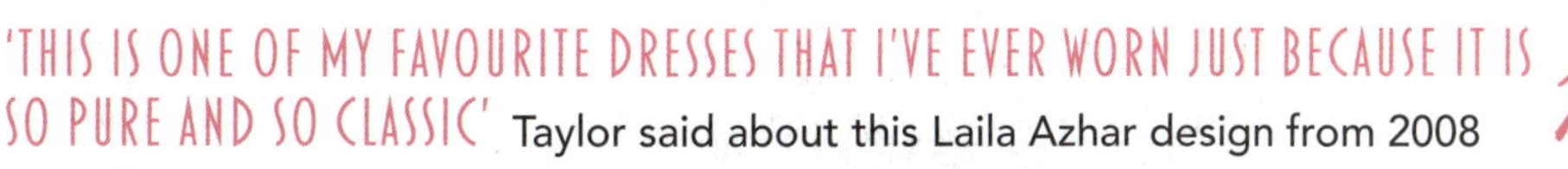

'THIS IS ONE OF MY FAVOURITE DRESSES THAT I'VE EVER WORN JUST BECAUSE IT IS SO PURE AND SO CLASSIC' Taylor said about this Laila Azhar design from 2008

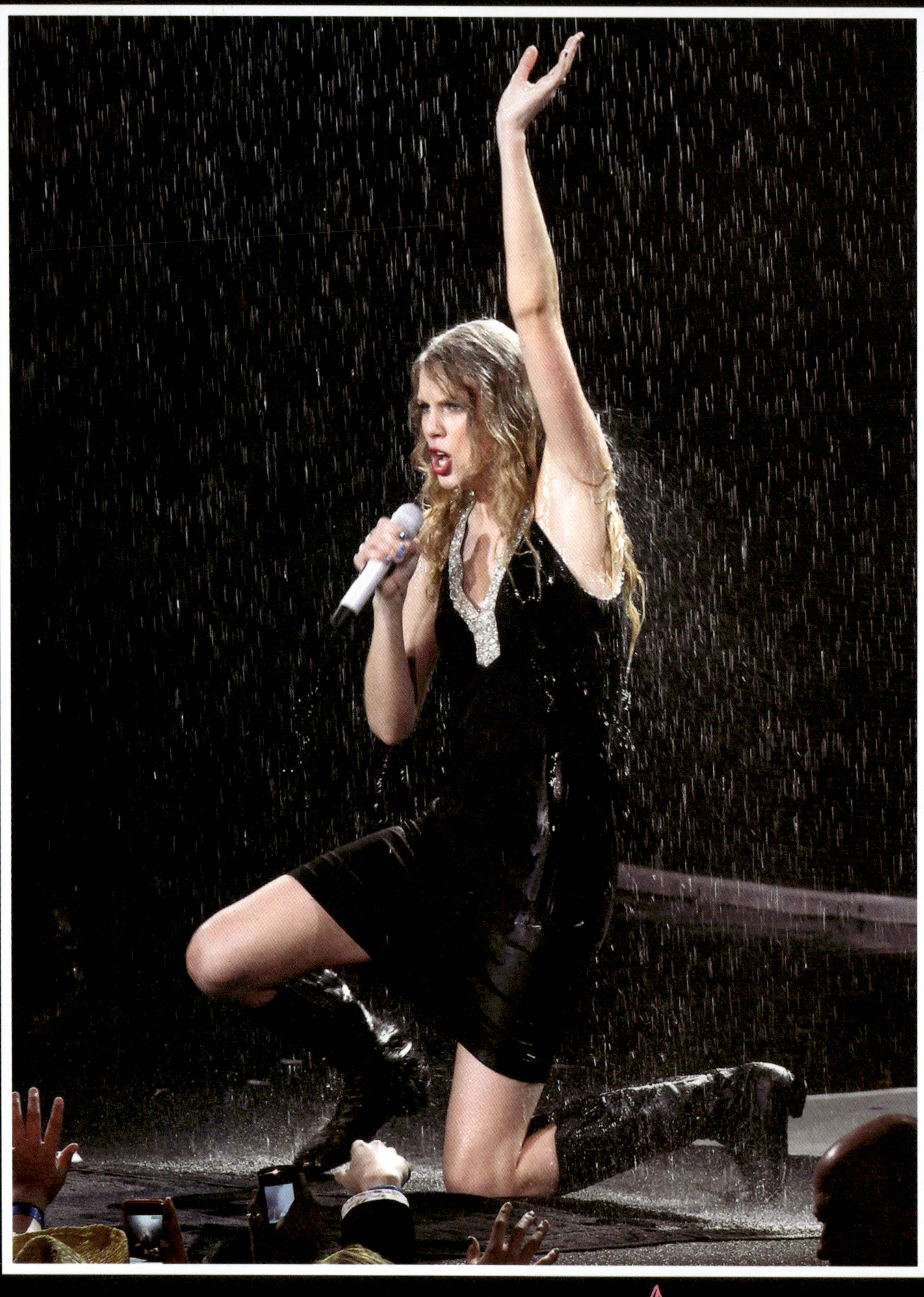

Taylor delivering typically fearless performances in vintage black dresses during her Fearless Tour (above) and at the CMA Music Festival in 2009 (right)

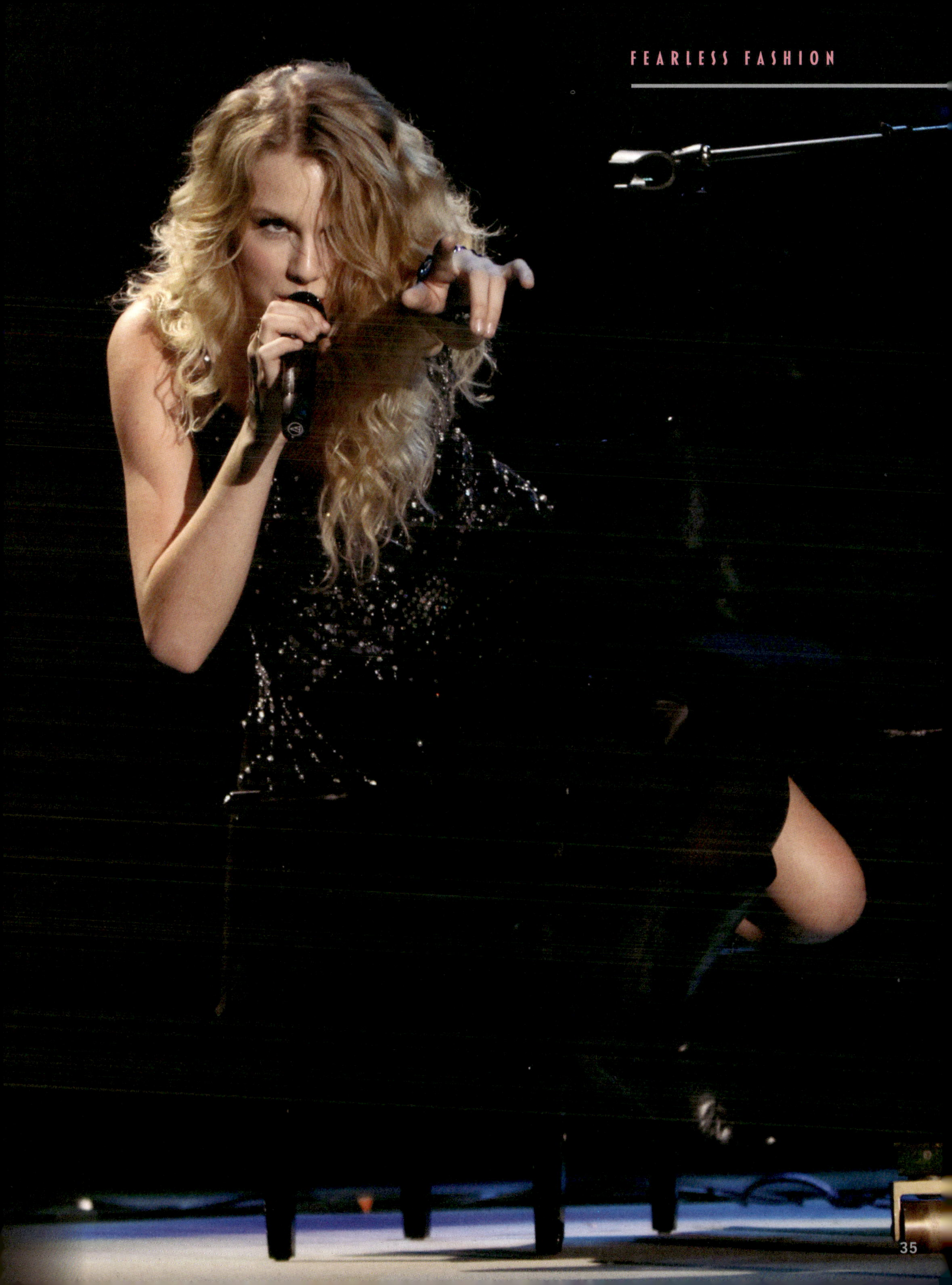

HAIR AND MAKEUP

Her signature long, curly hair was styled with soft, voluminous waves. This hairstyle enhanced the fairy-tale aesthetic of the *Fearless* era. Taylor frequently wore her hair in half-up, half-down styles, often adorned with subtle accessories like headbands or clips. With regards to make-up, Taylor featured a fresh and dewy look, emphasizing a youthful glow. Her makeup often included rosy blush and soft pink or peach lipstick, which complemented her soft, romantic fashion. Eye makeup was generally natural, with neutral eyeshadows and minimal eyeliner to maintain that bright-eyed, radiant look.

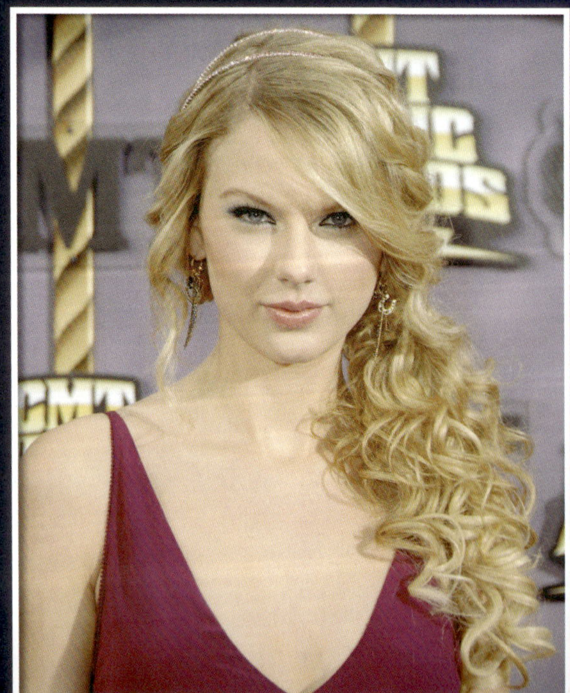

Taylor adds the youthfully freshness to the vintage look

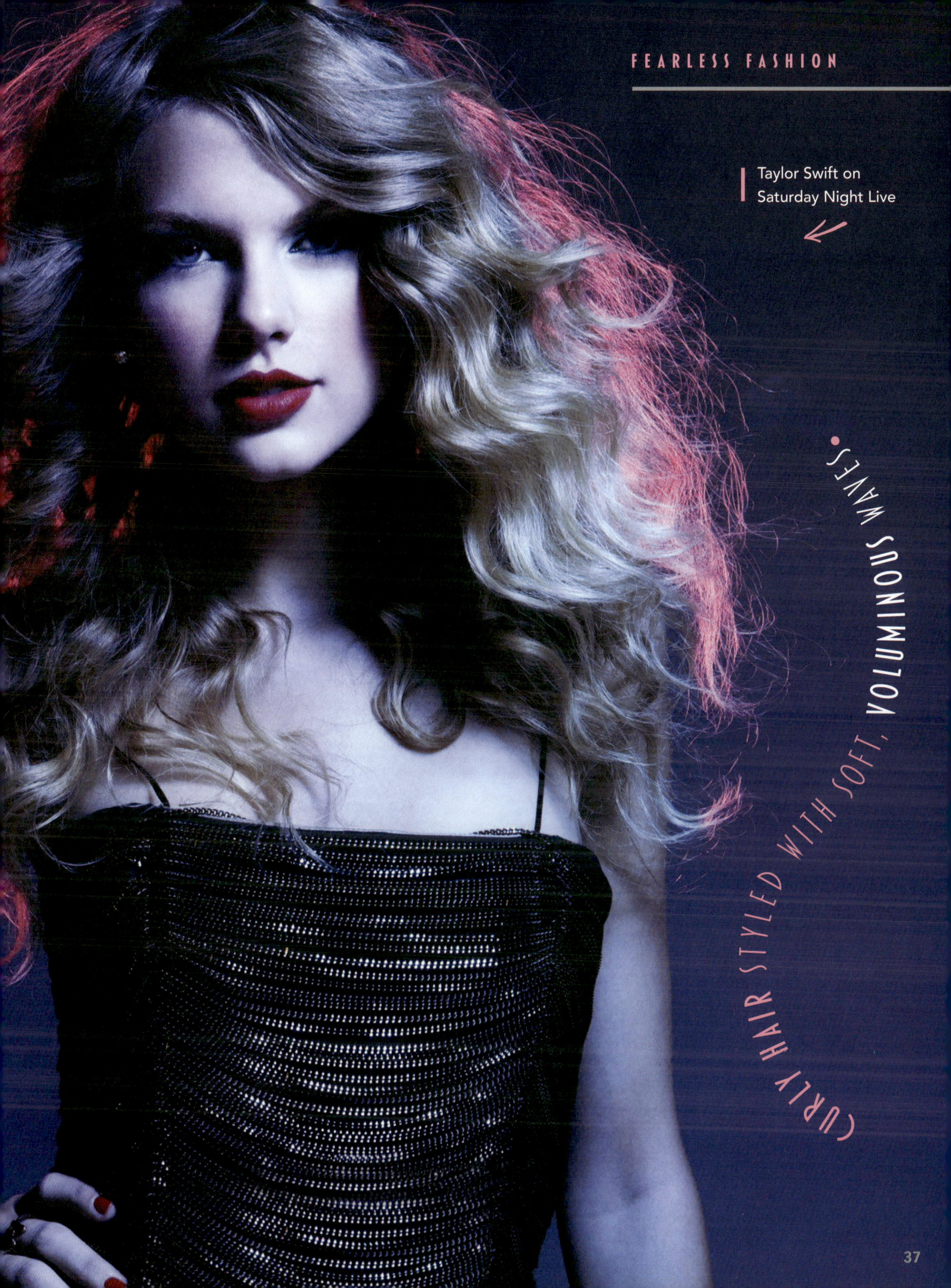

FEARLESS FASHION
Taylor Swift on
Saturday Night Live
CURLY HAIR STYLED WITH SOFT, VOLUMINOUS WAVES.

SPEAK NOW

CHAPTER THREE

STYLE

2010-2011

During Taylor's *Speak Now* **era (2010-2011), her fashion choices reflected the album's themes of love, drama, and theatricality.** The era was marked by a true blend of vintage-inspired glamour and whimsical elements, aligning with the storytelling nature of the album. This period in Swift's sartorial journey showcased her ability to blend whimsical vintage and glamorous modern aesthetics, all while maintaining her classic and elegant style.

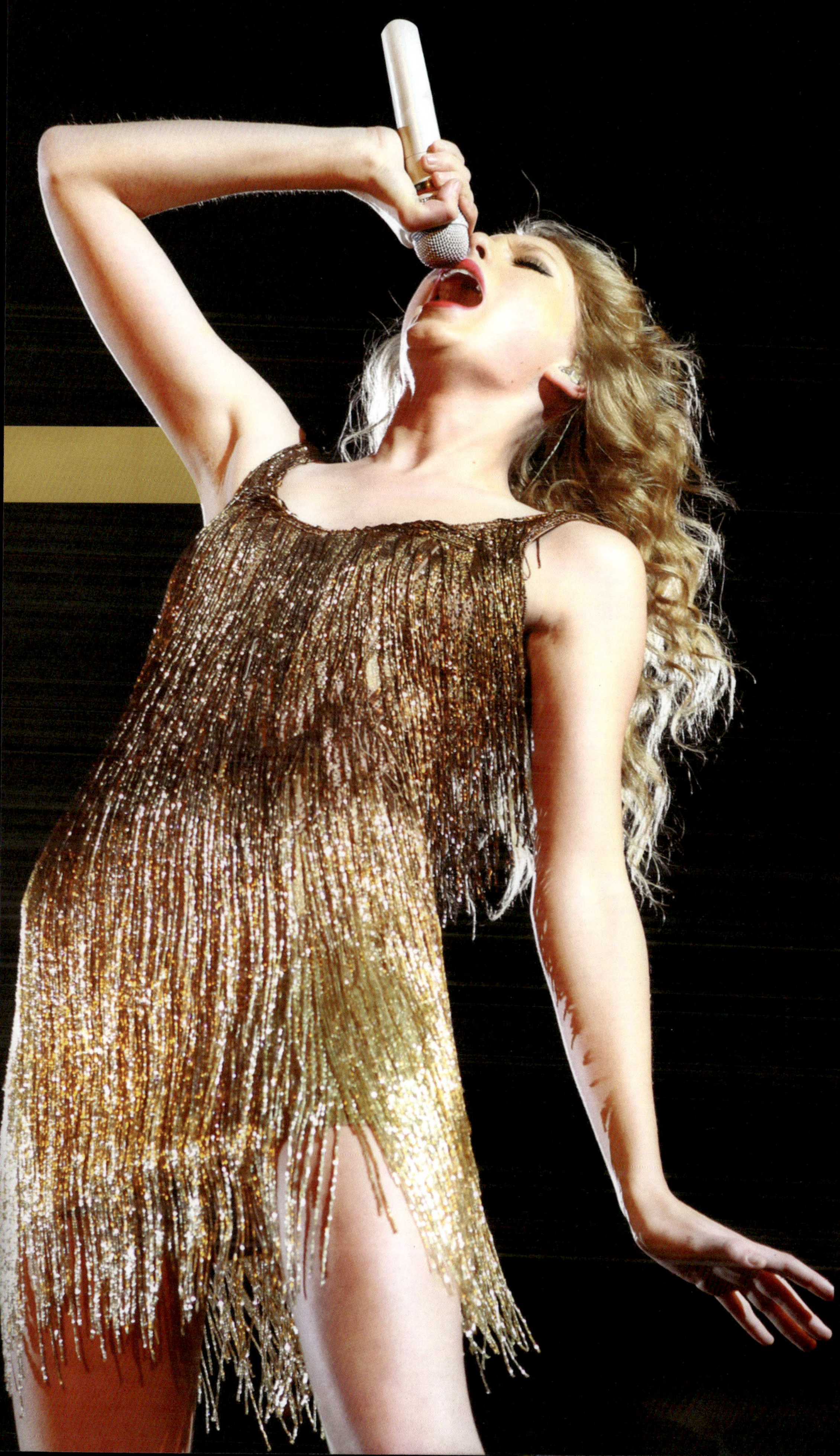

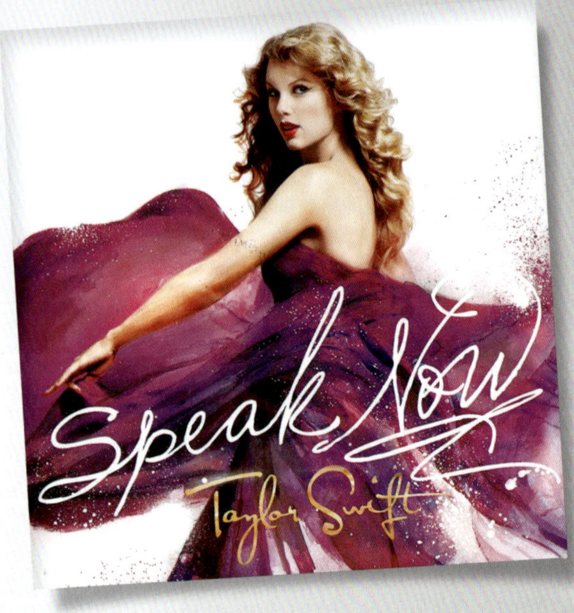

PURE THEATRE

The *Speak Now* era featured more elaborate, theatrical outfits. Taylor wore a lot of deep jewel tones, including purple and red, which matched the album's dramatic, love-laced storylines. Her stage outfits included flowing ballgowns made from luxurious fabrics like satin and tulle, with intricate embellishments such as beading and sequins.

Strapless deep lilac chiffon by Reem Acra worn by Taylor on the *Speak Now* cover

Taylor's Susan Hilferty dress with sweetheart neckline

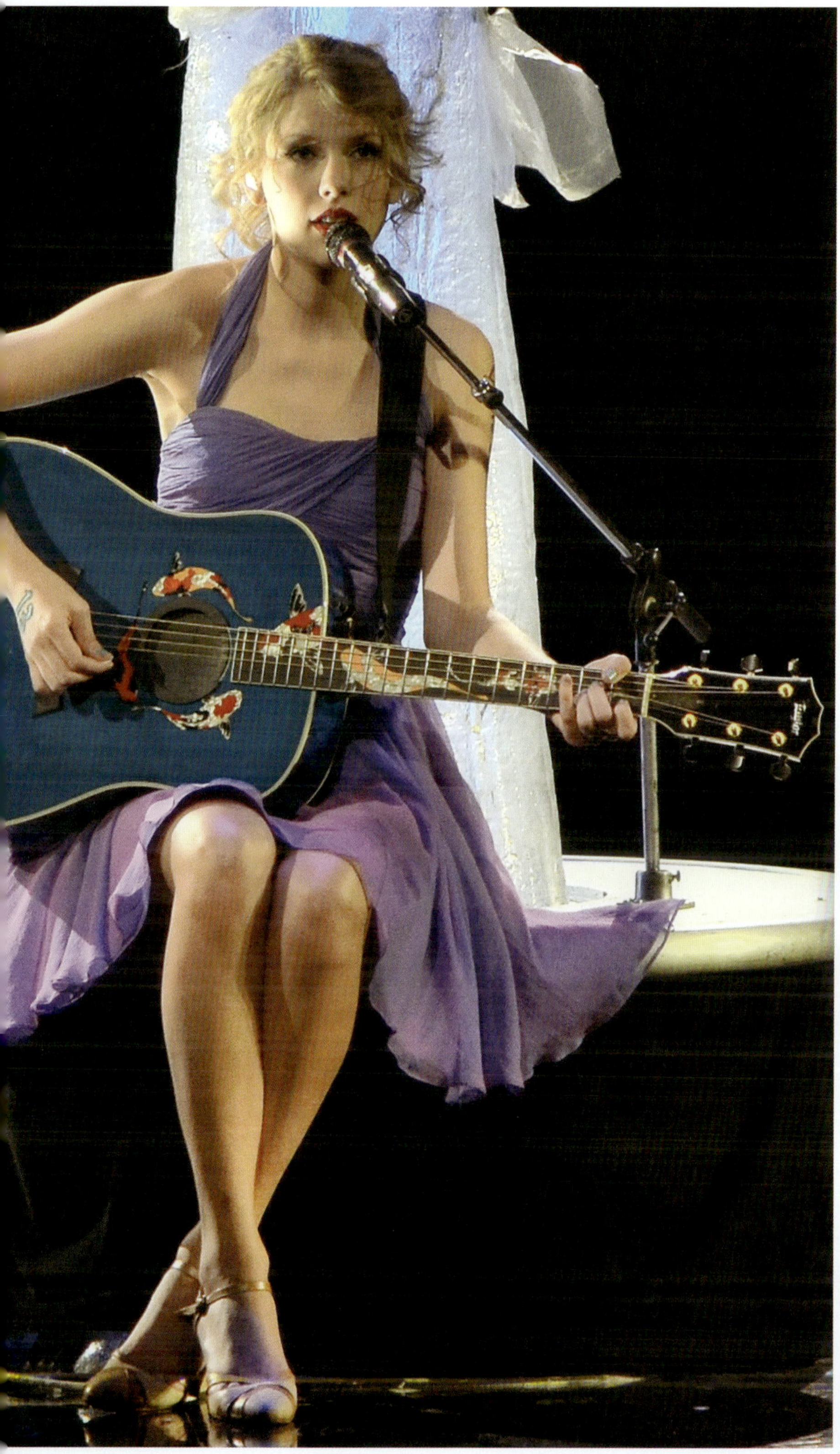

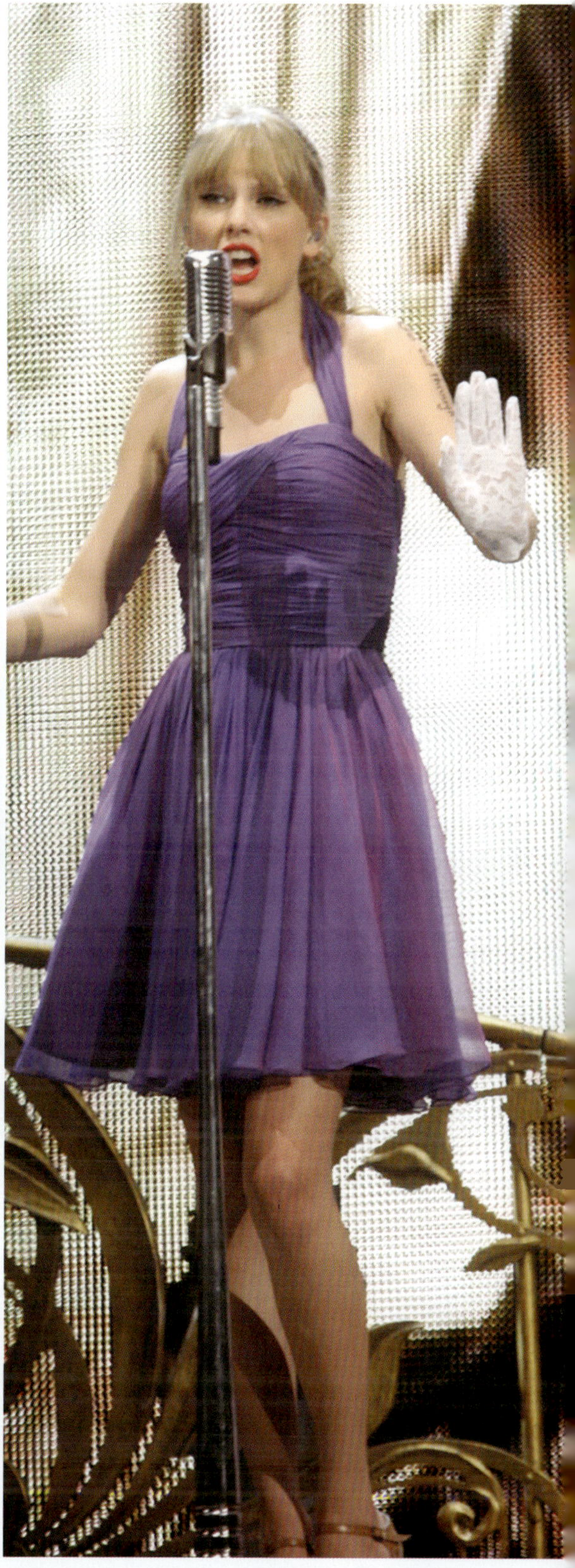

VINTAGE GLAMOUR

Away from the stage, Taylor began incorporating more vintage elements into her **style, embracing 1940s, 50s and 60s classically inspired silhouettes, including fitted bodices and full skirts.** She incorporated elegant details such as lace, ruffles, and bows into her outfits, adding an old-fashioned charm.

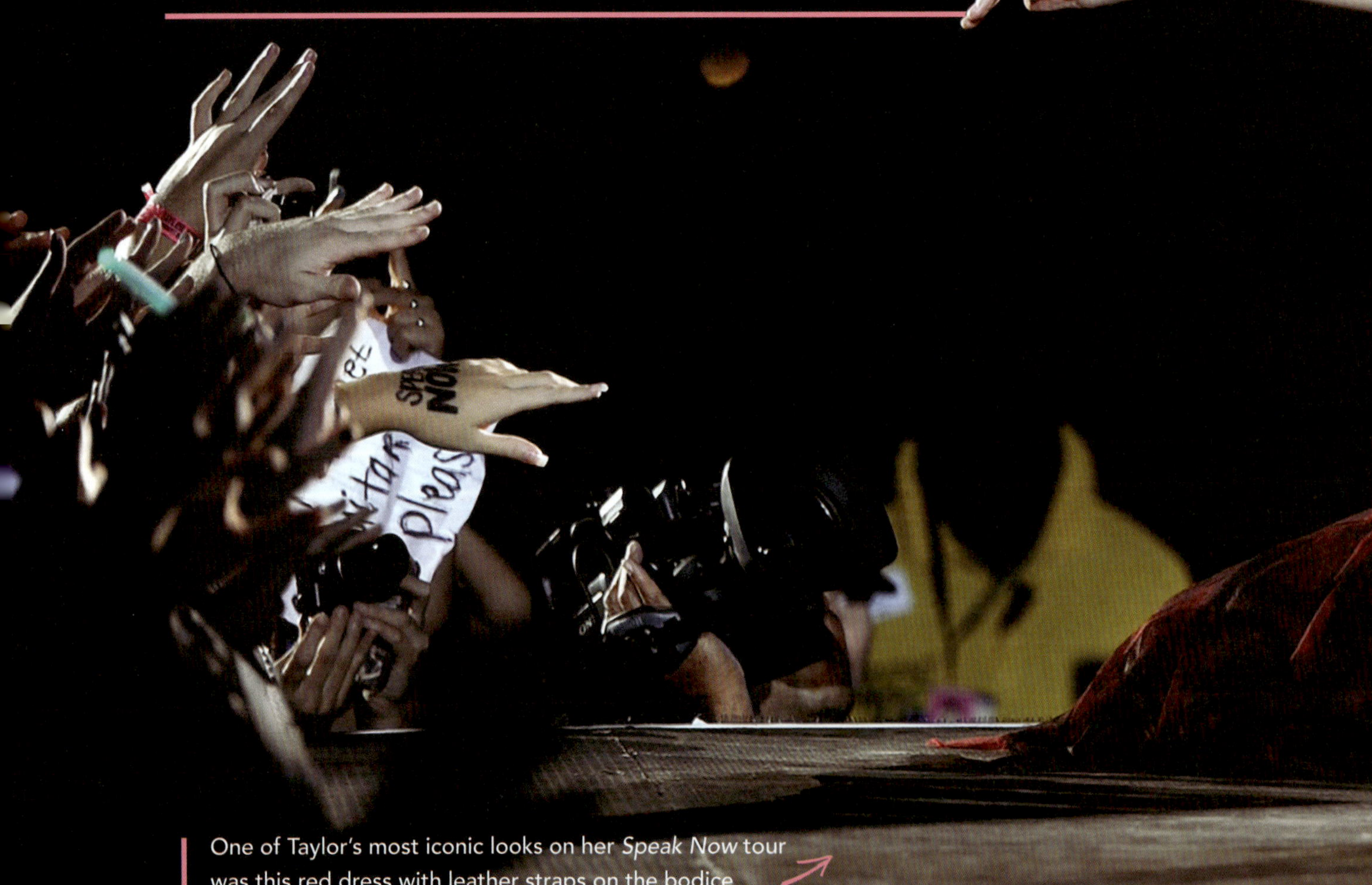

One of Taylor's most iconic looks on her *Speak Now* tour was this red dress with leather straps on the bodice

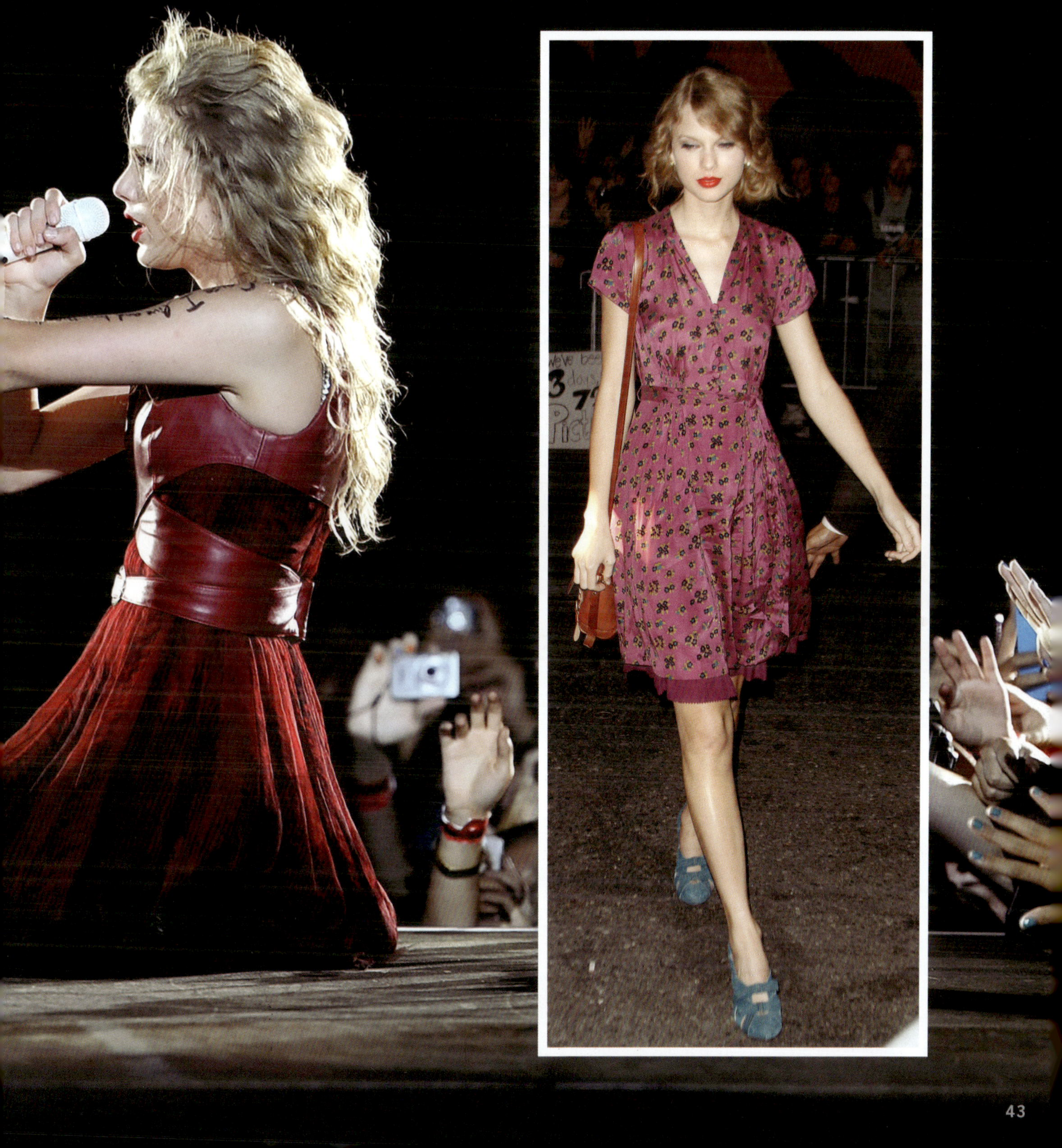

It's not often that Tay has worn Betsey Johnson, but back in 2010, she embraced a '40s-style frock from the designer in a pink-and-green floral print

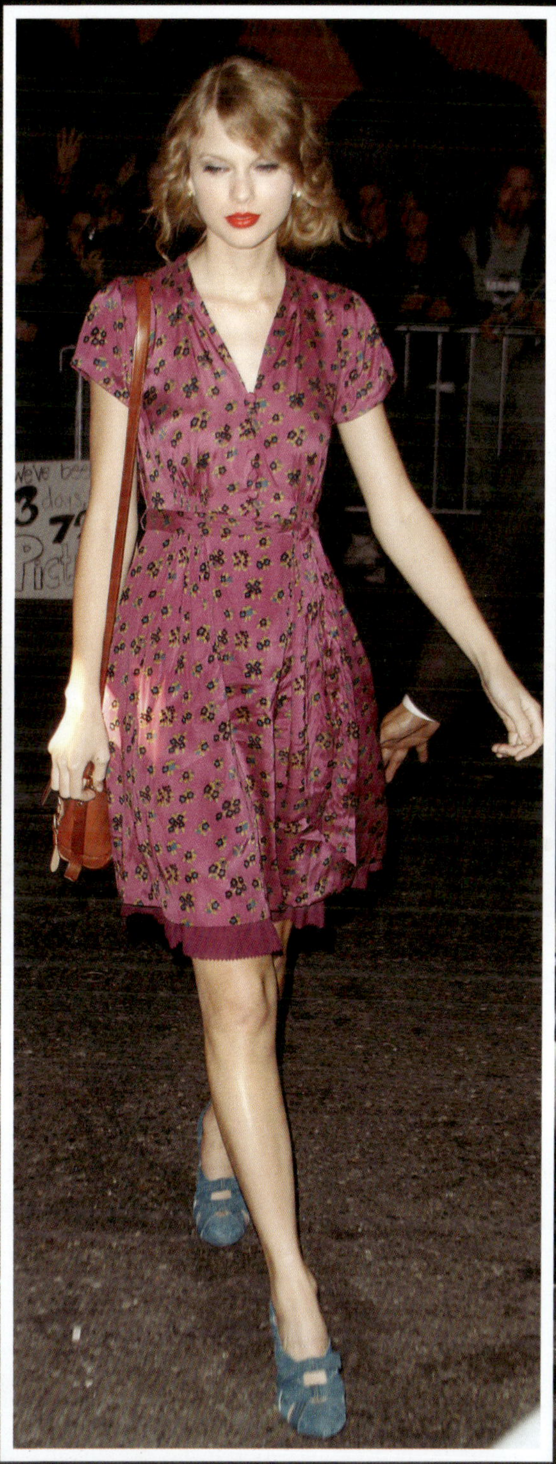

DAY-TO-DAY CHIC

For everyday looks, Taylor wore pretty, feminine dresses with floral prints or delicate **patterns.** These were often paired with cardigans or denim jackets for a casual touch. She also wore high-waisted trousers paired with blouses or sweaters, reflecting a classic and polished style.

Swift looked effortlessly put-together while leaving her hotel in London in 2011. She paired an oversized cream sweater with billowing sleeves over a blue floral dress, creating a chic bohemian silhouette

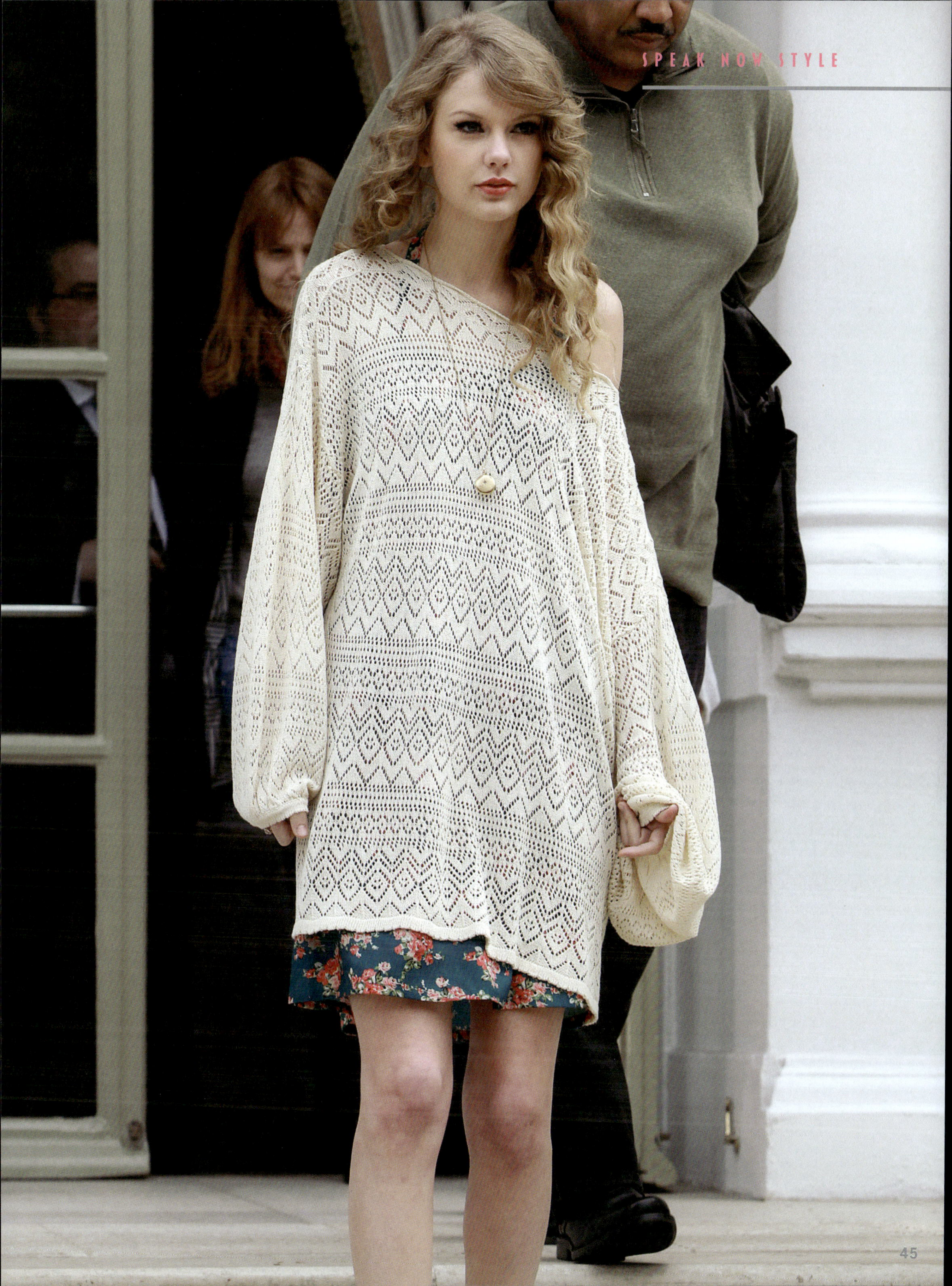

BEAUTY

Soft Waves and Elegant Updos were go-to looks for her locks. Taylor's hair was often styled in soft, romantic waves or glamorous curls. For formal events, she adopted elegant updos or classic chignons. Her makeup also stepped up a level, becoming dramatically different yet still maintaining a classic finish. Taylor often sported dramatic eye makeup, including smoky eyes or winged eyeliner, which complemented the theatrical nature of her outfits. Classic red lipstick became a staple, enhancing her glamorous and vintage-inspired looks, and quickly becoming her signature look of unmistakable style and confidence.

An elegant updo and statement crimson lips for the Met Costume Institute's Gala for Alexander McQueen: Savage Beauty in 2011

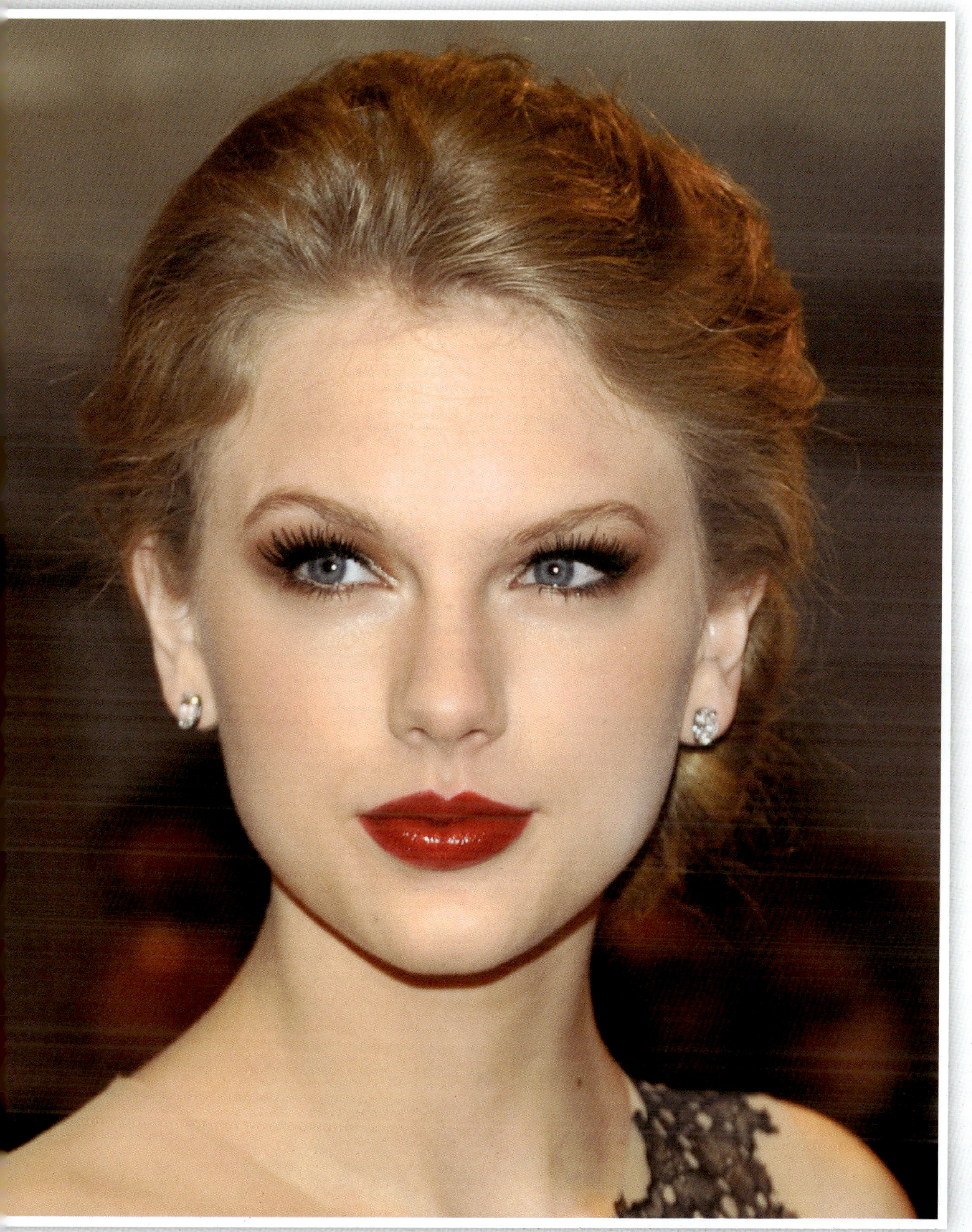

SOFT WAVES AND ELEGANT UPDOS.

TAYLOR'S SHOES

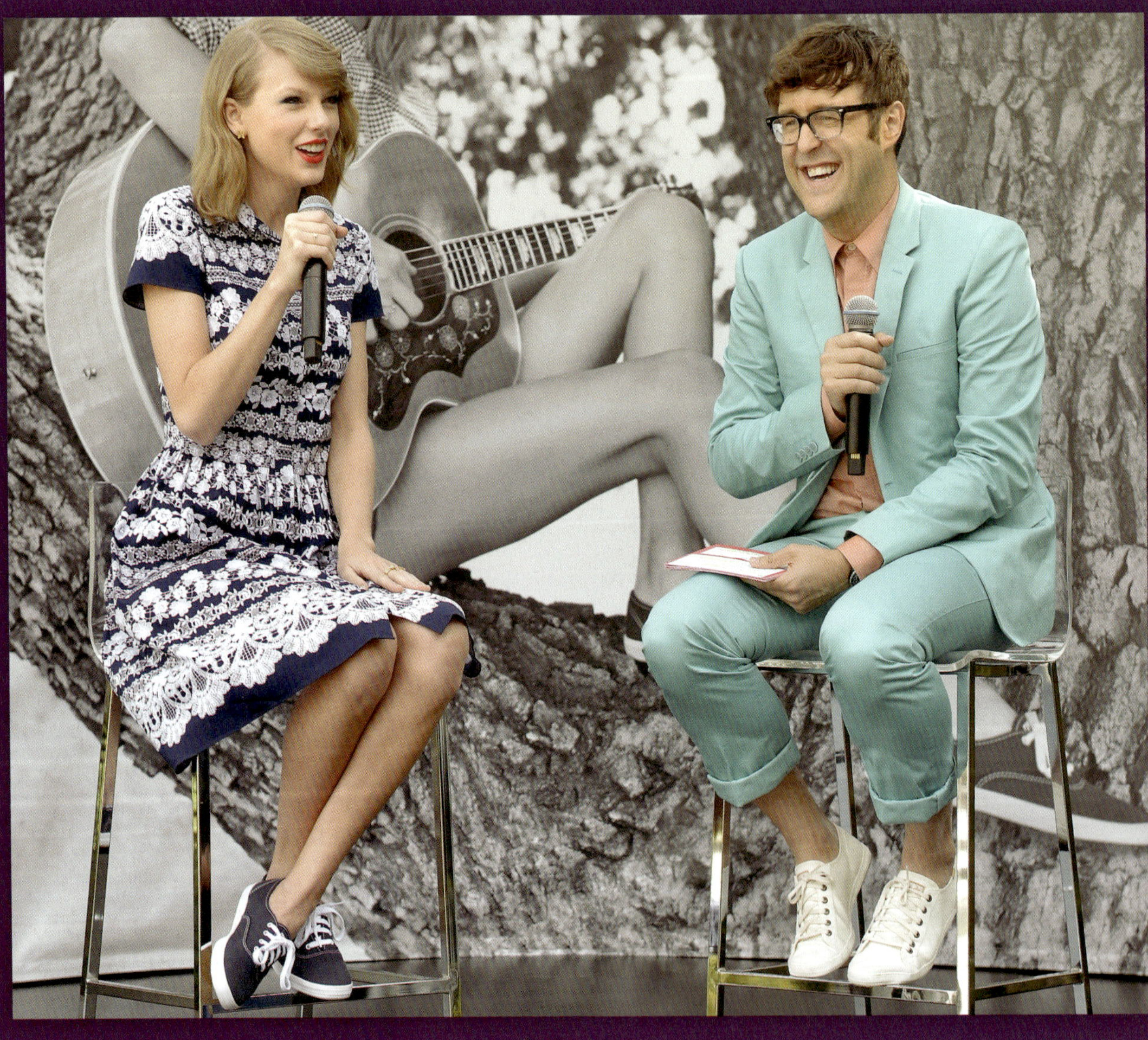

Taylor sits down with *Teen Vogue's* Style Features Director, Andrew Bevan, for an interview during the 'Taylor Swift for Keds: Style Icons' event in 2014

Taylor's collection brings on serious
footwear envy...

CHRISTIAN LOUBOUTIN

Louboutin boots and shoes are a TS favourite.
She often wears the brand on stage – check
out these gold boots. For the European leg of
Taylor's 2023 Eras Tour, Louboutin crafted the
custom footwear that perfectly complemented
her style and vision for each show.

Taylor also opts for Christian Louboutin heels for
her red carpet appearances. The signature red
soles and classic designs add an extra touch of
timeless elegance to her outfits.

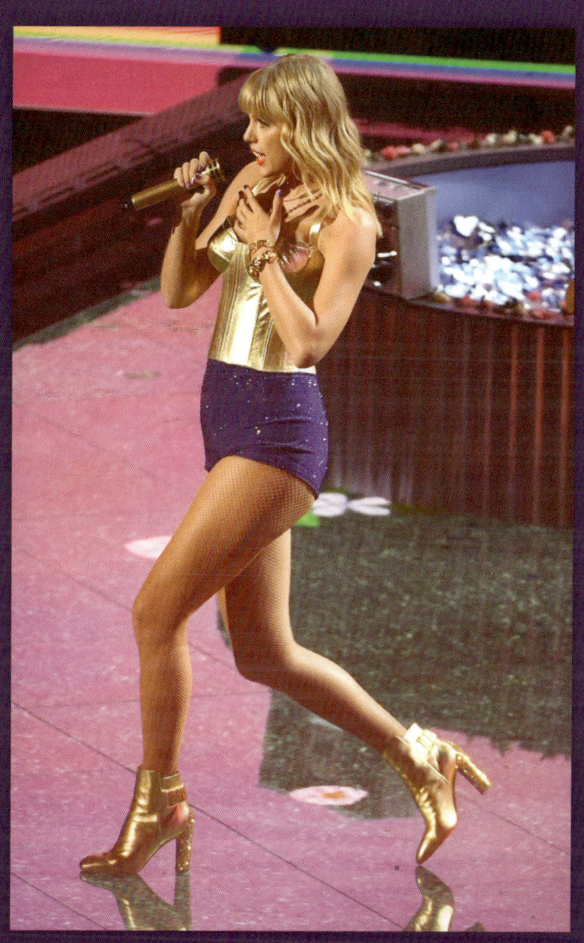

JIMMY CHOO

Taylor loves Jimmy Choo's glamorous sandals,
especially those embellished with crystals or
metallic finishes. These are often worn at awards
shows and high-profile events such as the 27th
annual GLAAD Media Awards in 2016.

GUCCI

Taylor sported these $2,400 Gucci knee-high
snake boots to an album listening party in 2017.

She also wears Gucci's more casual shoes, like
these loafers, during her off-duty days.

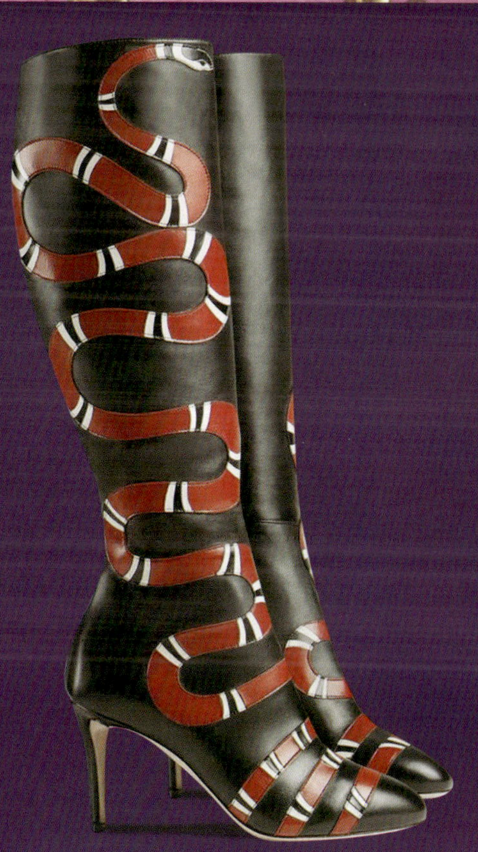

STUART WEITZMAN

Taylor often wears Stuart Weitzman's iconic over-the-knee boots, especially during the autumn and winter months. These boots pair well with mini dresses or skinny jeans.

For a sleek and minimalist look, she's a fan of Stuart Weitzman's Nudist sandals, which have a barely-there design that complements a variety of outfits.

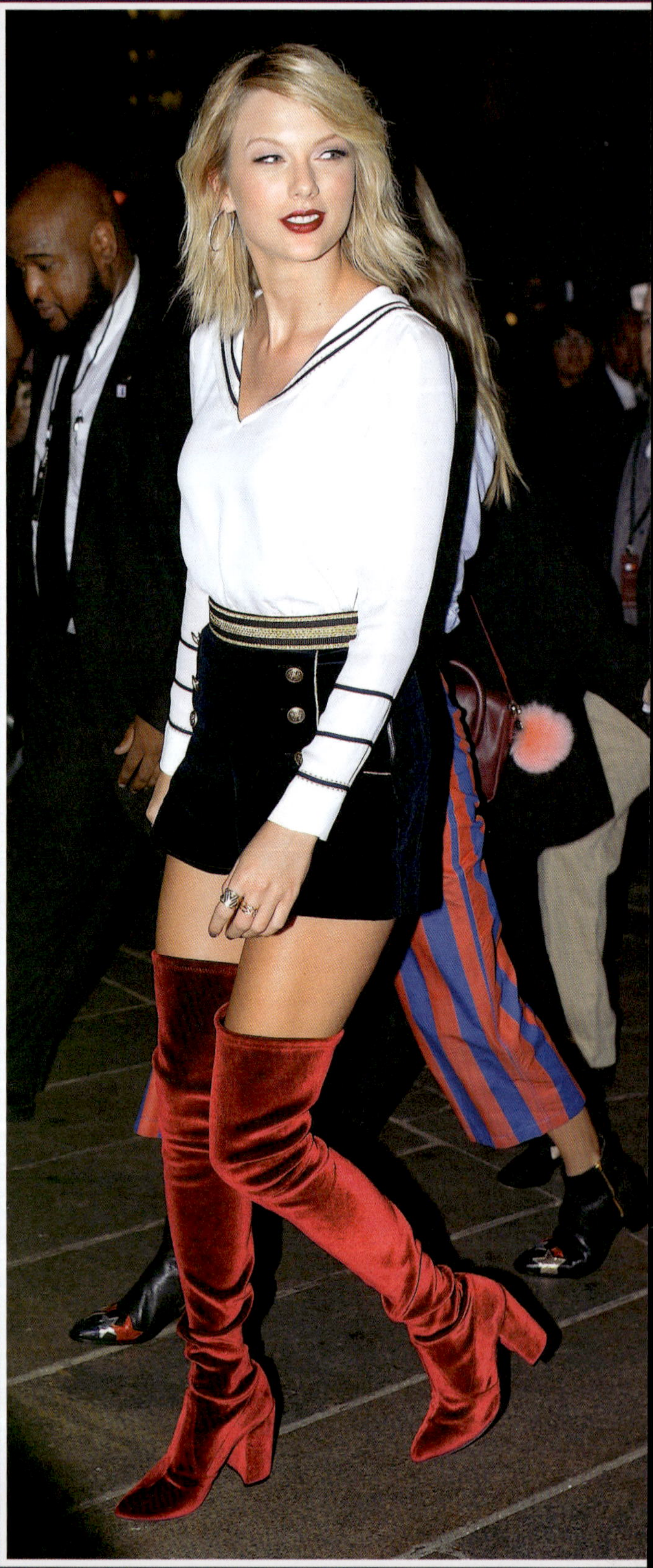

PRADA

Prada's elegant heels offer a mix of sophistication and modern style – just like Taylor herself.

Prada's chic ankle boots are a standout favourite, often worn during the cooler months.

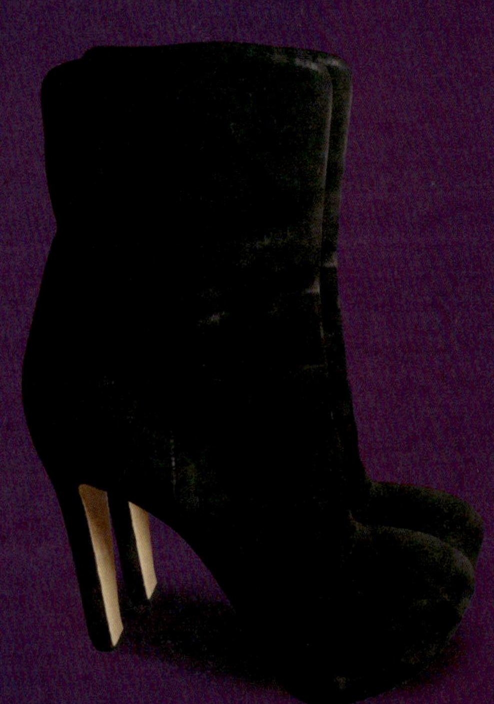

CHANEL

Taylor has been seen in Chanel's timeless ballet flats, which are perfect for adding a touch of polish to a casual look.

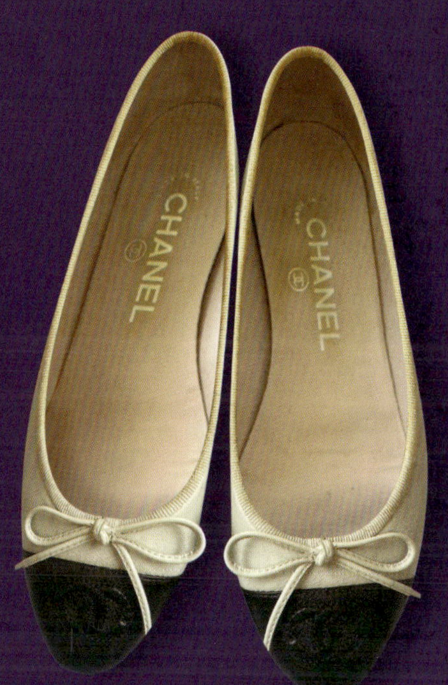

KEDS

Casual and cute! Taylor famously collaborated with Keds and often wears their classic sneakers, reflecting her girl-next-door charm. She even designed a line of Keds, featuring fun patterns and colours.

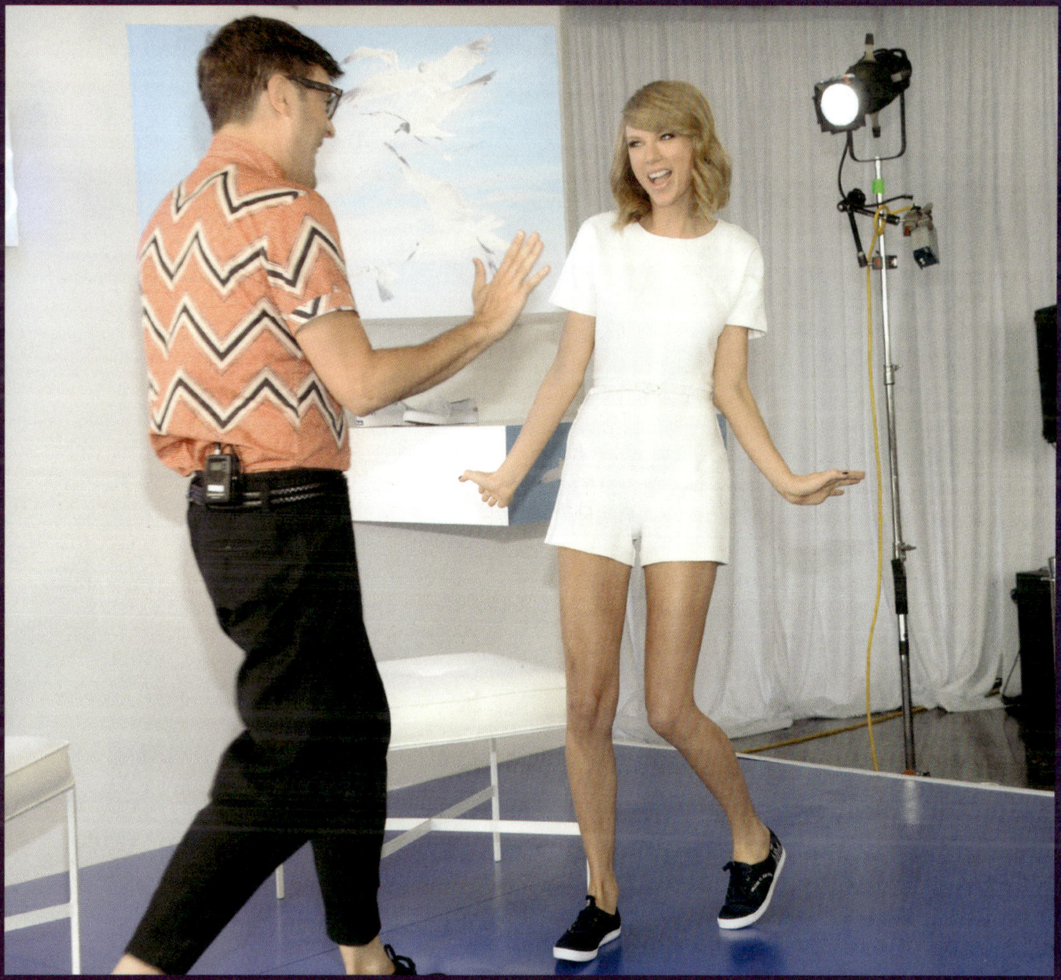

IN THE RED

CHAPTER FOUR

2012-2013

Taylor's *Red* era (2012-2013) was a time of significant evolution in her fashion sense, reflecting the bold and passionate themes of the album, entitled, of course, *Red*. Just as *Red* was a ground-breaking moment in Swift's musical transition from country star to pop star, it was also a pivotal time in her style evolution. Swift was 22 when the album came out, and when she started to leave behind some of the styles of her teenage years. She traded flowing curls for sharp, sharp, straight looks and princessy gowns for high-waisted short-shorts and edgy hats, and naturally, she wore lots of bright red — clothing and lipstick both. This period saw her embracing a mix of vintage glamour, modern chic, and sophisticated elegance, showcasing her ability to blend bold, glamorous elements with classic and modern styles. Her outfits from this period highlighted her transition into a more mature and sophisticated fashionista, reflecting the passionate and dynamic themes of her music.

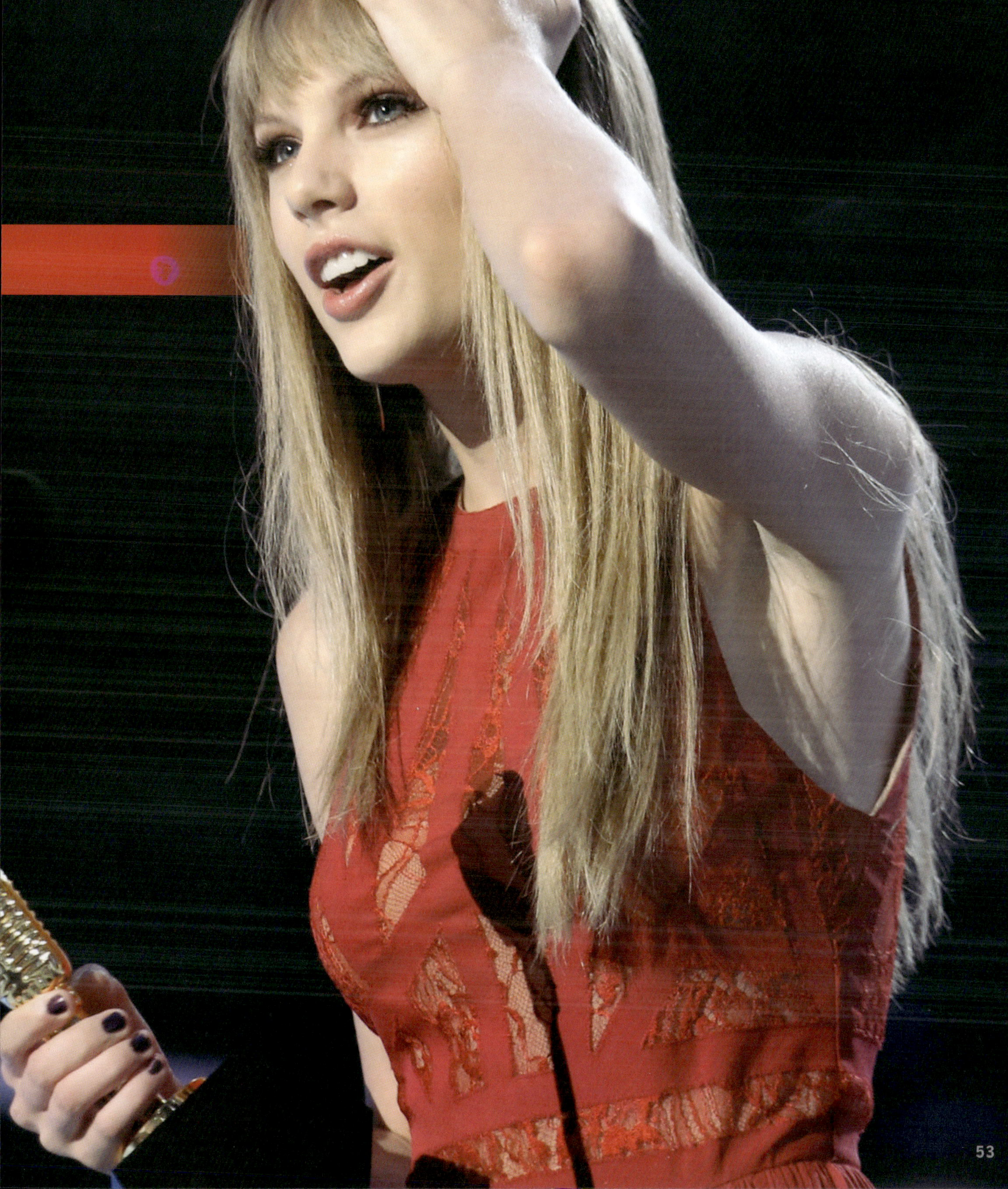

RED DRESSES

True to the album's title, Taylor frequently wore striking red dresses **during this time.** These dresses often featured bold cuts and designs that made a statement on the Red Carpet and during performances. They ranged from sleek, fitted styles to flowing gowns with dramatic skirts, showcasing a versatile approach to glamorous dressing.

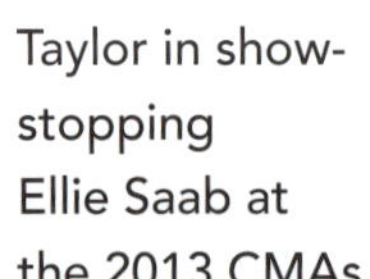

Taylor in show-stopping Ellie Saab at the 2013 CMAs

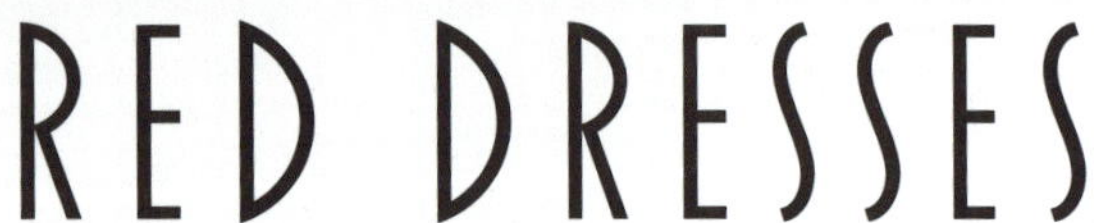

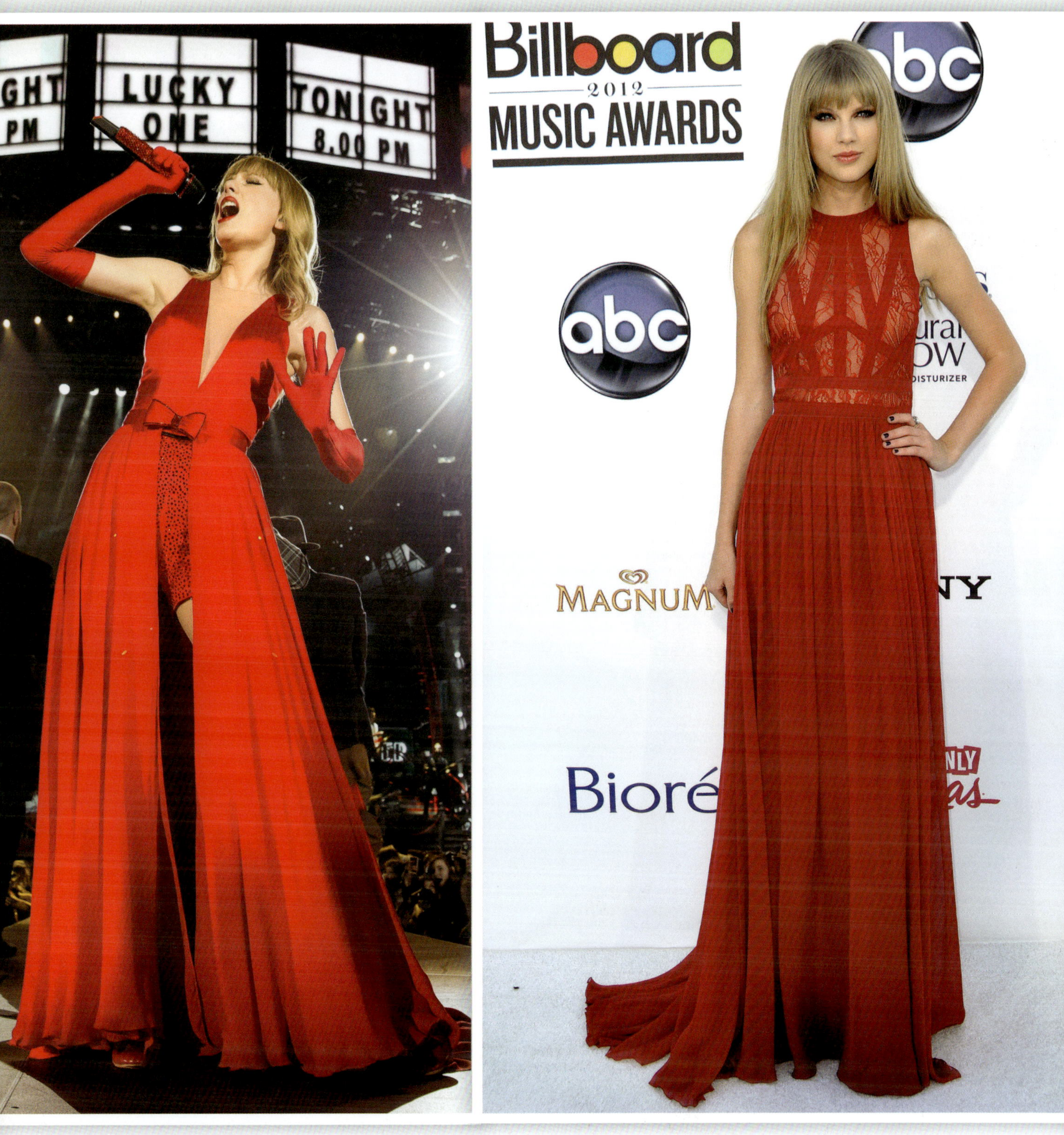

A Marina Toybina-designed costume on the *Red* Tour

Billboard Music Awards 2012 - Once known for her blond curls, Swift's 'do is now bone-straight, paired with a lacy red Ellie Saab gown featuring a trailing skirt and finished with a dark manicure

SOPHISTICATED LADY

At the 2012 MTV Video Music Awards, Taylor donned a sleek white pantsuit by J. Mendel, marking a sophisticated departure from her earlier girly dresses and establishing herself as a versatile fashion chameleon.

In a floor-length, nude-coloured gown embellished with intricate gold beading and embroidery by Ellie Saab at the ARIA Awards in 2012

Taking sophistication to a new level in a sleek white pantsuit by J. Mendel at the 2012 MTV Video Music Awards

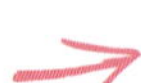

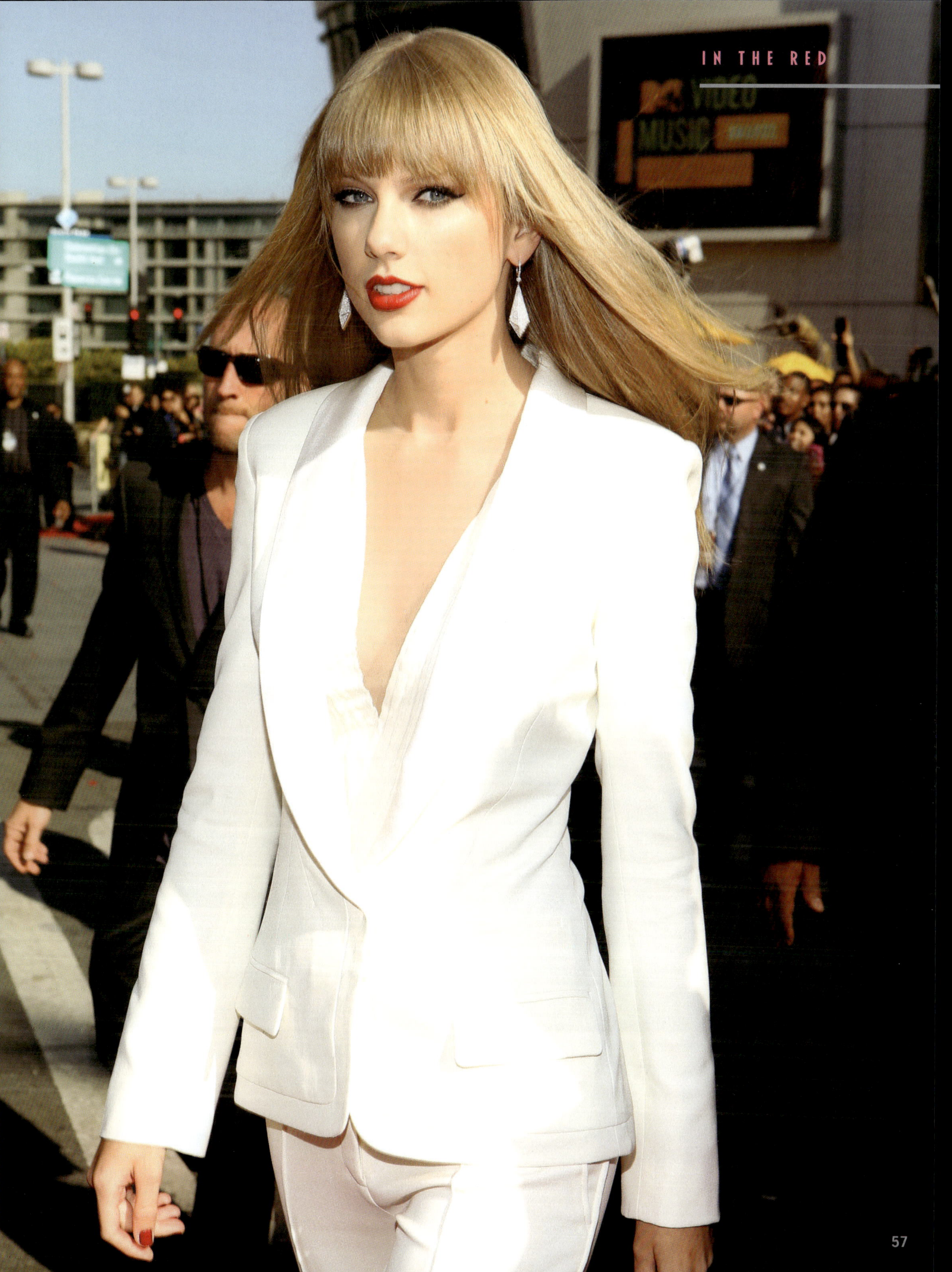

VIDEO
MUSIC

SHORTS!

Taylor often wore high-waisted shorts during her *Red* tour. These shorts became a signature part of her stage outfits during this era, reflecting a fun and youthful vibe that matched the energetic and vibrant feel of the album. She paired the shorts with various tops, including striped T-shirts, sequined or glittery tops, and tailored blouses, often completing the look with her signature red lip and a choice between ankle boots or oxford shoes.

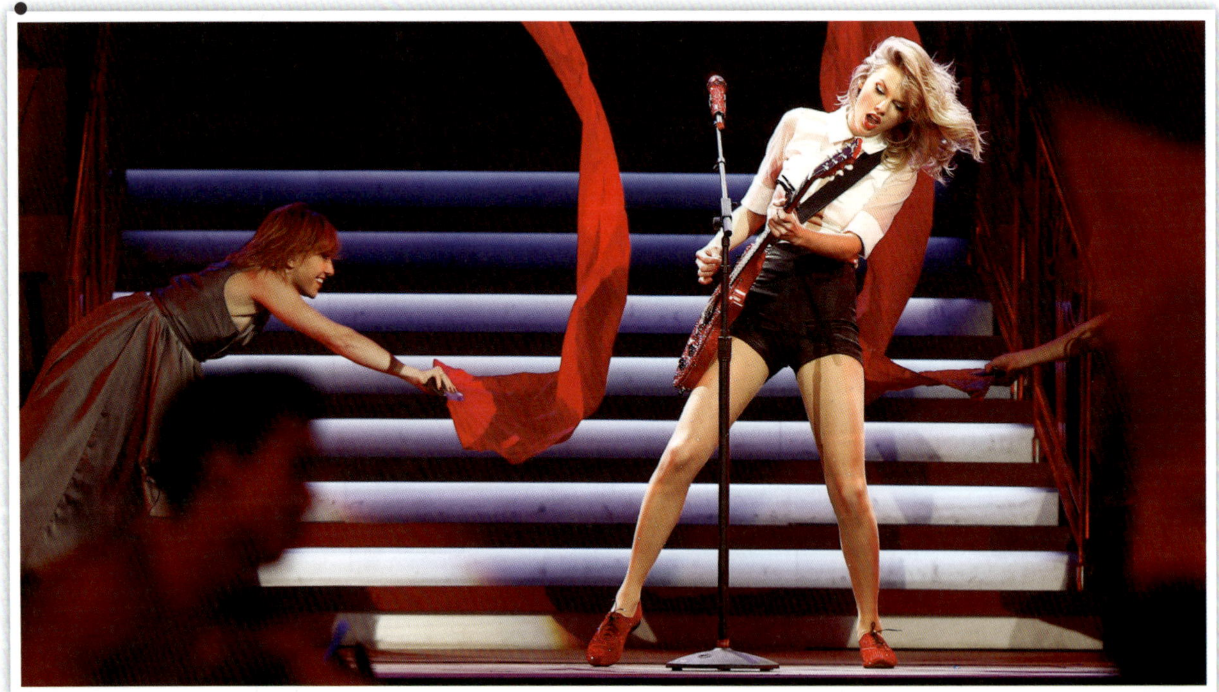

Taylor paired black shorts with a white blouse in Germany during the European leg of The Red Tour

Sparkles and shorts on stage. In December 2012 at the Jingle Ball Performance, New York City, Taylor rocked a pair of high-waisted shorts and a sparkly top

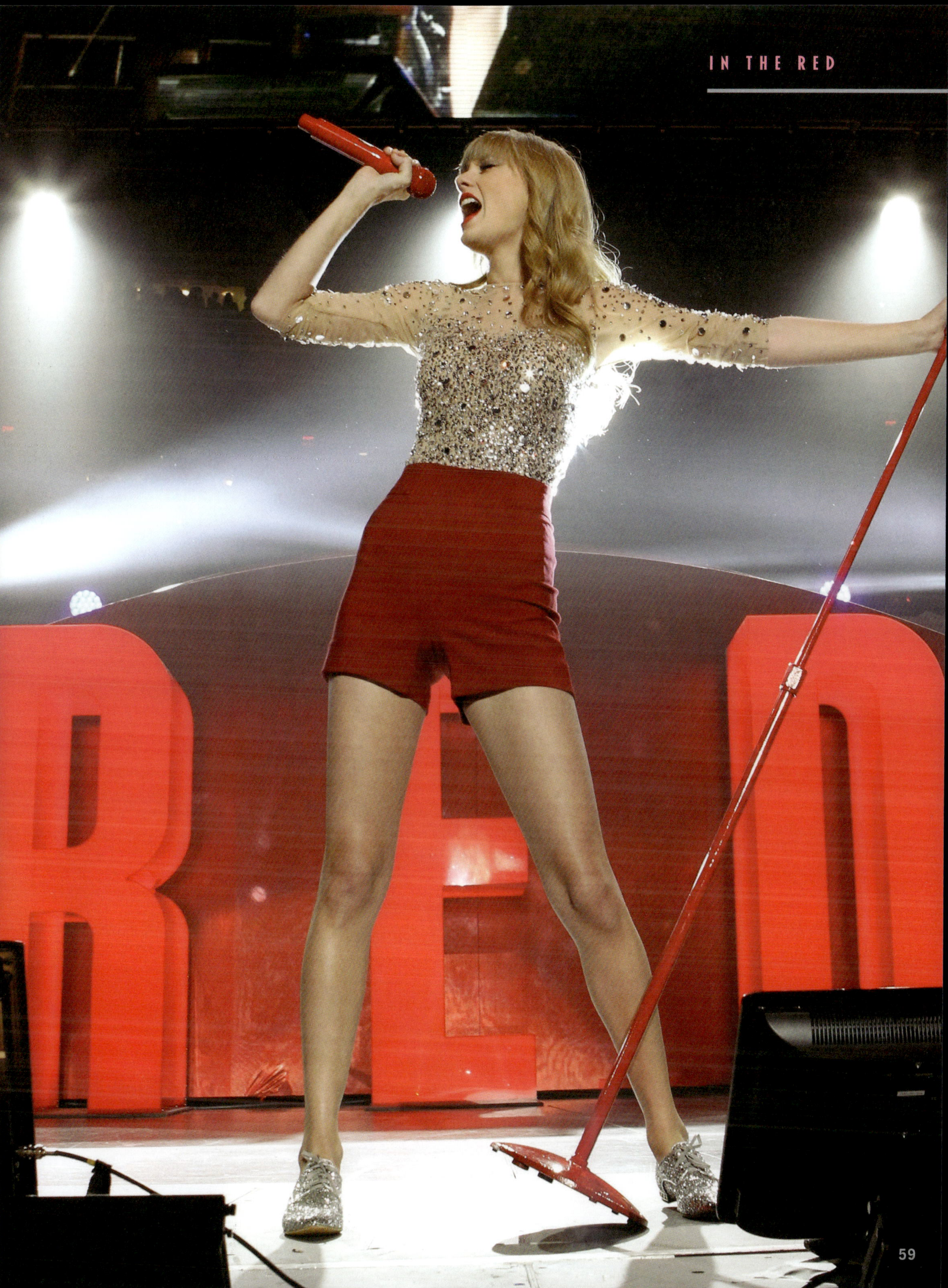

HAIR

During the *Red* era, Taylor often wore her hair straight and sleek, reflecting a more polished and sophisticated look. However, she occasionally reverted to her old ways, styling her hair in 'old school' soft waves.

MAKEUP

We're talking bold and dramatic. The lips? Red of course! The shade perfectly complemented her outfits and matched the album's theme. Brand favourites were said to be Mac's Ruby Woo, NARS Velvet Matte Lip Pencil in Dragon Girl and Cover Girl's Exhibitionist Cream Lipstick in Hot. Eyebrows were well groomed and defined, adding to her polished appearance. The eyes themselves enhanced with smoky eye makeup or winged eyeliner, enhancing her dramatic and glamorous look.

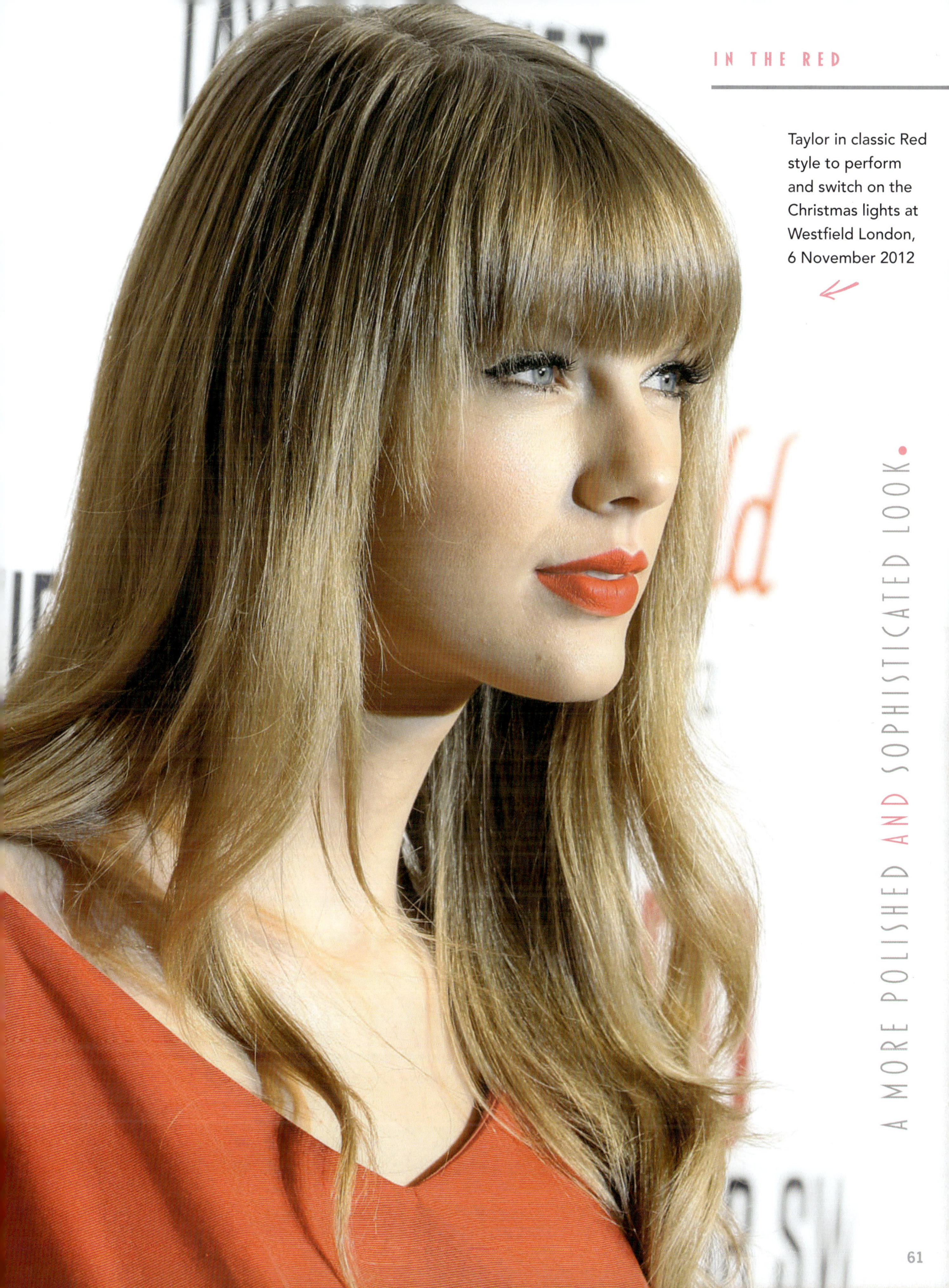

Taylor in classic Red style to perform and switch on the Christmas lights at Westfield London, 6 November 2012

A MORE POLISHED AND SOPHISTICATED LOOK.

IT'S 1989

CHAPTER FIVE

2014-2015

Taylor's *1989* era (2014-2015) marked a significant shift in her fashion journey, **reflecting her transition from US country star to global superstar.** Embracing the vibrant and youthful energy of the 1980s and paying tribute to the decade of her birth – which she had just managed to squeeze into – this era was characterized by a more modern and edgy style, both on and off stage, which also influenced her more formal appearances.

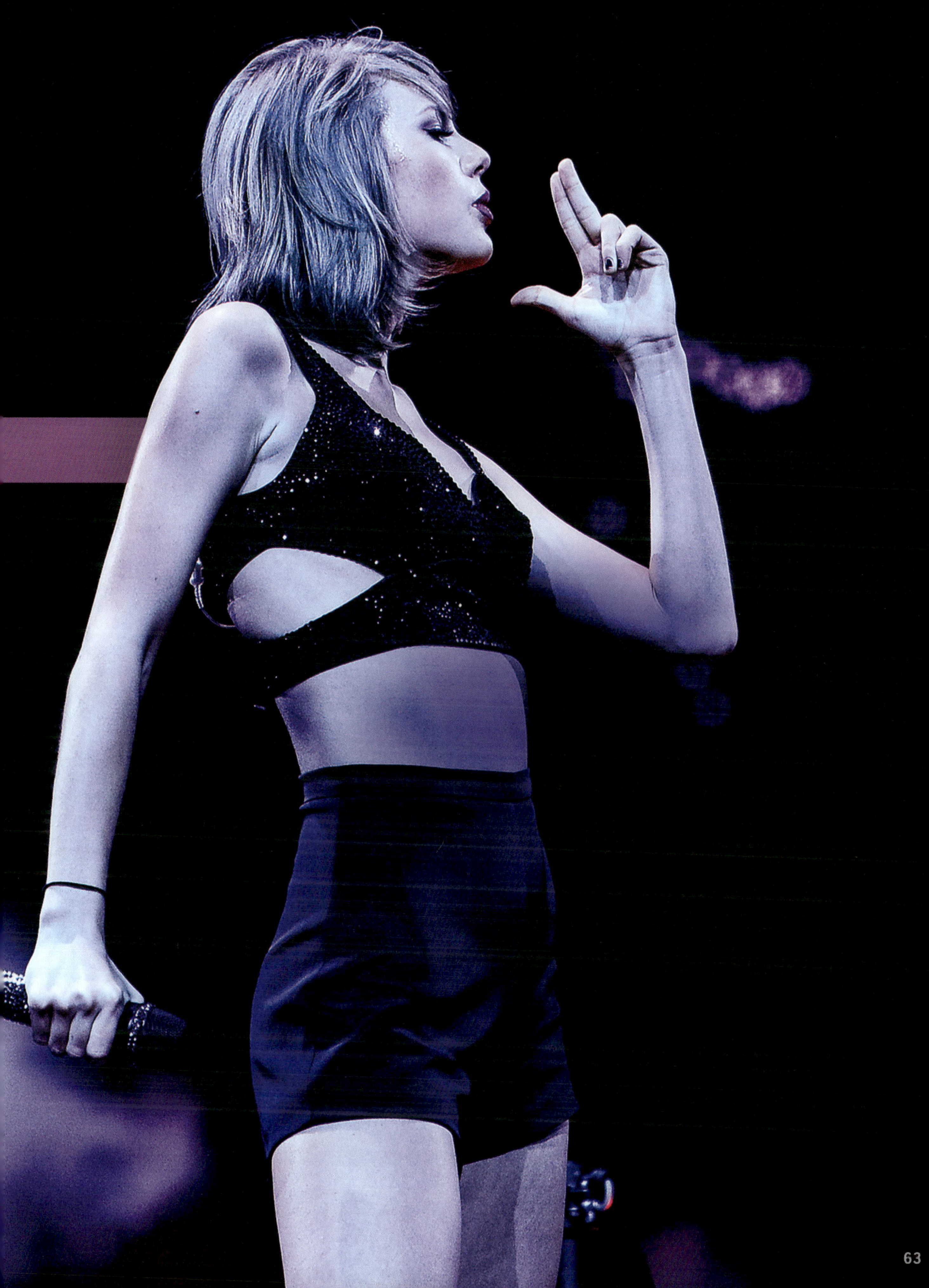

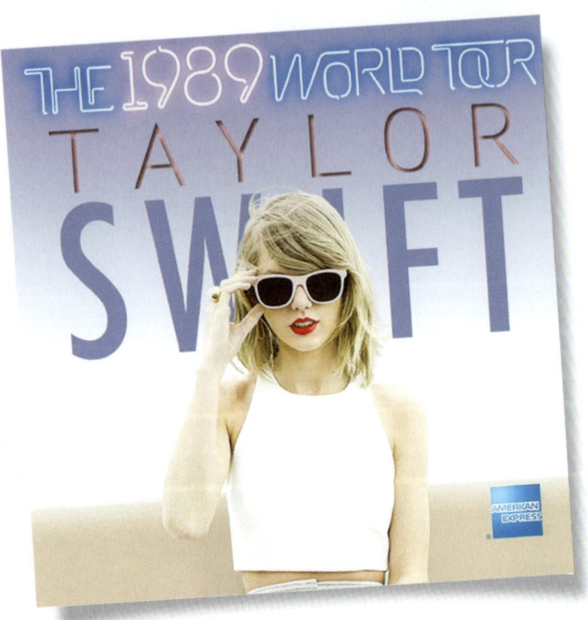

BOLD AND EDGY

Taylor embraced the trend of crop tops, often pairing them with high-waisted skirts or trousers. These ensembles – some matching some not – featured bold patterns, bright colours, shiny fabrics and sleek designs, reflecting the fun aspect of the 1980s. The combination created an uber stylish and retro-themed silhouette. She wore pieces with bold patterns, such as stripes, polka dots, and geometric designs to give a certain edge. The costumes for Taylor Swift's *1989* World Tour were designed by a combination of high-profile fashion designers in including Taylor's go-to costume designer Jessica Jones; British designer Ashish Gupta who created several sequined pieces for the tour; Arab designer Yousef Aljasmi; and Lebanese designer Zuhair Murad.

The *1989* World Tour promotional artwork 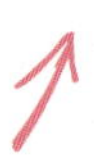

More purple and multicoloured shimmers in a Jessica Jones sequined jacket, skirt and crop top at the *1989* World Tour in St Louis, 2015

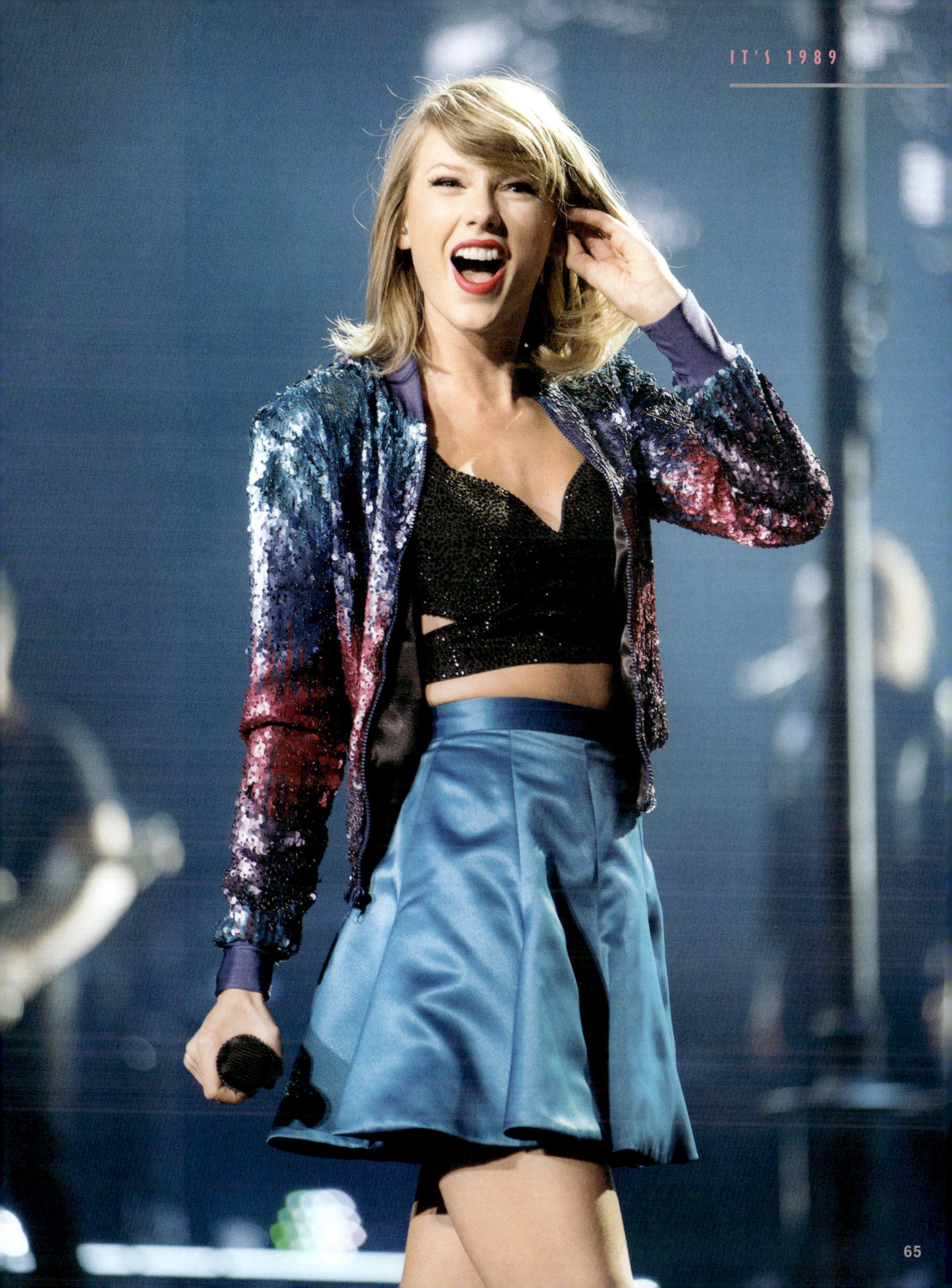

SUITS YOU!

Taylor wore tailored blazers and matching skirts, trousers and even shorts, often featuring sleek, monochrome colours. This added a sophisticated touch to her modern, pop-inspired wardrobe. She also wore structured dresses with clean lines and minimalistic designs, reflecting a chic and polished look.

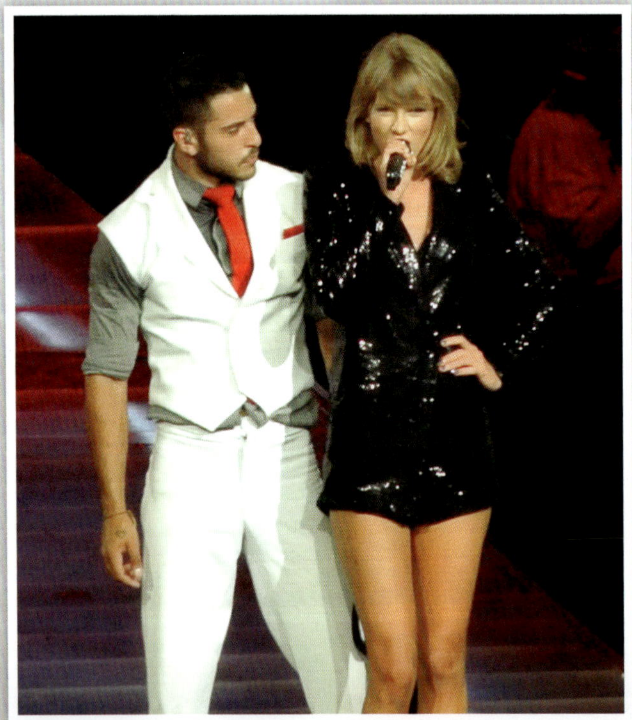

Taylor performs in a black, fully sequined suit ensemble by Kaufman Franco during The 1989 World Tour, 2015

Taylor steps out in New York City looking chic in a tailored blazer, 1 April, 2014

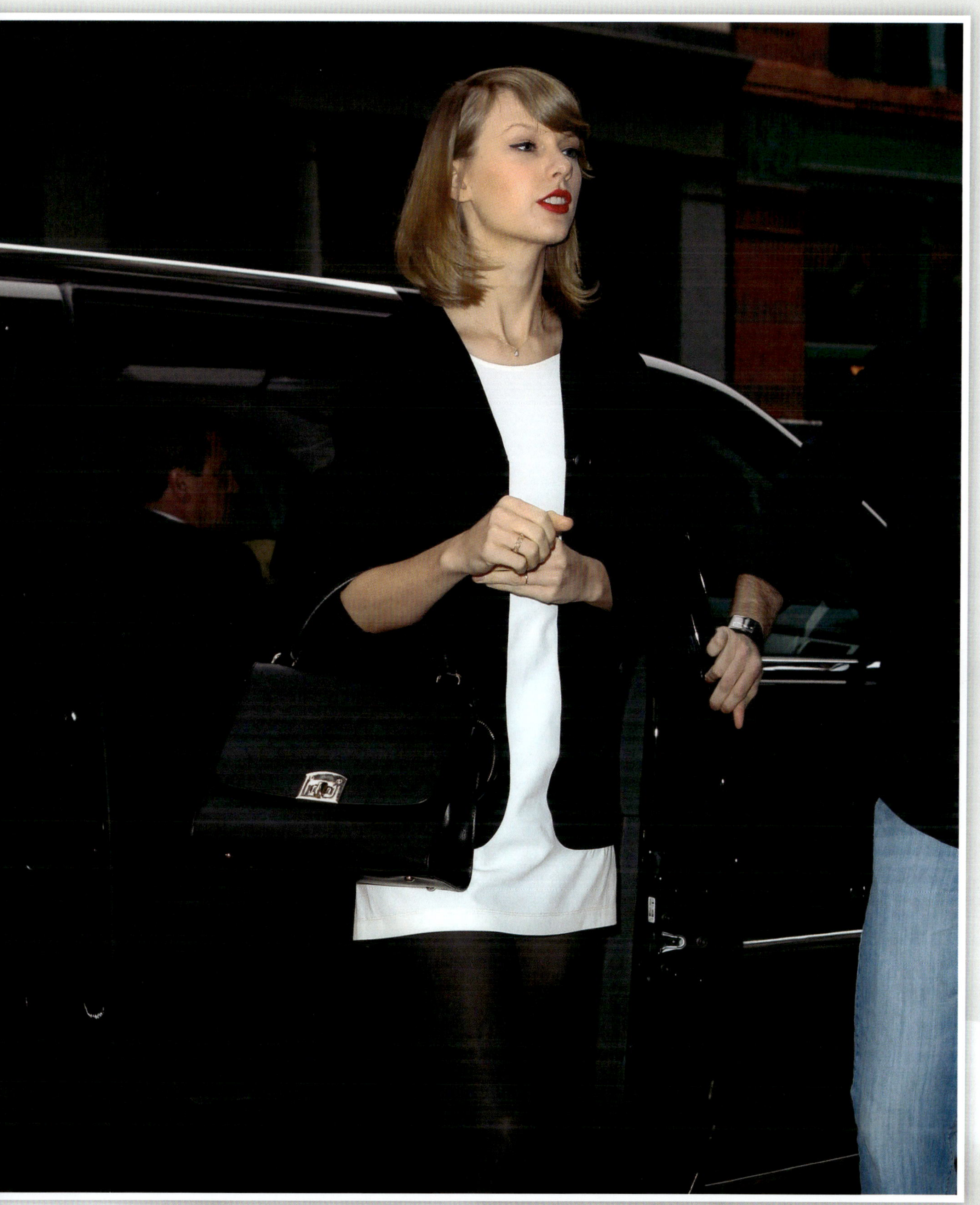

EVENT DRESSING

The minimalist theme extended to Taylor's red carpet and more formal appearances. While often drawn to sparkle, Swift embraced simplicity and classic elegance for many events, opting for clean, structured silhouettes. She often kept accessories understated, choosing statement rings and bold earrings over more elaborate jewellery.

Taylor is the epitome of sleek sophistication in this stunning metallic, floor-length gown by Julien Macdonald at the 2014 Vanity Fair Oscar Party

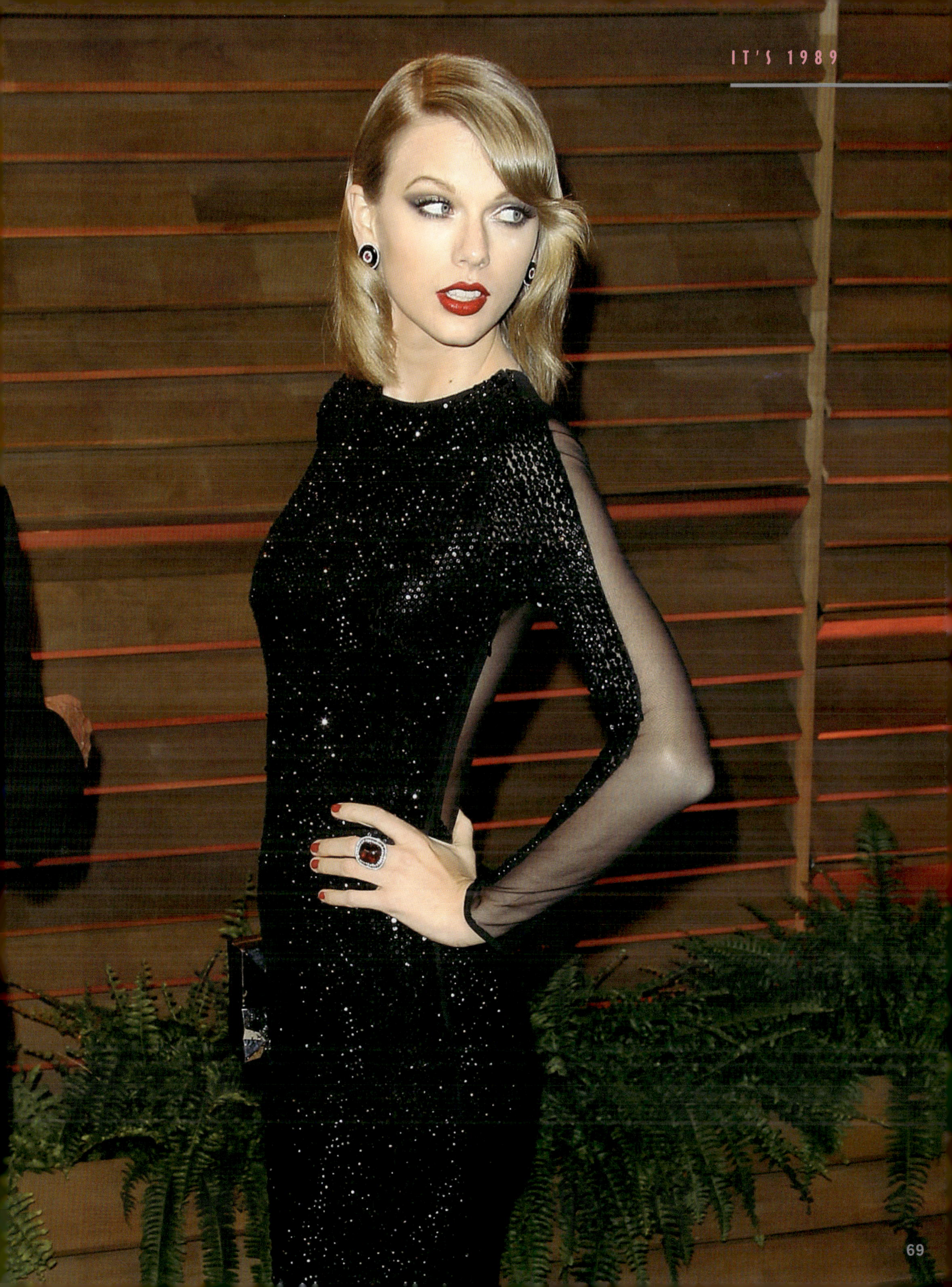

HAIR

During the *1989* era, Taylor debuted a chic bob with a sleek, **straightened look.** She often styled her bob with a deep side parting, adding to its modern aesthetic.

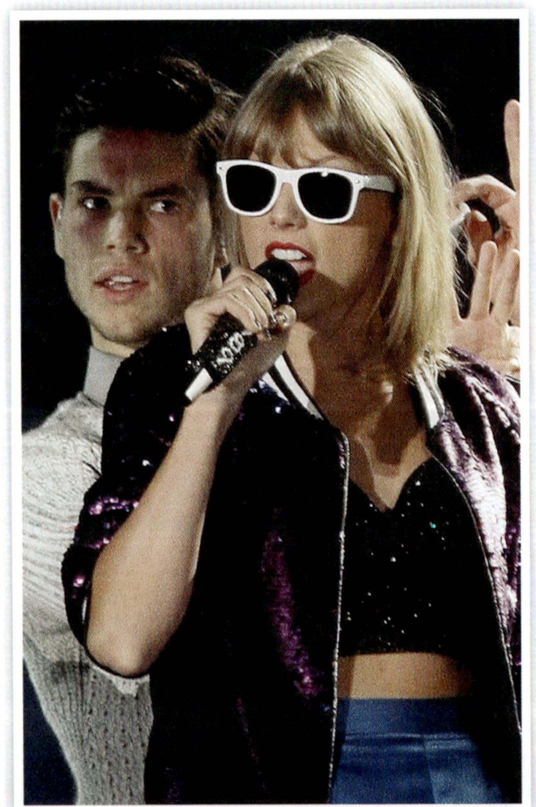

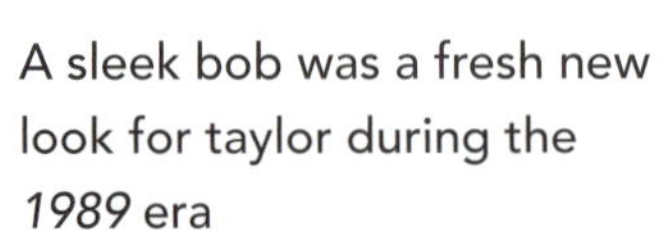

A sleek bob was a fresh new look for taylor during the *1989* era

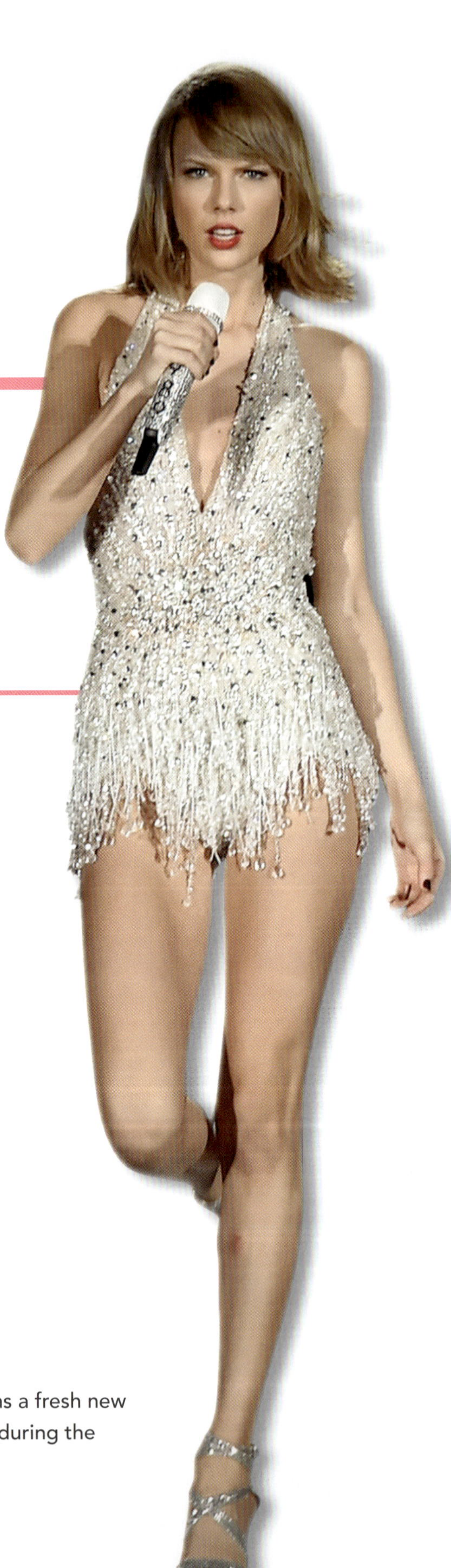

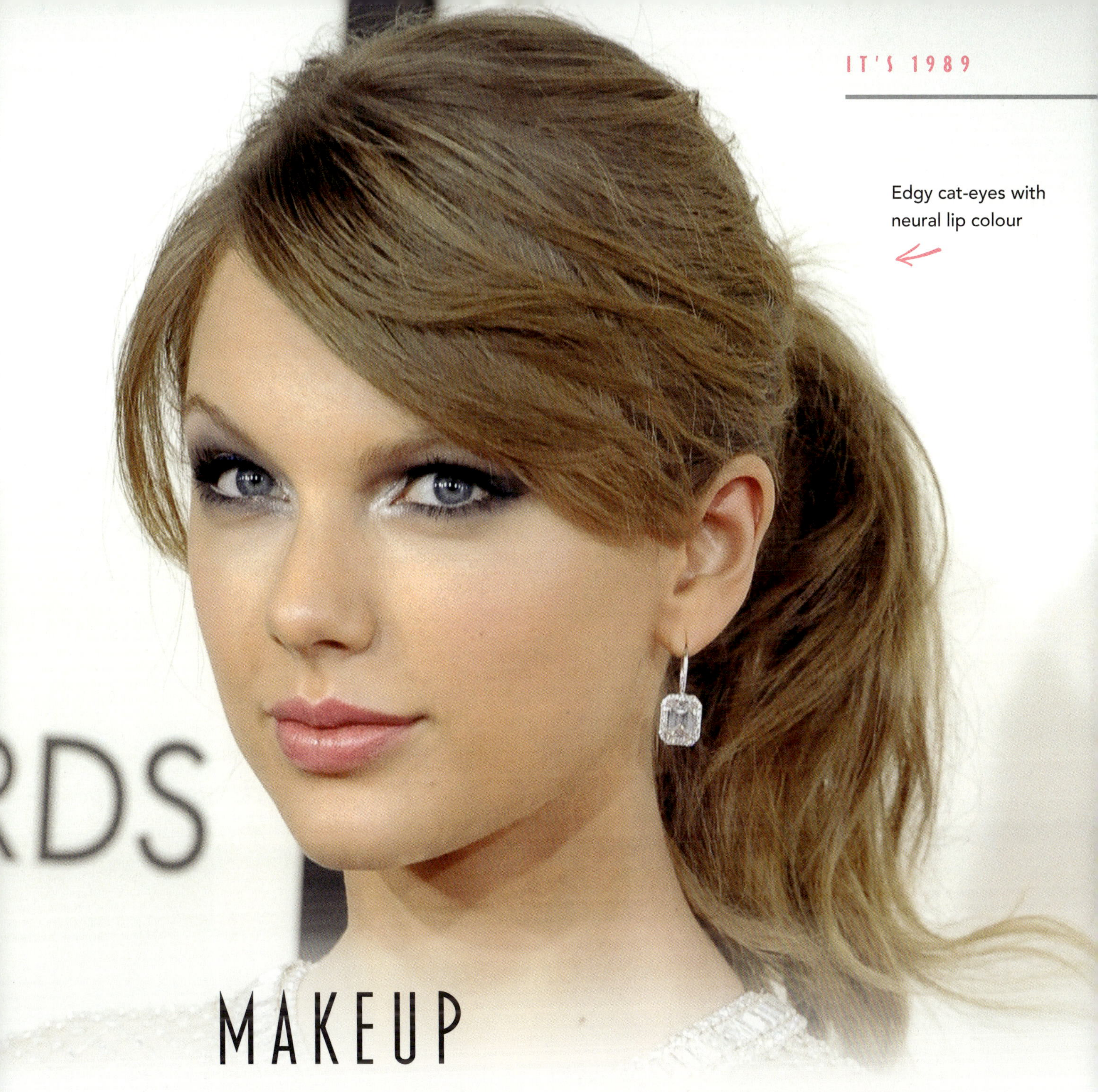

MAKEUP

Taylor frequently wore bold eyeliner, including winged and cat-eye styles, which **complemented the edgy, 1980s-inspired fashion.** Her lip colour during this era was usually neutral or nude, balancing the dramatic eye makeup.

BAG LADY!

Taylor's diverse and stylish handbag collection is the stuff of dreams! The girl is a genius when it comes to selecting purses that complement her outfits - whether that be on the Red Carpet, performing on stage, or out and about in her everyday life.

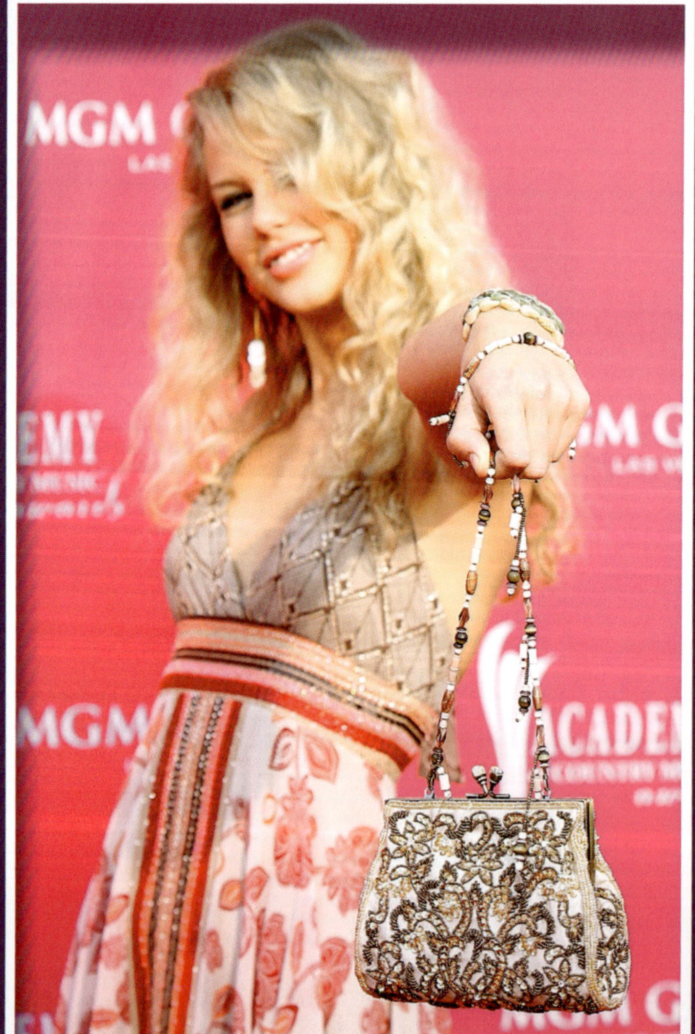

Taylor shows off her bag when arriving at the Country Music Awards at the MGM Grand Garden Arena in Las Vegas, 2006

PRADA

Taylor often opts for Prada's classic tote bags, which are both functional and stylish, perfect for her more polished, sophisticated looks. The Prada Galleria bag, known for its timeless design, is one of her go-to choices for a sleek and elegant appearance.

DOLCE & GABBANA

Taylor often carries the Dolce & Gabbana Sicily bag, which is a structured top-handle bag that adds a touch of even more class.

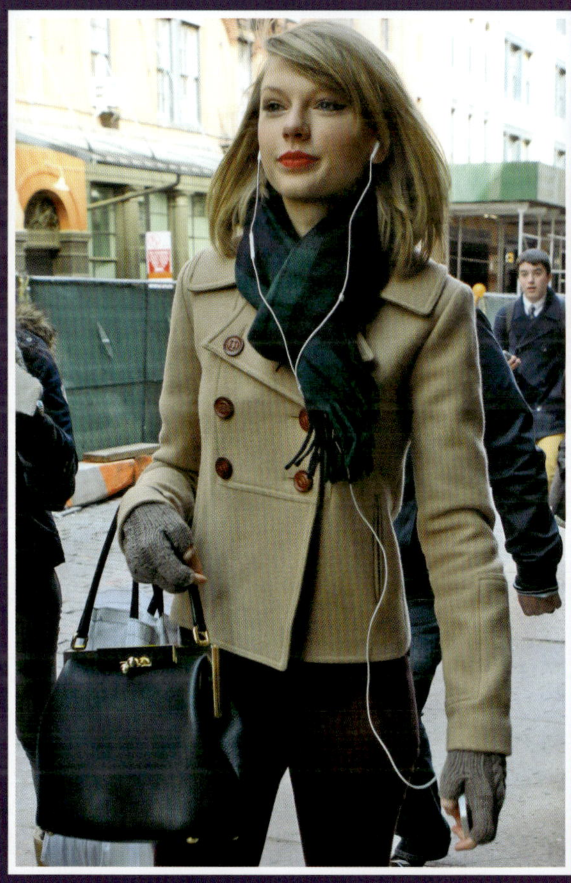

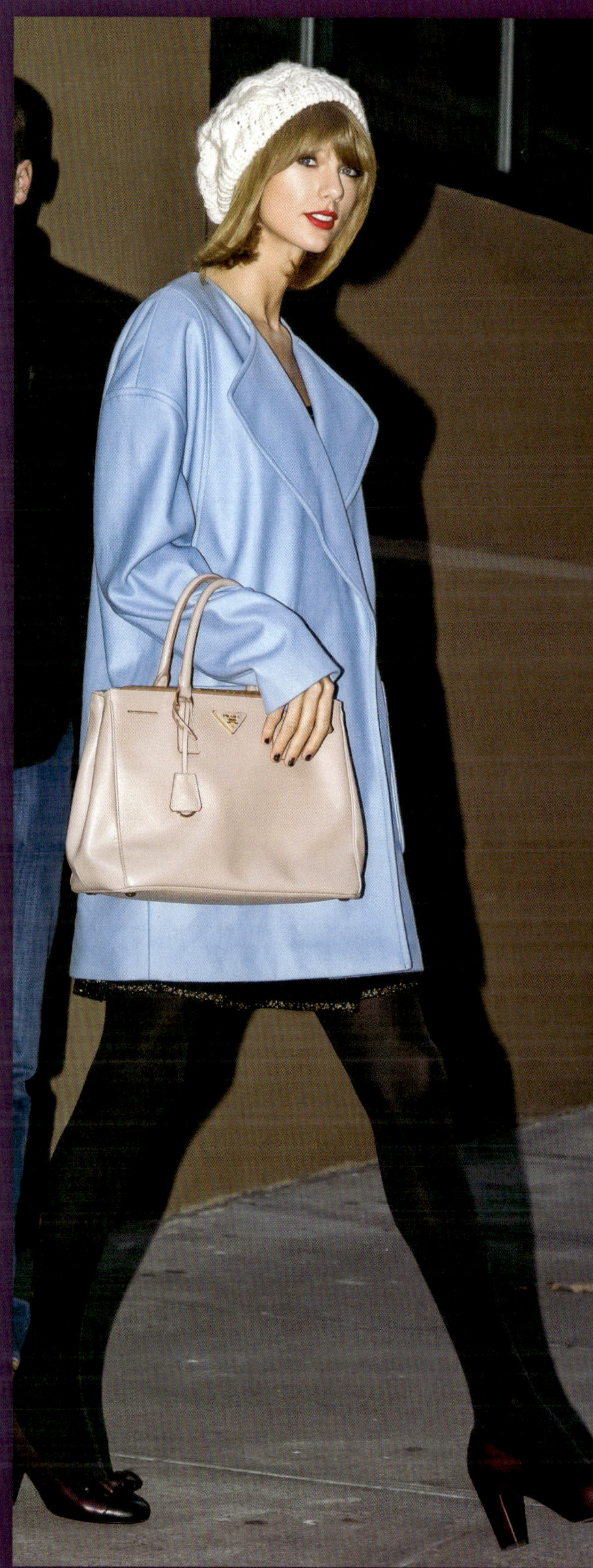

GUCCI

Taylor has a penchant for Gucci's vintage-inspired handbags that add a retro-chic vibe to her outfits.

She's been spotted with the GG Marmont bag, a versatile piece that works well with both casual and dressed-up looks.

LOUIS VUITTON

TS is fan of LV. She has been seen carrying the Louis Vuitton Limited Edition Shopping Bag, which was designed in a collaboration with Christian Louboutin. Taylor is also a fan of the classic Louis Vuitton Capucine bag, which is known for its understated luxury and timeless style.

Another favourite is the LV Petite Malle, as seen here, a mini trunk-inspired bag that adds an edgy and fashionable touch to her outfits.

TOD'S

Taylor is also a fan of the Tod's crossbody bag. Other TS favourites in the brand's range include the understatedly elegant Wave bag and Tod's D-Styling bag.

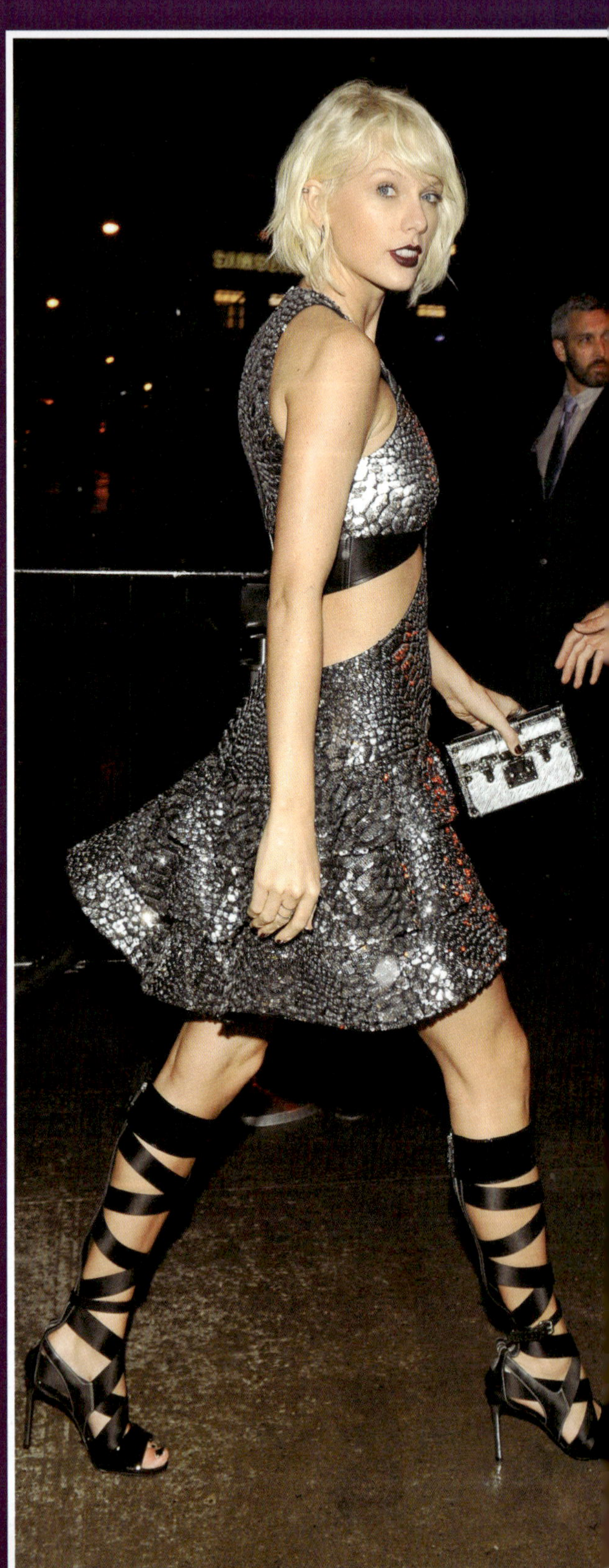

MICHAEL KORS

Taylor has been known to carry Michael Kors bags, particularly the Jet Set Tote, which is perfect for travel and everyday use. The bag is practical yet stylish, aligning with her on-the-go lifestyle.

She's also worn Michael Kors crossbody bags, ideal for casual outings and adding a touch of effortless chic.

MULBERRY

Taylor has shown a fondness for Mulberry's Bayswater bag, a British classic known for its craftsmanship and timeless design. It complements her love for vintage-inspired fashion.

She's also been seen with the Mulberry Alexa bag, which has a more relaxed and youthful feel, fitting her street style.

STELLA MCCARTNEY

As a friend and collaborator of Stella McCartney, Taylor has often been seen carrying Stella's Falabella bag, known for its chain detailing and eco-friendly design. It's a stylish and ethical choice that aligns with Taylor's values.

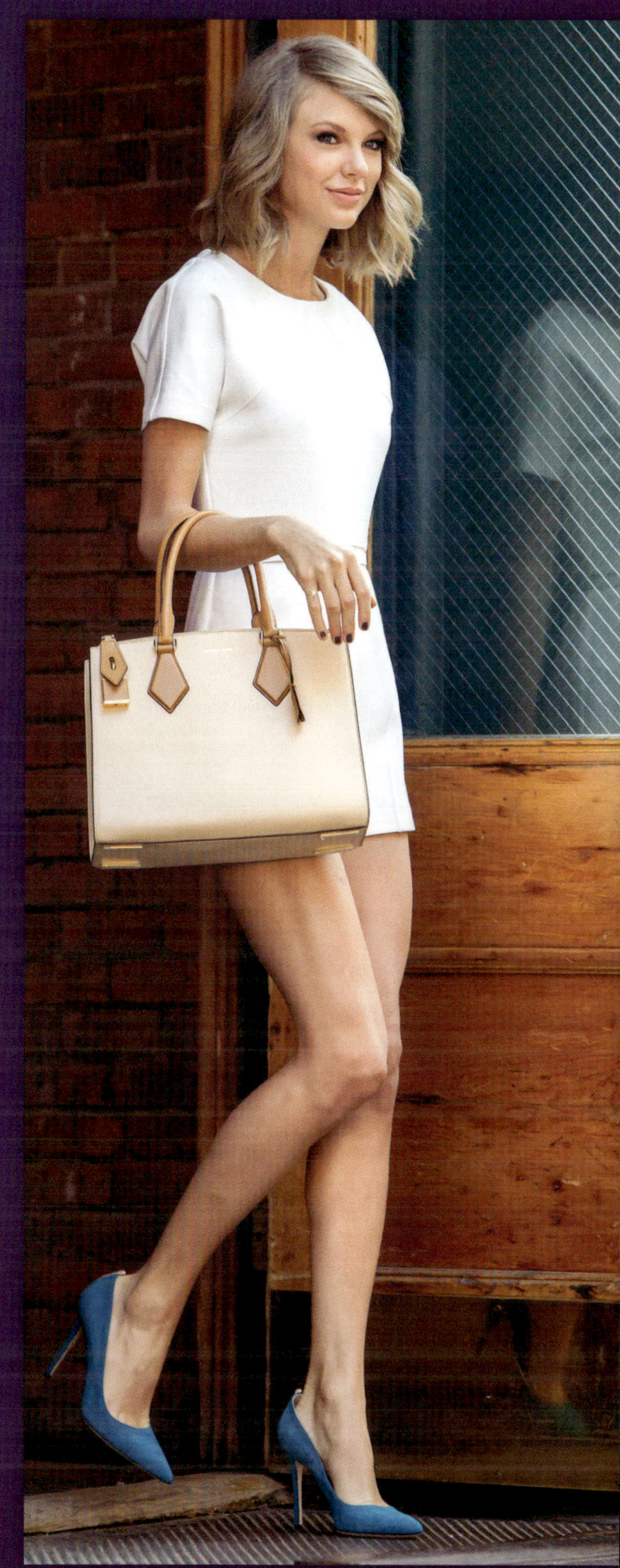

REPUTATION

ROCKS

2017-2018

Circa 2017-2018 were Taylor's *Reputation* years with her fashion undergoing a dramatic shift to match the darker, edgier tone of the album. This period was marked by a more assertive, fierce style that sharply contrasted with the more romantic and polished looks of her previous eras. Think confidence, power and a modern, rebellious spirit.

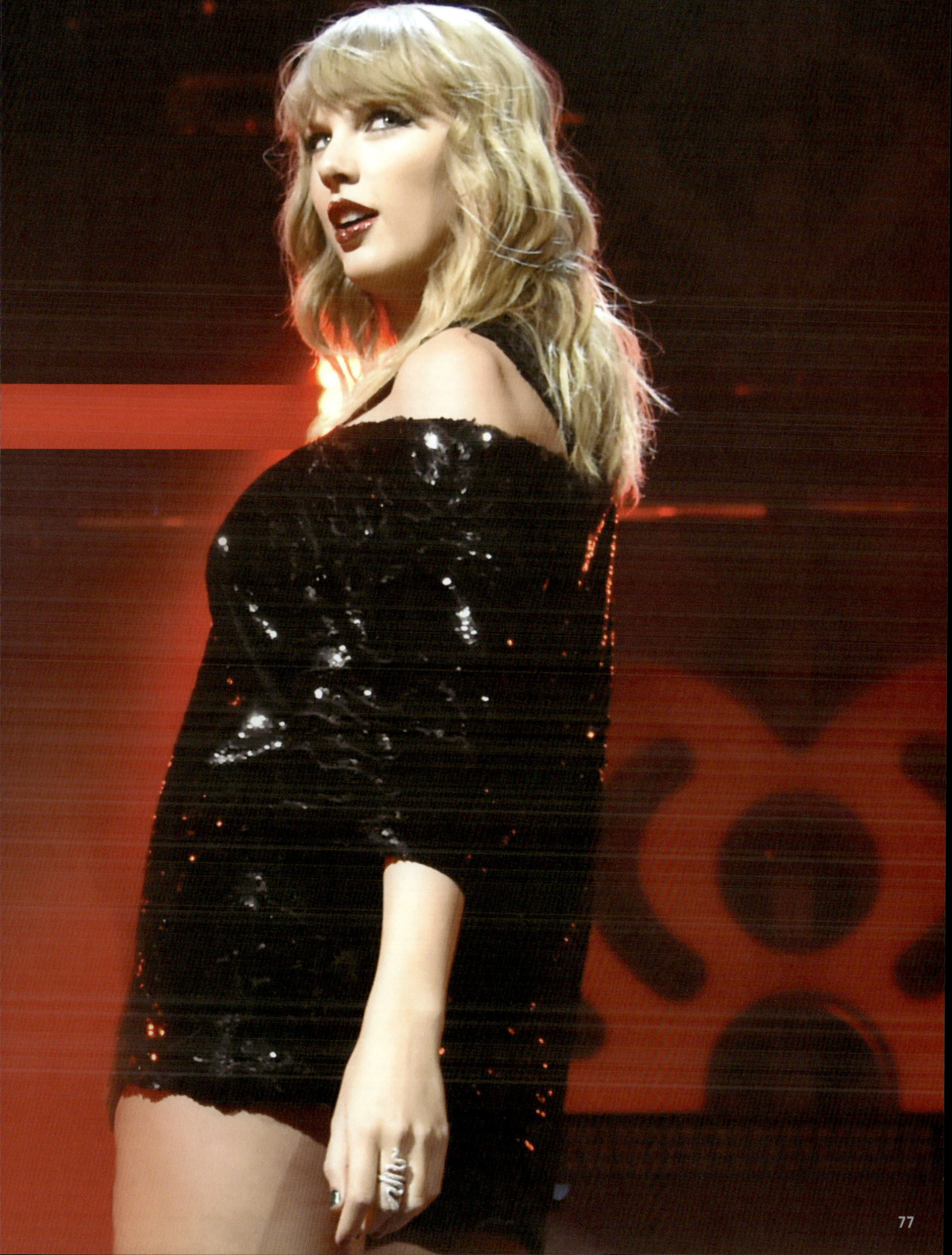

PAINT IT BLACK!

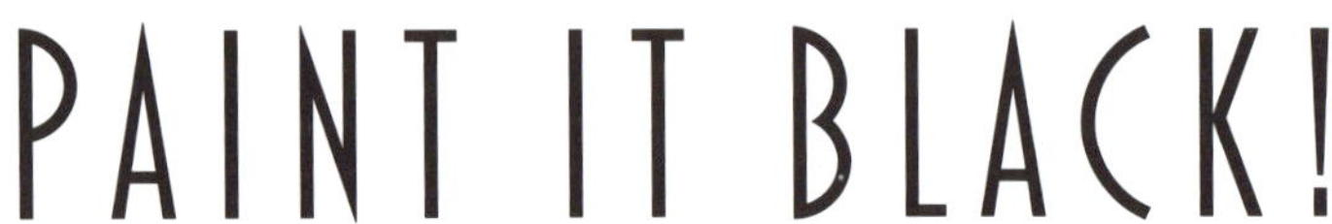

Black was a dominant colour in Taylor's wardrobe, reflecting the album's themes of reinvention and empowerment. She also incorporated metallics, such as silver and gold, adding a futuristic vibe. The use of leather and vinyl contributed to the edgy and rebellious aesthetic of the era. Taylor favoured form-fitting bodycon dresses and jumpsuits that accentuated her figure and projected confidence. Statement pieces with unique designs, such as cut-outs, embellishments, and bold patterns were also to be found in her closet. Meanwhile she was all about the boots when it came to footwear, favouring knee-high and over-the-knee boots, often in black leather or suede. Combat boots also featured prominently.

Taylor performing in a stunning black-and-gold gown embroidered with glittery chainlink details and featuring a unique split hemline

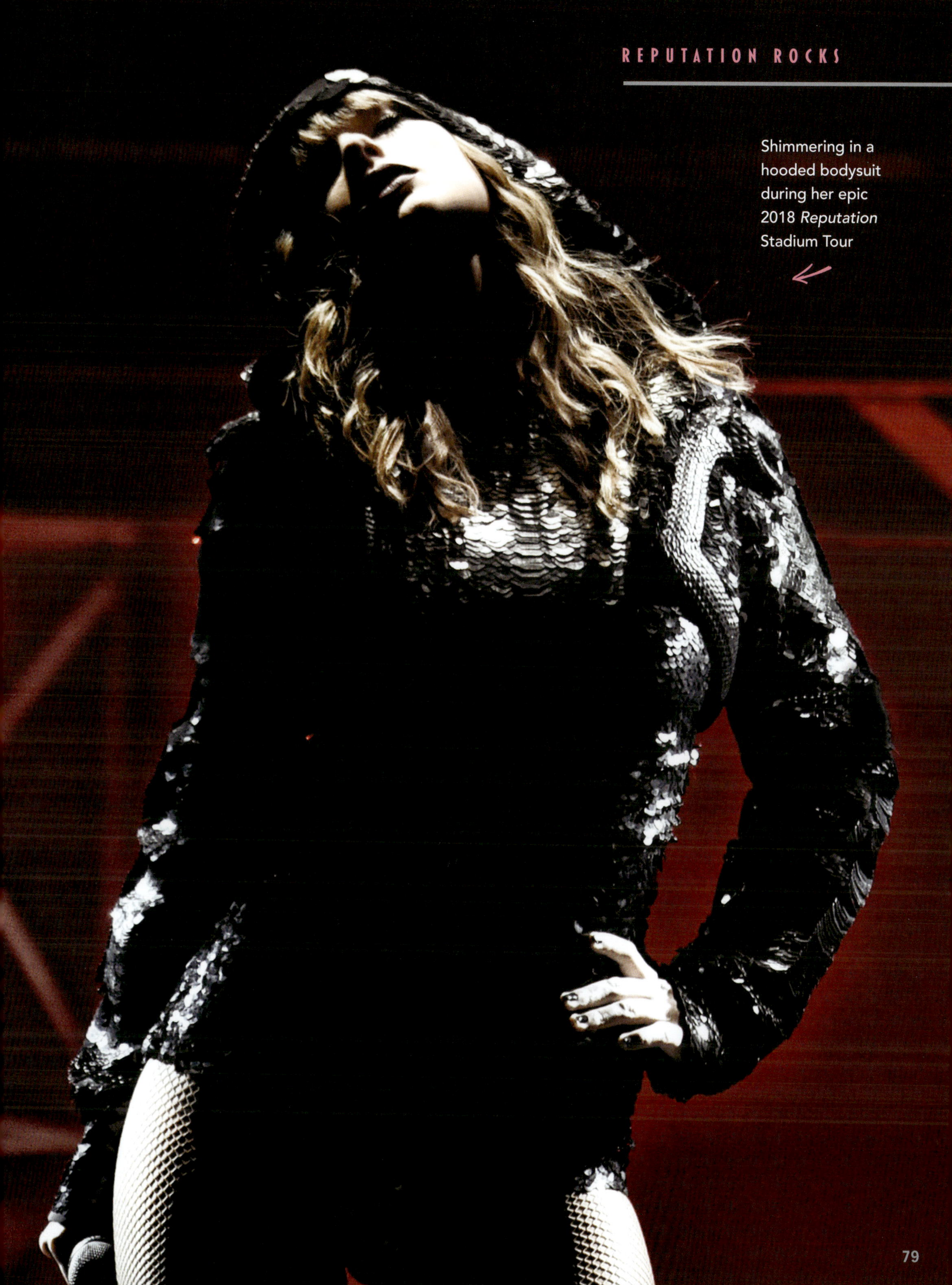

Shimmering in a hooded bodysuit during her epic 2018 *Reputation* Stadium Tour

STREET STYLE FASHION

Graphic tees were part of Taylor's street-inspired looks, often paired with leather skirts or high-waisted jeans for an edgy-meets-casual appearance. These pieces often featured bold logos or slogans, aligning with the album's themes of boldness and self-assuredness.

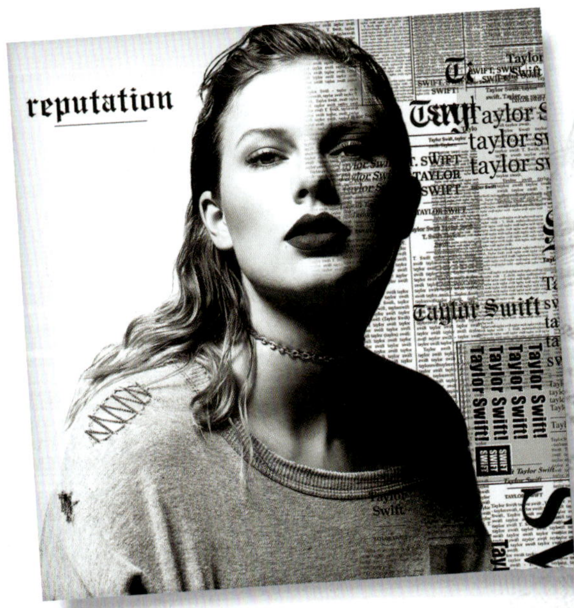

Taylor's cover shot for the *Reputation* album featuring a casual street look

Taylor out and about in New York in 2018 in a leopard-print miniskirt, worn with a loose lace tee

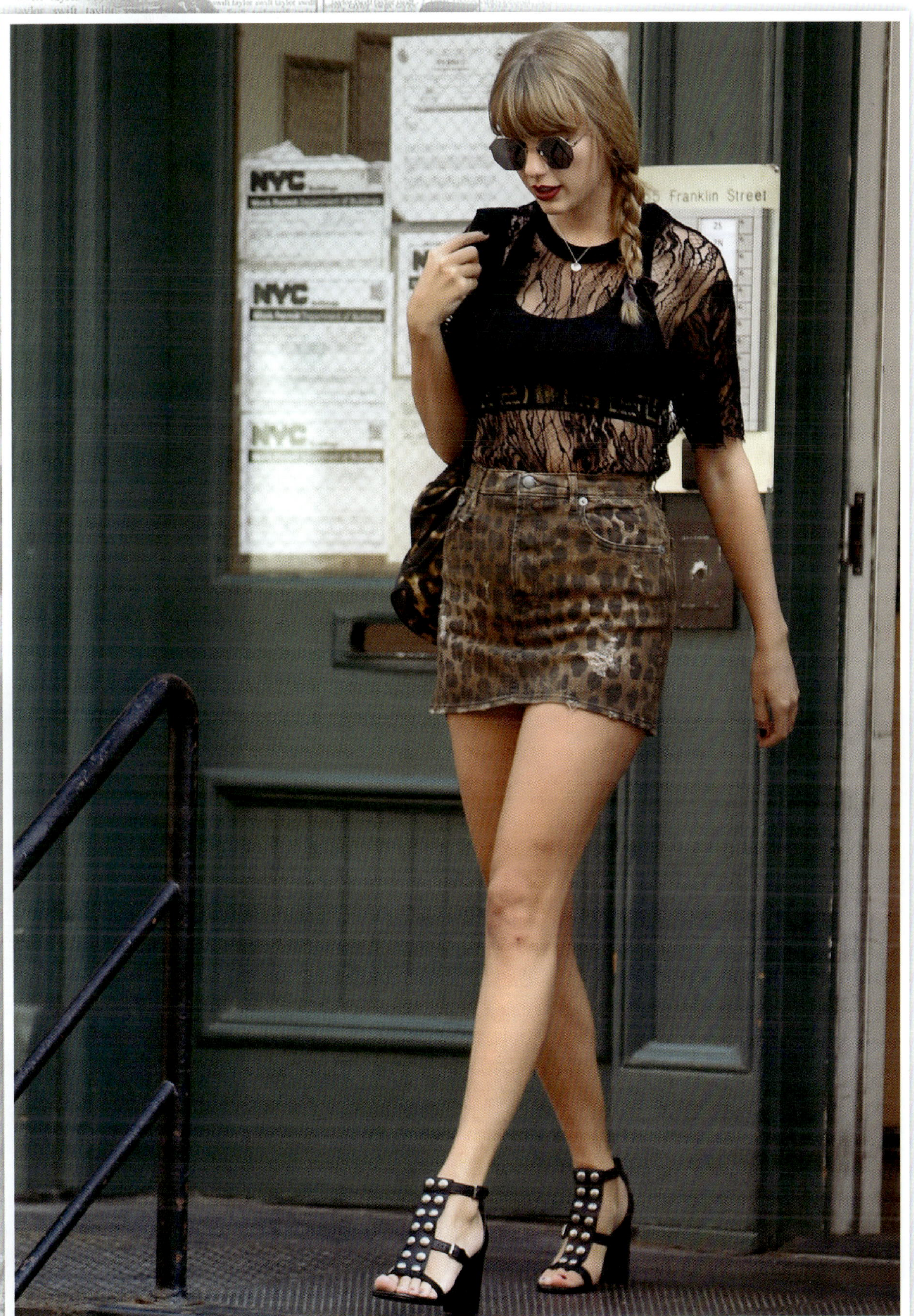
NYC
NYC
NYC
Franklin Street

HIGH FASHION

For Red Carpet events, Taylor wore glamorous gowns with intricate detailing, including sequins, feathers, and dramatic silhouettes by couture designers. These gowns maintained an edgy yet elegant look.

Taylor literally shone in a holographic silver Balmain minidress and matching thigh-high boots at the American Music Awards in 2018

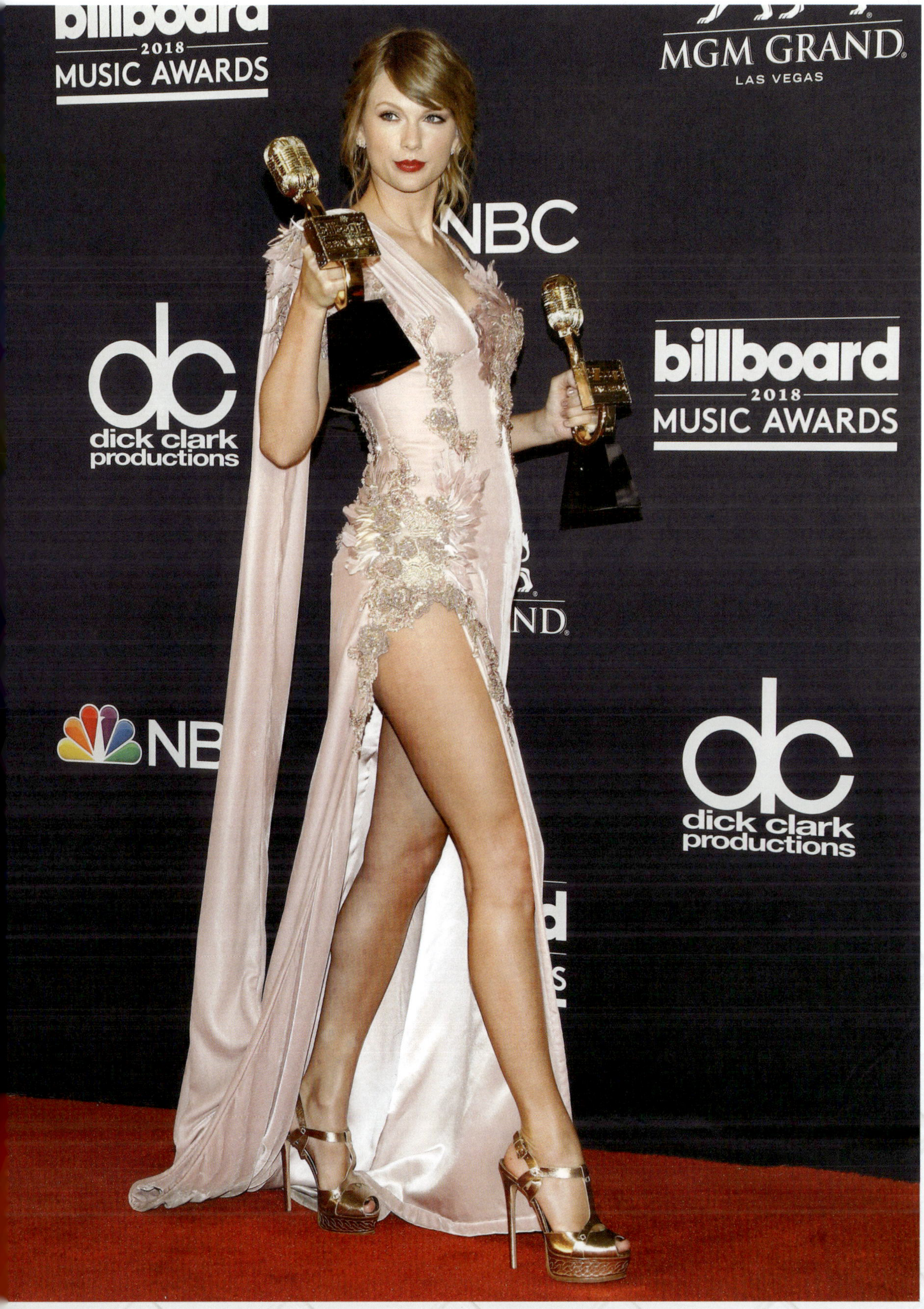

In show-stopping, thigh-splitting Atelier Versace at the 2018 Billboard Music Awards

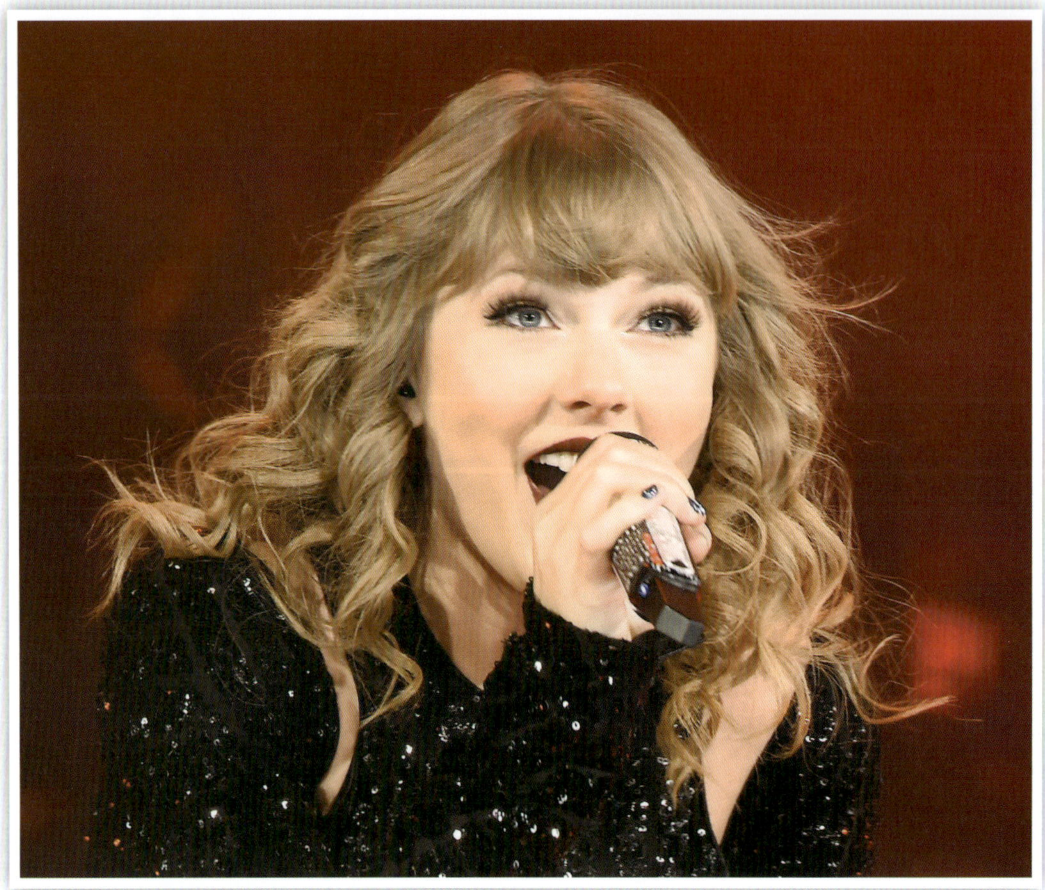

HAIR

Taylor got experimental. Sometimes going for sleek and straight, and other times styling her hair in loose waves for a more laid-back yet glamorous appearance.

Taylor's classic wavy hair as she performs in Tokyo, 2018

Berry lips on the *Reputation* stadium tour

MAKEUP

Dramatic and Bold! Think smoky eye shadow and heavy eyeliner. As for lips, Taylor ditched the pink for deep reds and berry shades.

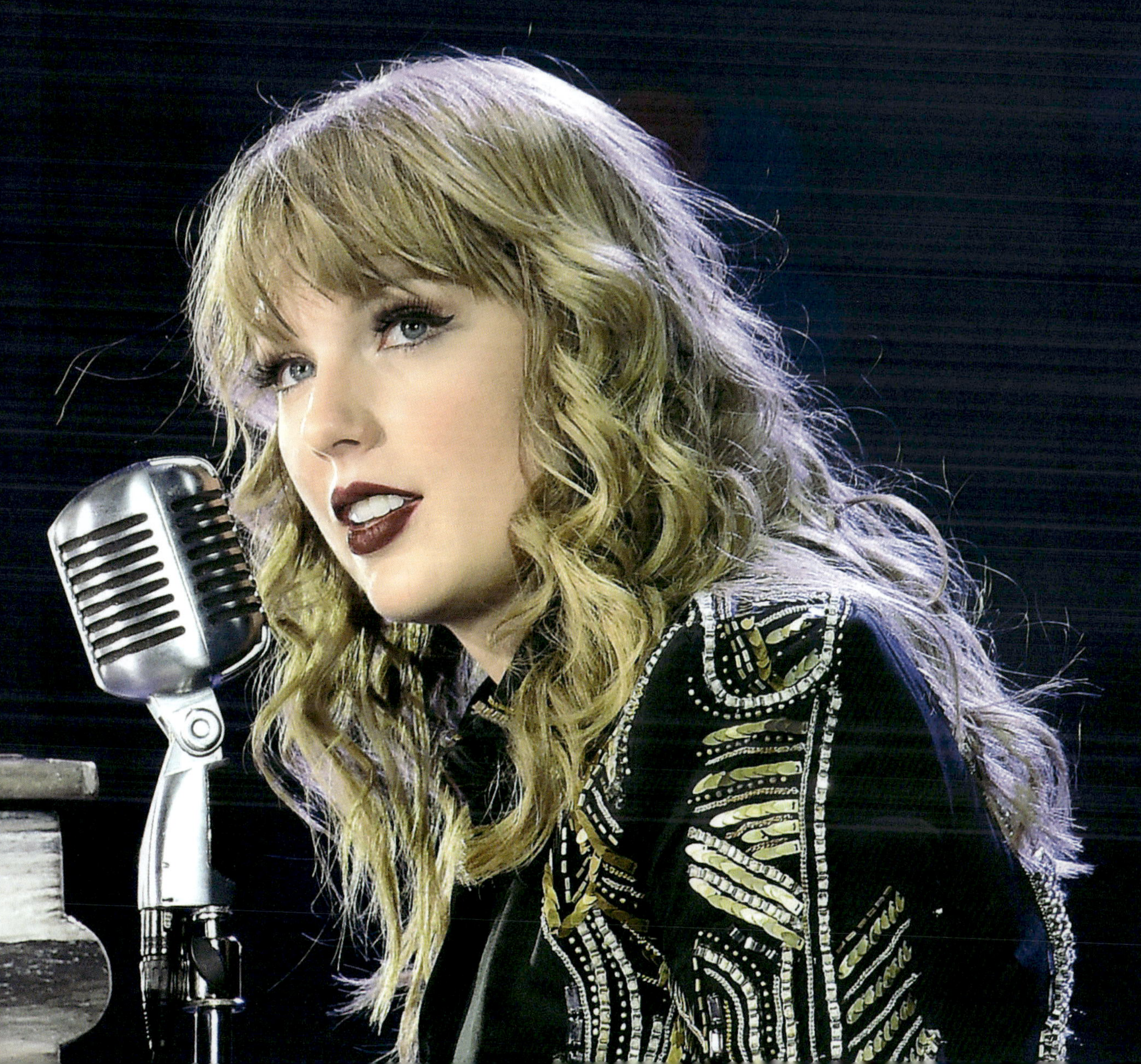

LOVER

CHAPTER SEVEN

LOOKS

2019-2020

Two Thousand and Nineteen saw a return to uber romantic fashion for Taylor as she embraced her *Lover era*, encompassing love, joy and self-expression. Her fashion choices reflected this beautifully as she teamed pastel colours, floral prints, heart motifs and an altogether dreamy aesthetic with a nostalgic 60s and 70s vibe — all while incorporating her beloved sparkles and sequins. Feel-good fashion at its best.

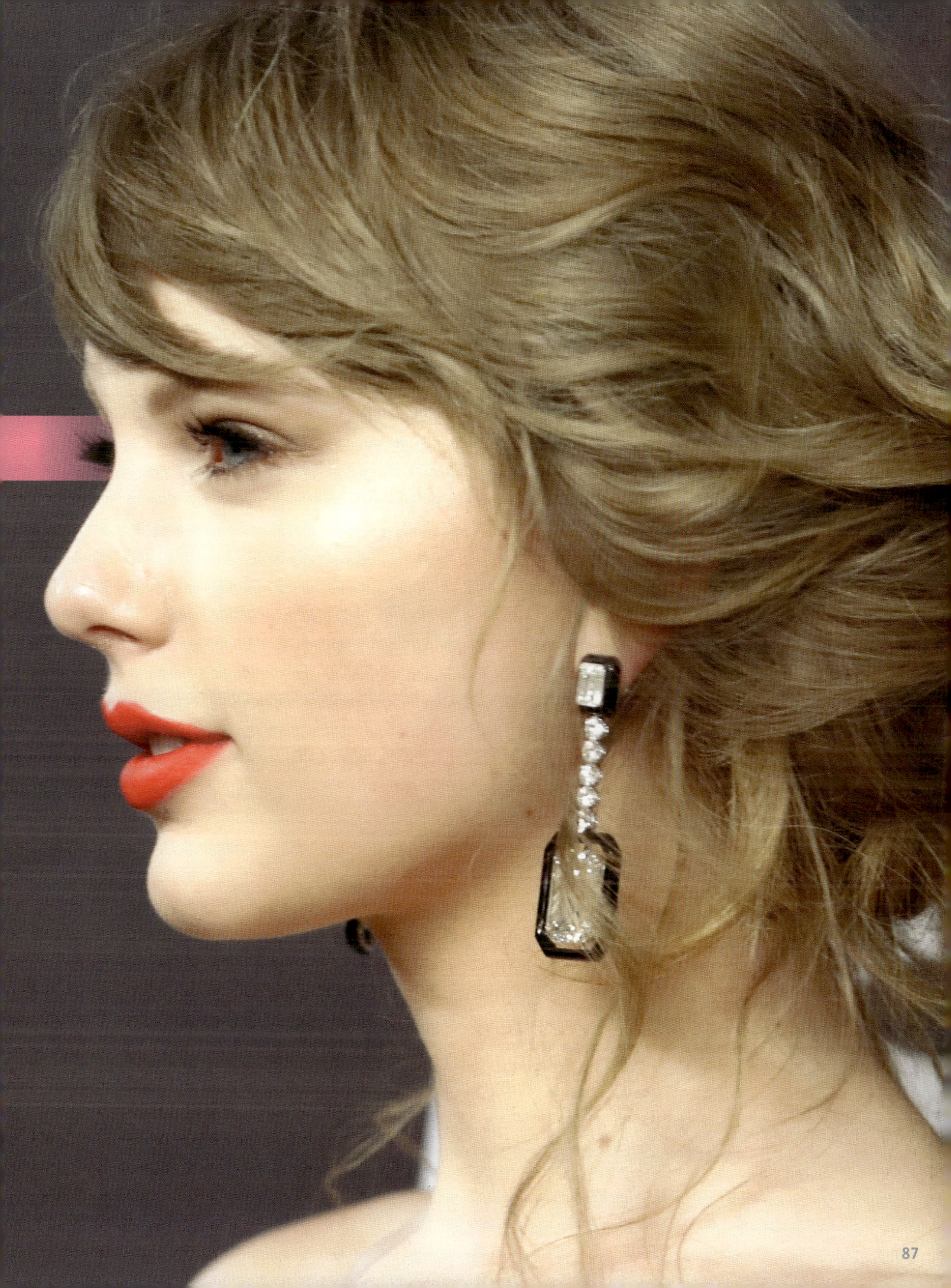

PRETTY AS A PICTURE

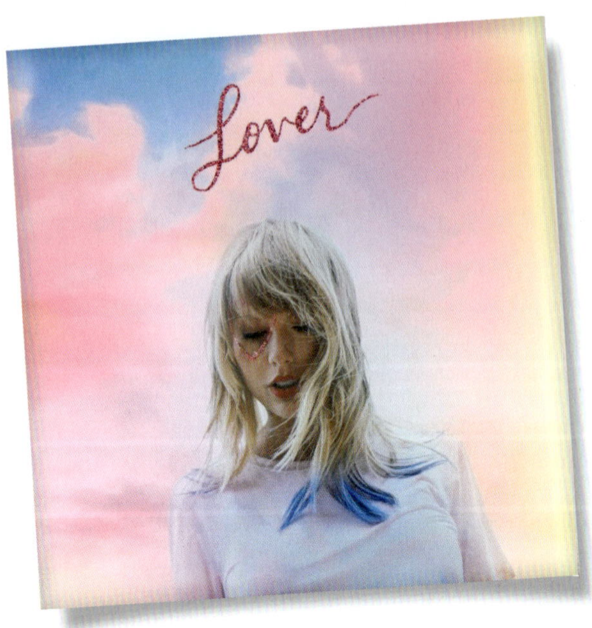

The *Lover* era was dominated by soft, pastel hues such as baby pink, lavender, sky blue, and mint green. These colours were seen in Taylor's outfits, accessories, and even her album's cover art. Florals were a significant motif in this era, appearing on dresses, tops, and accessories. The prints were often delicate and feminine, evoking a sense of springtime and romance.

The cover of Taylor's *Lover* album showcasing the pastel hues that defined the *Lover* era

Taylor backstage at the 2019 Billboard Music Awards in a custom single-sleeved, sherbet-coloured, fringed bodysuit by Jessica Jones, finished with a pair of sequined Stuart Weitzman boots

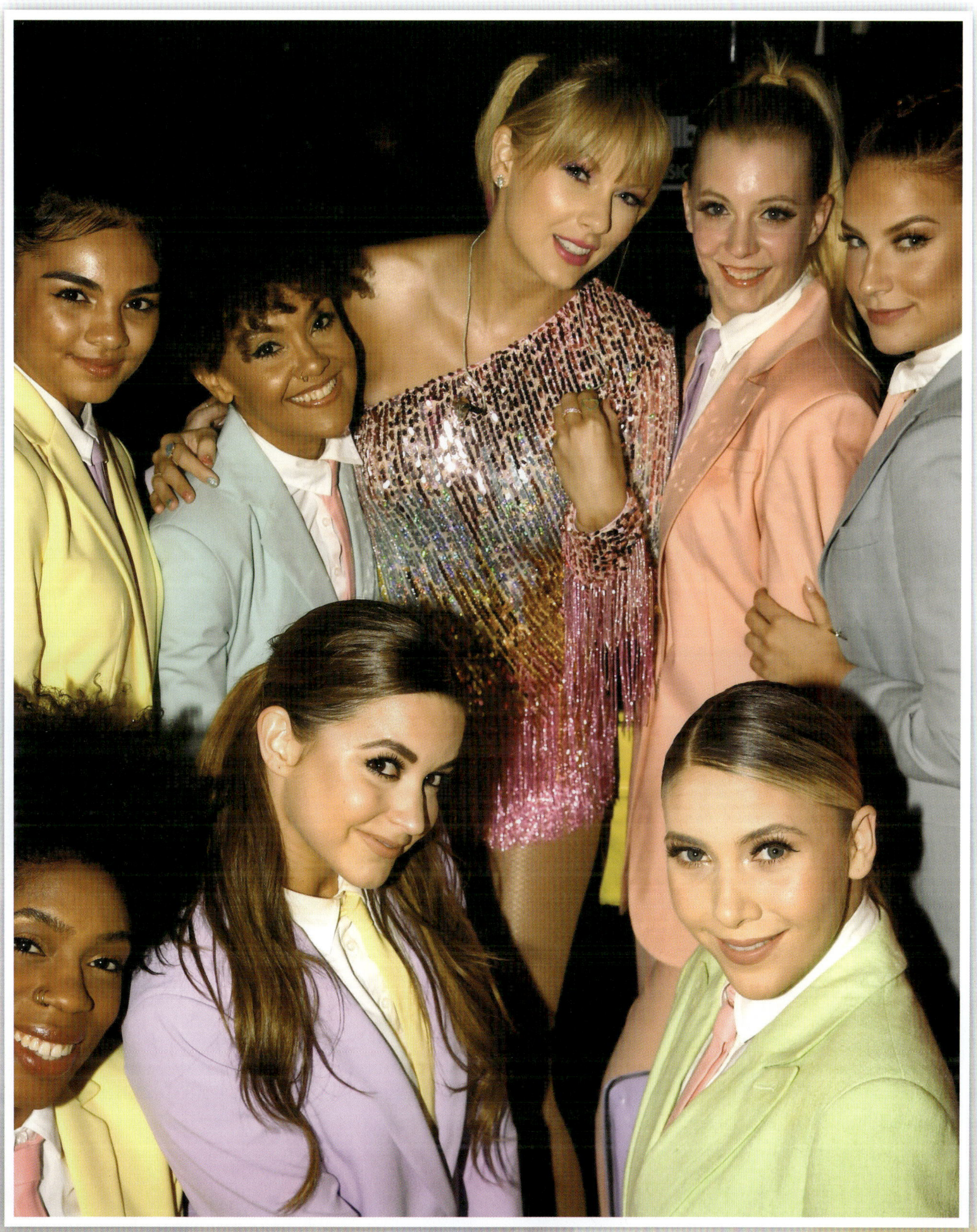

THE LOOK OF LOVE

Flowing, romantic dresses were a staple of this era, often featuring lace, ruffles, and **soft fabrics**. These dresses were perfect for both stage performances and red carpet events.

Bringing the pastel hues to the Billboard Music Awards 2019 with a Raisa & Vanessa Ruffled Dress in soft lilac and Casadei Glitter Ankle Strap Sandals

Turning up to the Time 100 Party in 2019 with a perfect, dreamy blend of pastel pink and yellow in a stunning J Mendel gown paired with Chloe Gosselin Tori sandals

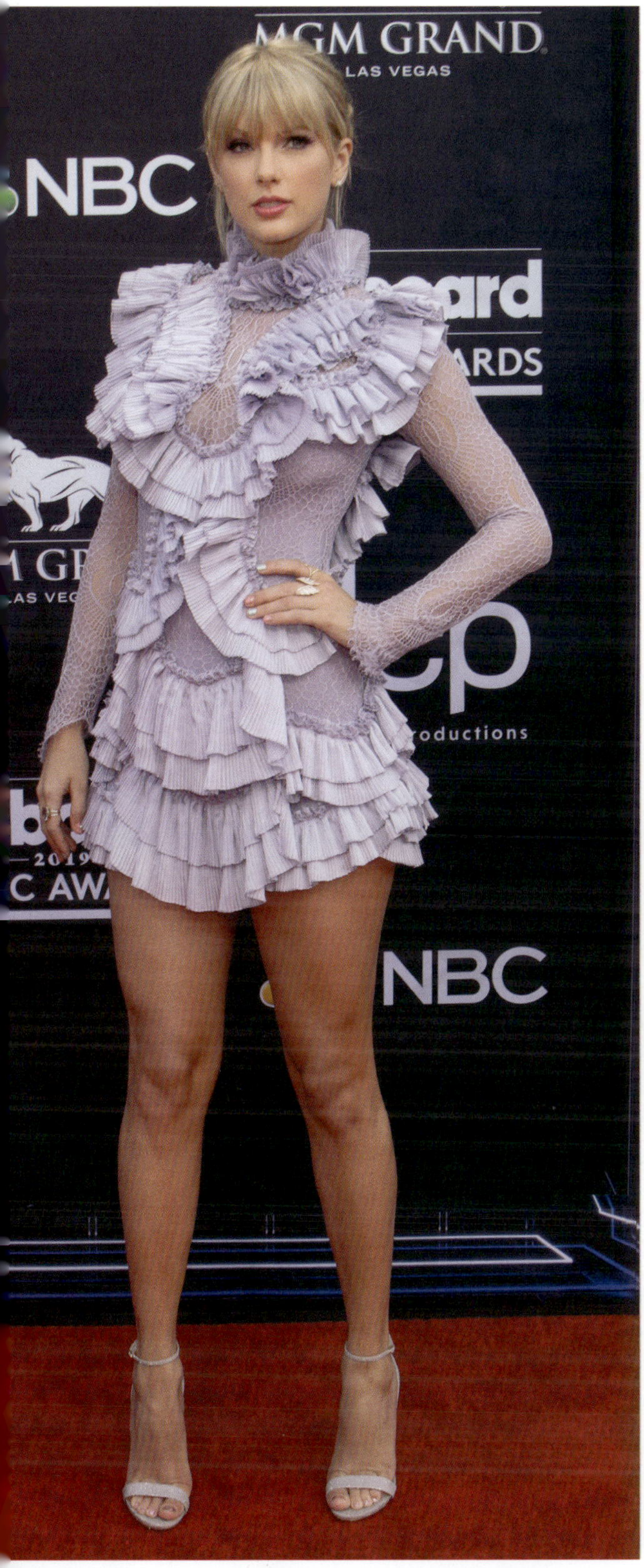
MGM GRAND
LAS VEGAS
NBC
NBC

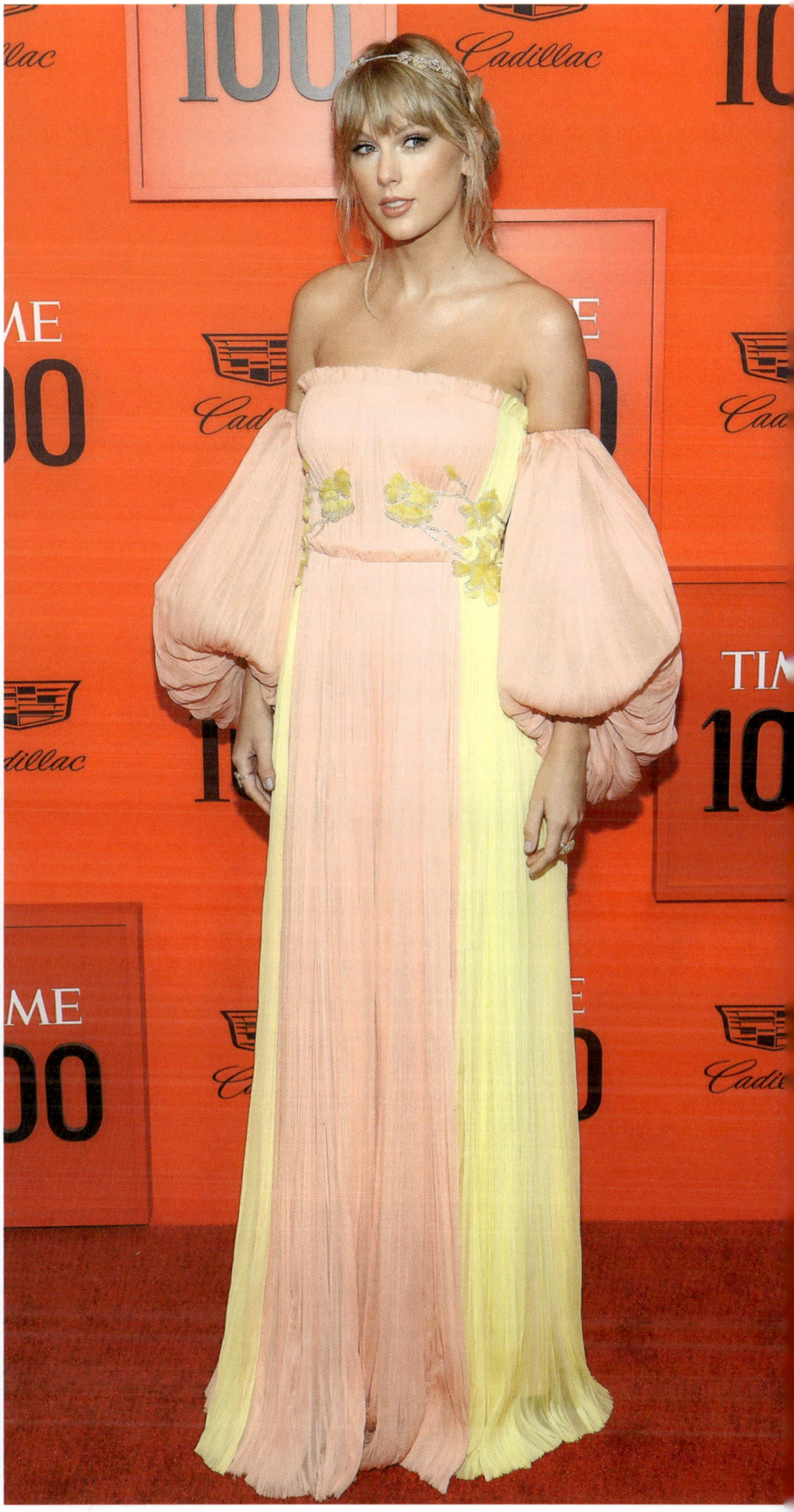
100
Cadillac

SPARKLES

Taylor frequently incorporated sequins, shiny fabrics and sparkly embellishments into her Lover outfits, adding a touch of glamour to the love!

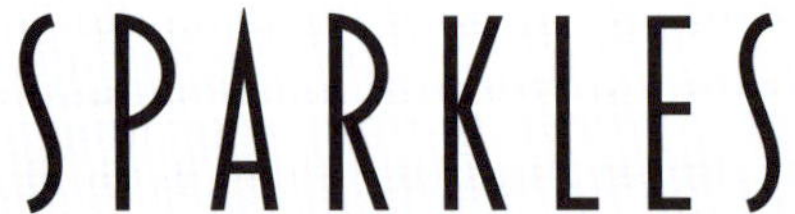

Bright, colourful, joyous energy in China, 2019, in this sequin Ashish dress

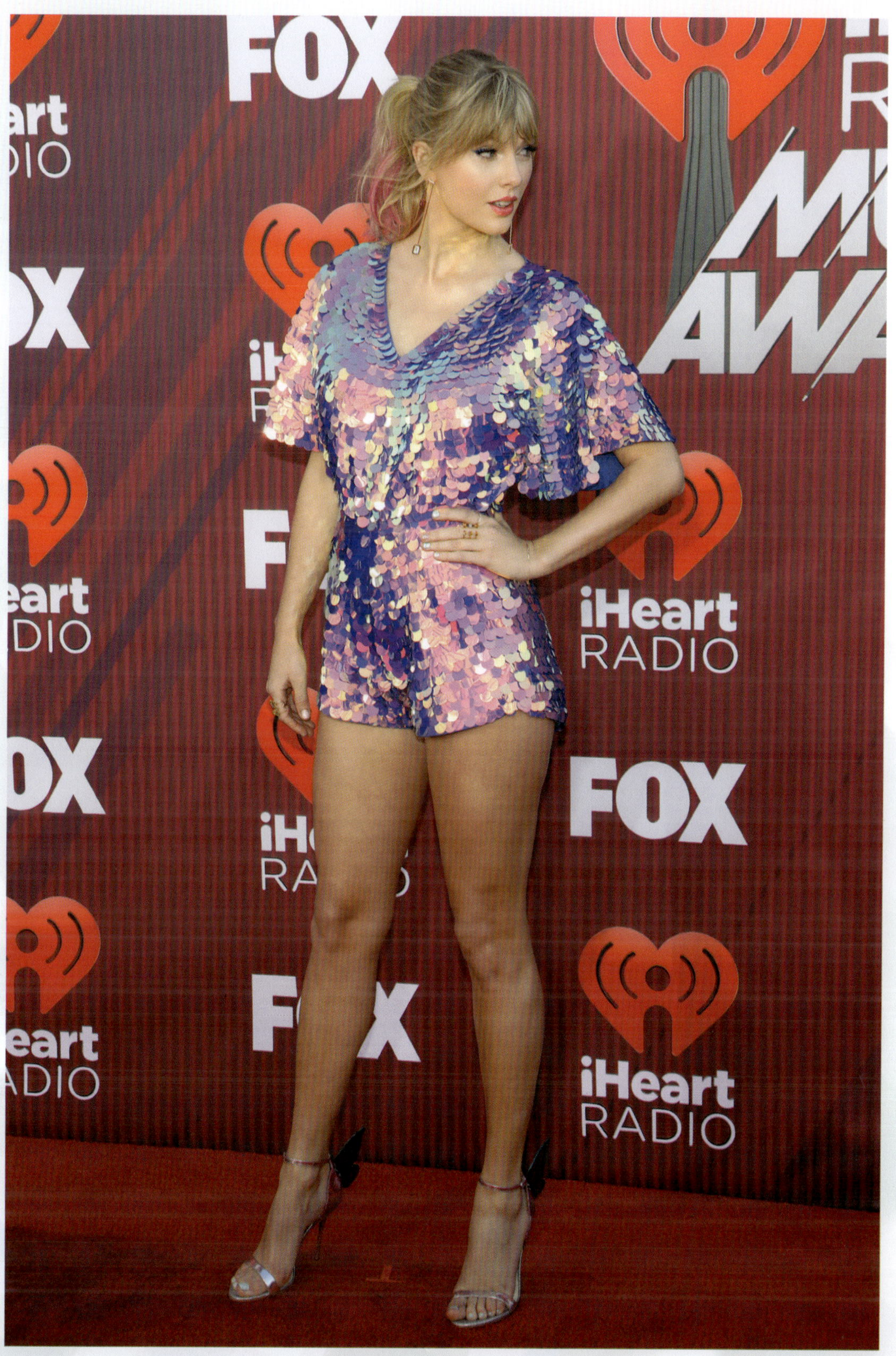

Bringing the sequins back at 2019 iHeart Radio Music Awards wearing a Rosa Bloom Mella Cape Playsuit and butterfly embellished Sophia Webster Chiara Sandals

HAIR AND MAKEUP

Taylor's hair was often styled in loose waves or tied up in a cute ponytail or bun, often with a pastel-coloured scrunchie or headband. Her makeup was soft and natural, with a focus on pink tones, shimmering eyeshadows, and her signature red or pink lip.

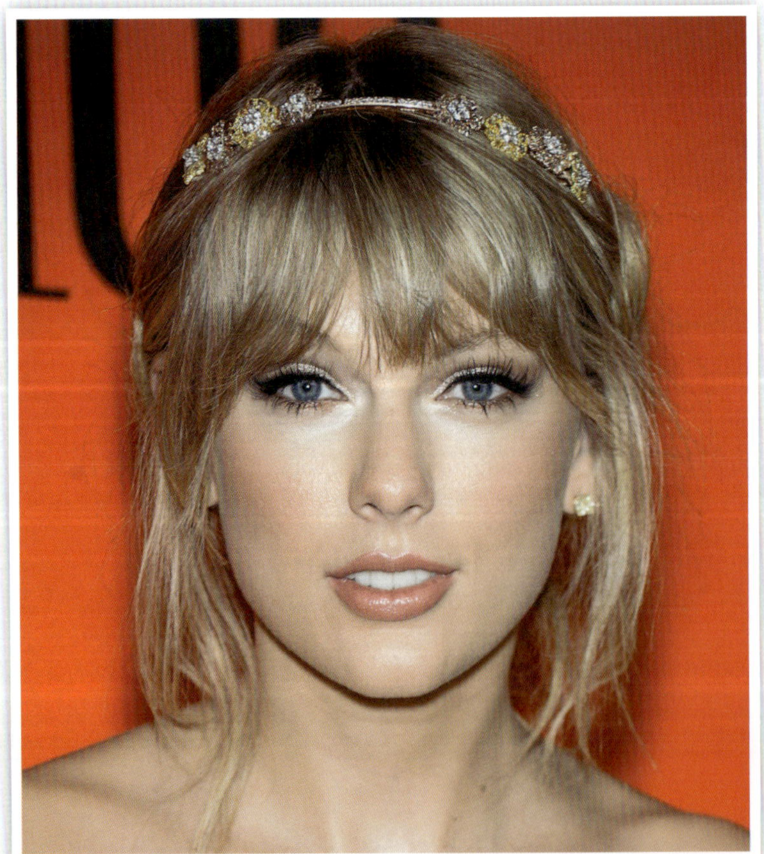

Delicate headband and natural makeup

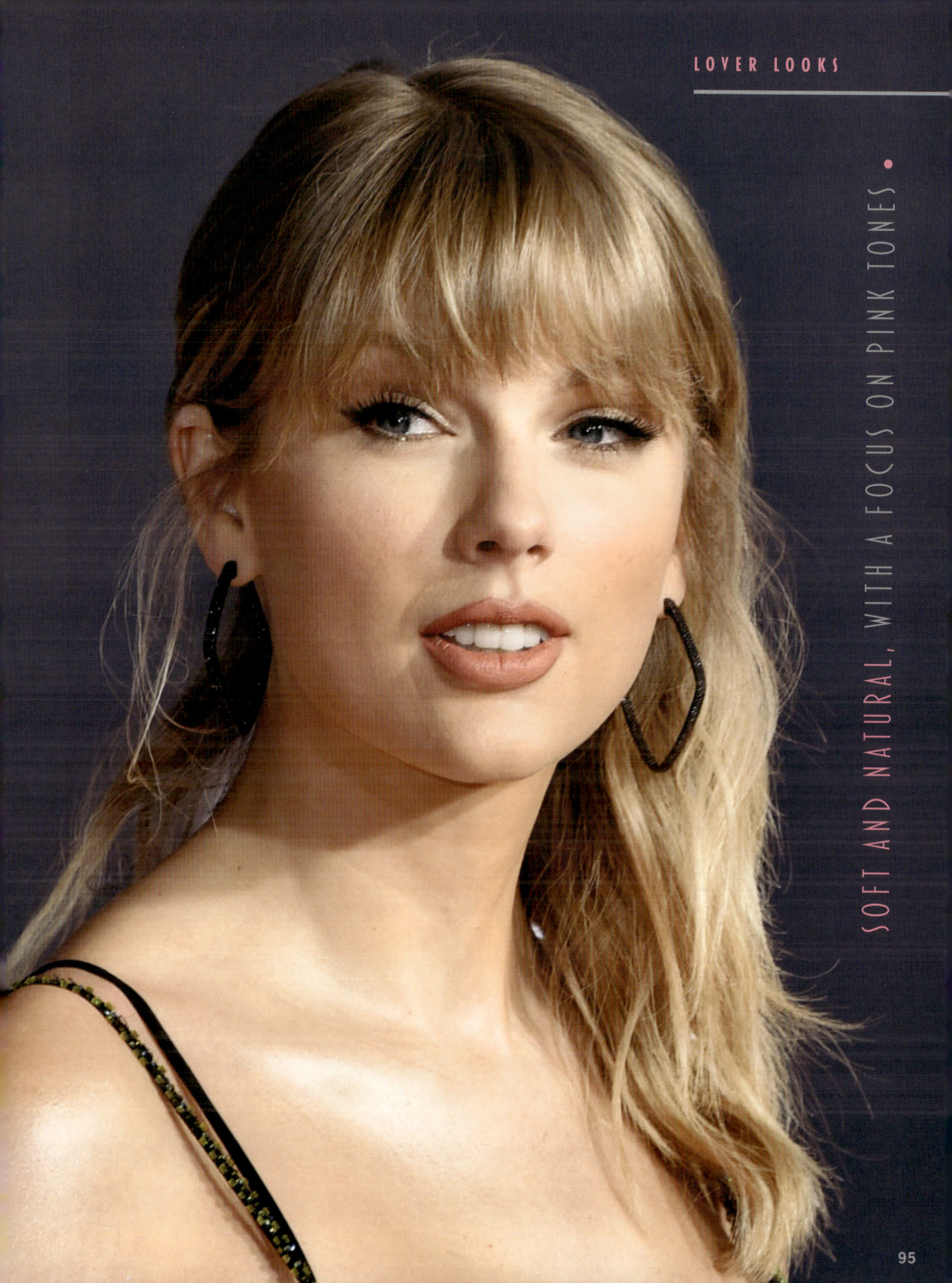

SOFT AND NATURAL, WITH A FOCUS ON PINK TONES

SWIFTIE FASHION

Never has there been such a dedicated group of fans as Taylor's 'Swifties', as they are globally known. They're famous for their dedication to 'Tay-Tay' and their fashion choices are greatly influenced by their heroine's iconic styles. Never is this more apparent than when they go to a TS concert.

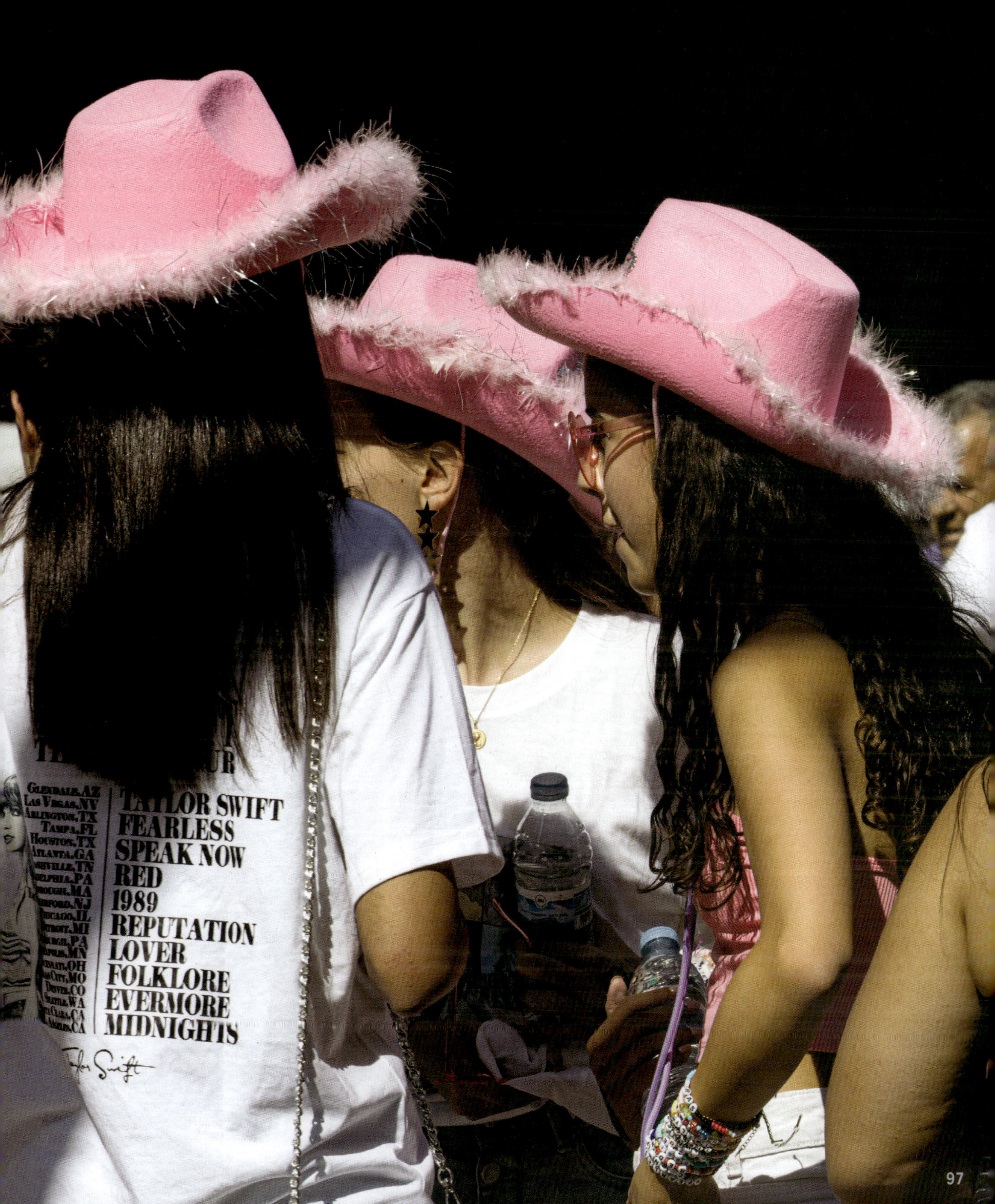
TAYLOR SWIFT
FEARLESS
SPEAK NOW
RED
1989
REPUTATION
LOVER
FOLKLORE
EVERMORE
MIDNIGHTS

ERA-INSPIRED OUTFITS

Fans choose their favourite TS fashion era and dress accordingly. So that's cowboy boots and hats for the Debut years; glittering and glitzy fairy-tale looks for the *Fearless* chapter; deep jewel tones and vintage inspired looks for the *Speak Now* years; high-waisted shorts, striped shirts, red lip, and Taylor's signature heart-shaped sunglasses from the *Red* era; bobbed hairstyles, crop-tops and skater skirts from 1989; a darker, edgier look with black garments, snake motifs, leather jackets, bold eye make-up for the *Reputation* era; romantic, flowing outfits in baby blues, soft pinks and lavender, and pastel sparkles for lovers of the Lover period; a cottage-core vibe for the Swiftie folk who are drawn to *Folklore* and *Evermore* era fashion – ie, oversized cardigans, prairie dresses, plaid patterns, earthy tones and a soft, natural make-up; a glitzy, glam, retro vibe for *Midnights* era Swifties - shimmering dresses, velvet fabrics, and deep blue or purple tones, often with celestial or star motifs; while fans of the *Tortured Poets Department* era favour monochrome short skirts with sheer black tights, loafers, oversized sweaters and blazers, and '70s-inspired trousers.

CUSTOM TEES

Fans often create custom T-shirts with lyrics, album titles, or references to Taylor's songs.

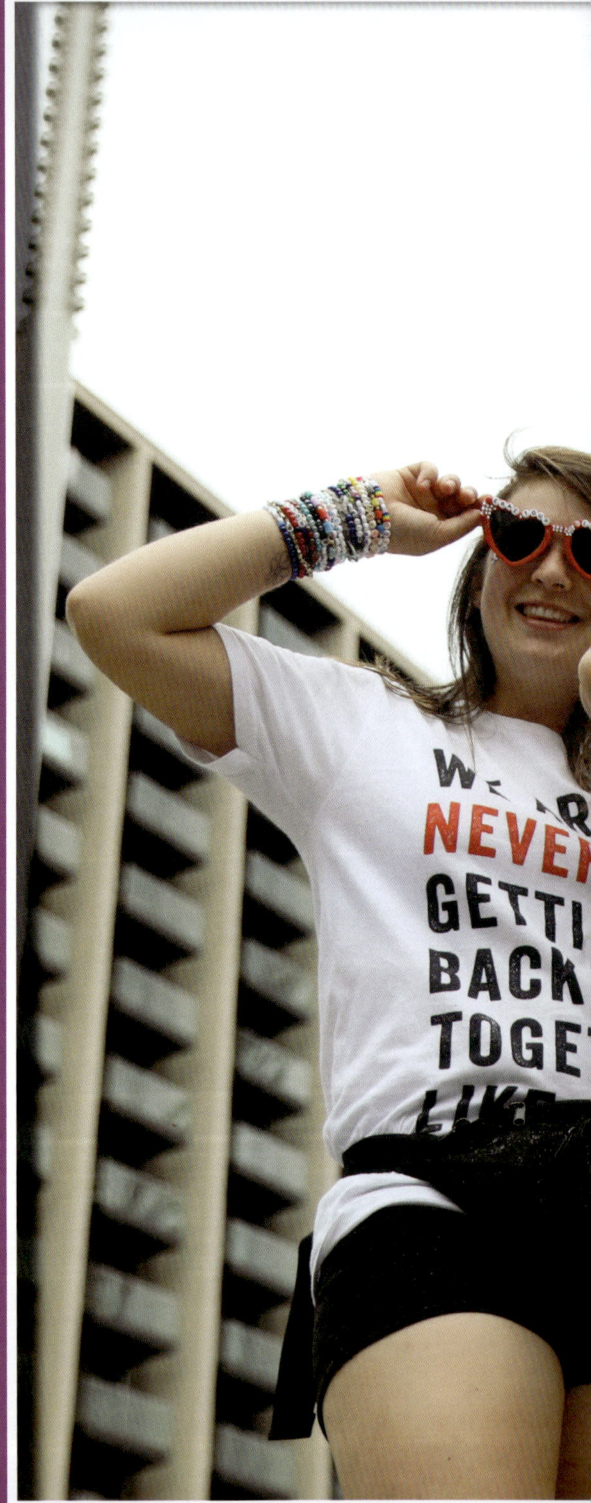

Custom T-shirts, heart-shaped sunglasses, sparkly skirts and friendship bracelets. They've got it all!

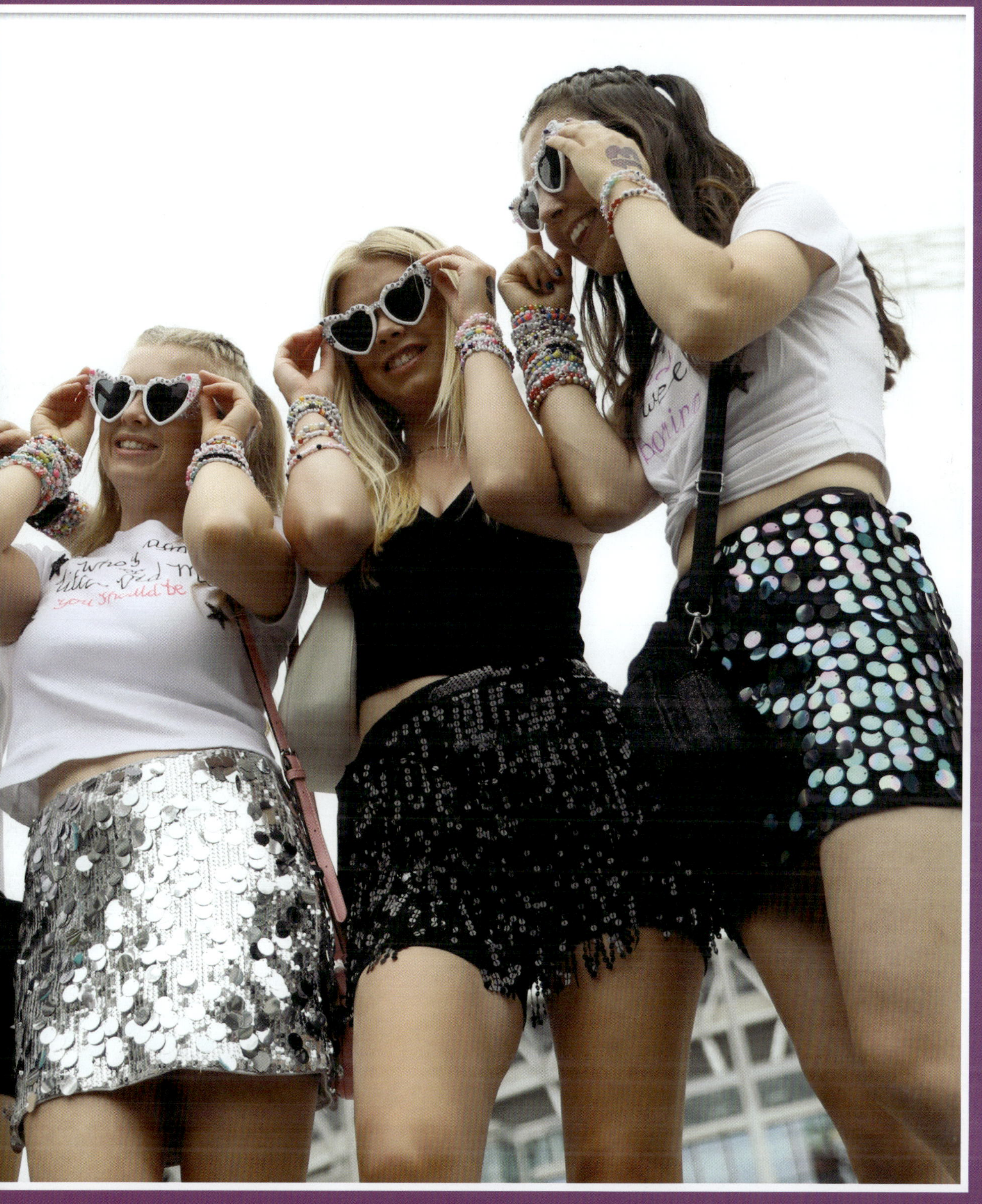

HEART-SHAPED SUNGLASSES A NOD TO THE 22 MUSIC VIDEO •

SEQUINS AND GLITTER

It goes without saying that Swifties love to wear sequin dresses, glittery tops, and shiny accessories a la Taylor!

THEMED COSTUMES

Many fans dress up as specific looks from Taylor's music videos, performances, or iconic appearances. EG, a Swiftie might wear a marching band outfit from *You Belong with Me* or a cheerleader uniform from *Shake It Off*.

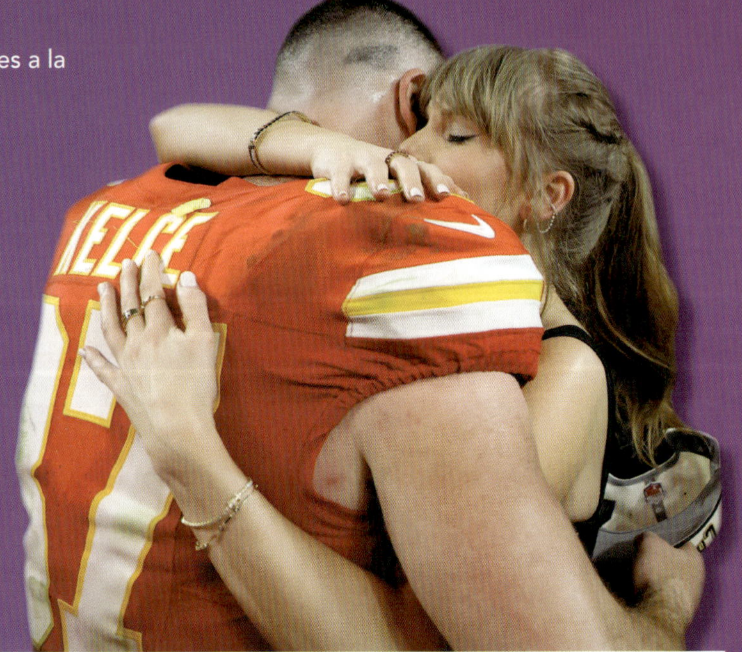

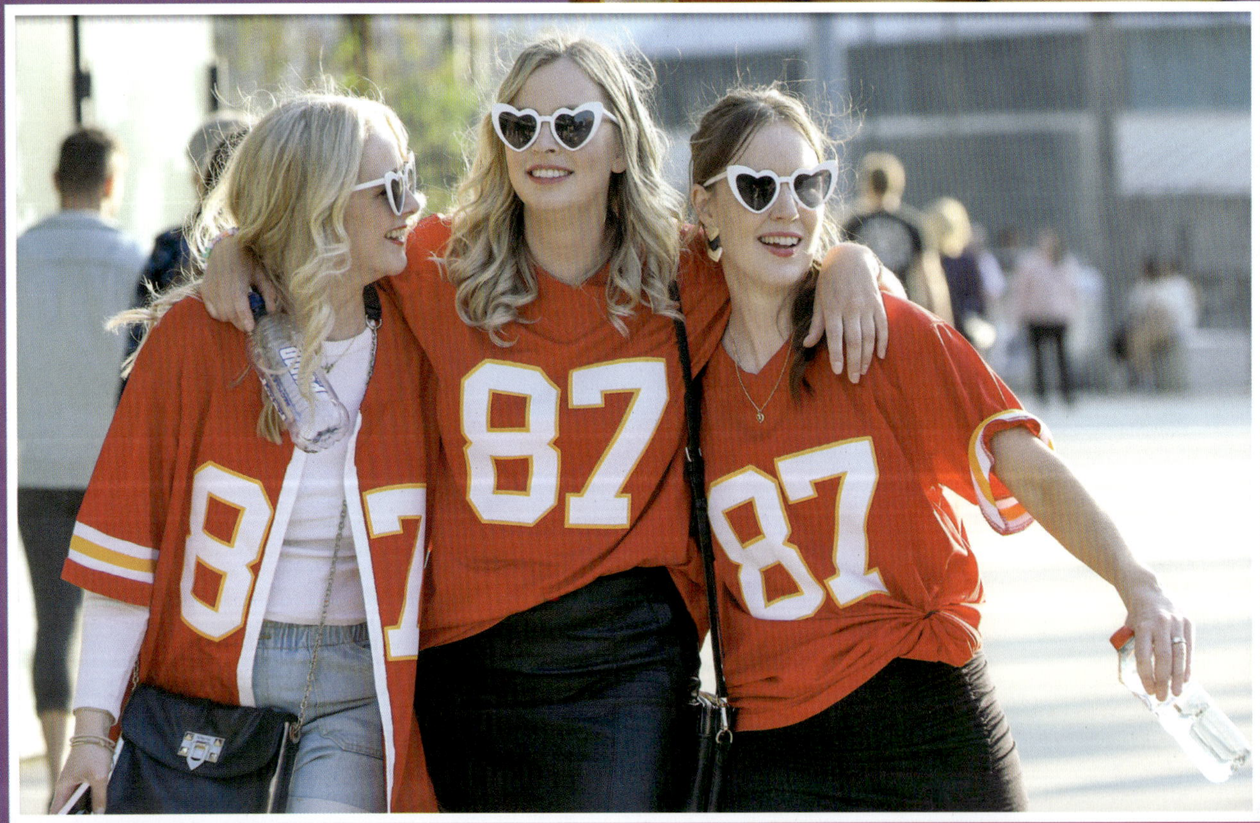

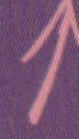

Fans pair iconic heart-shaped glasses with football jerseys in a nod to Taylor's relationship with Kansas City Chiefs' number 87, Travis Kelce

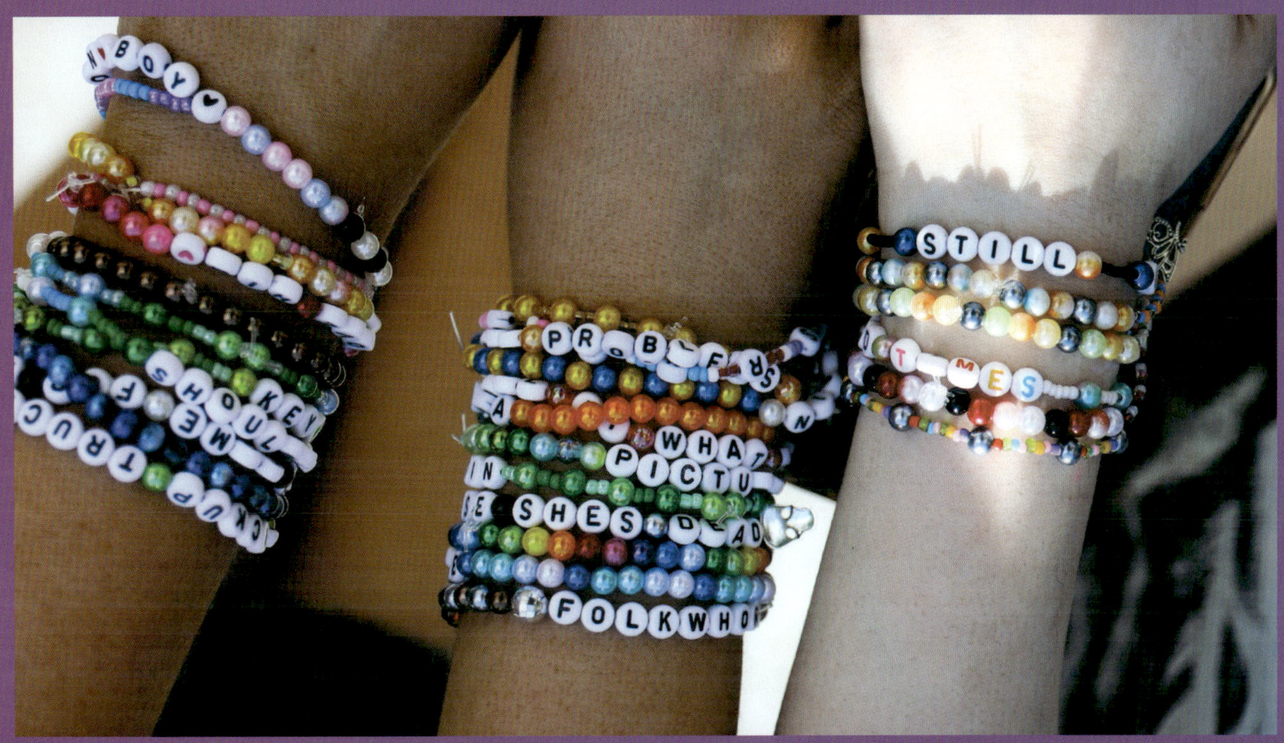

SWIFTIE FRIENDSHIP ↗ BRACELETS

Inspired by the *Eras* Tour, Swifties often exchange and wear friendship bracelets featuring lyrics, album titles, or inside jokes from the fandominium.

SWIFTIE ACCESSORY

Heart-Shaped Sunglasses. In a nod to the *22* music video, heart-shaped sunglasses are a popular accessory among Swifties. It goes without saying that red lips are a must with many Tay Tay looks. Swifties also often pay homage to Taylor's cats – Olivia, Meredith and Benjamin – by adopting cat-themed accessories.

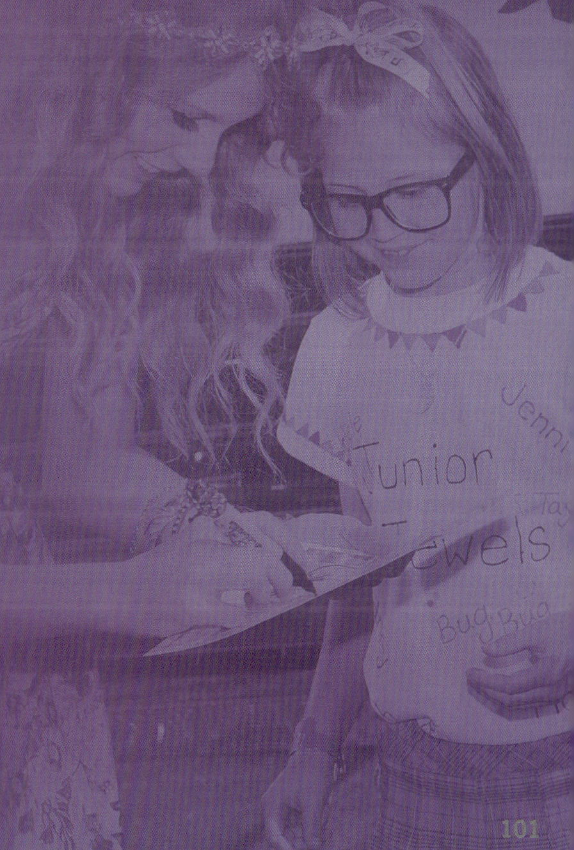

FOLKLORE &

CHAPTER EIGHT

EVERMORE

Overall, Taylor's fashion during the *folklore* and *evermore* eras can be described as a blend of vintage-inspired, cottage-core, and rustic styles – but a touch of understated elegance. The fashion, much like the sister albums, emerged as a result of the COVID-19 pandemic. Taylor had been due to tour *Lover* in 2020 but the pandemic put a stop to that. As world priorities changed, so did Taylor's music and style.

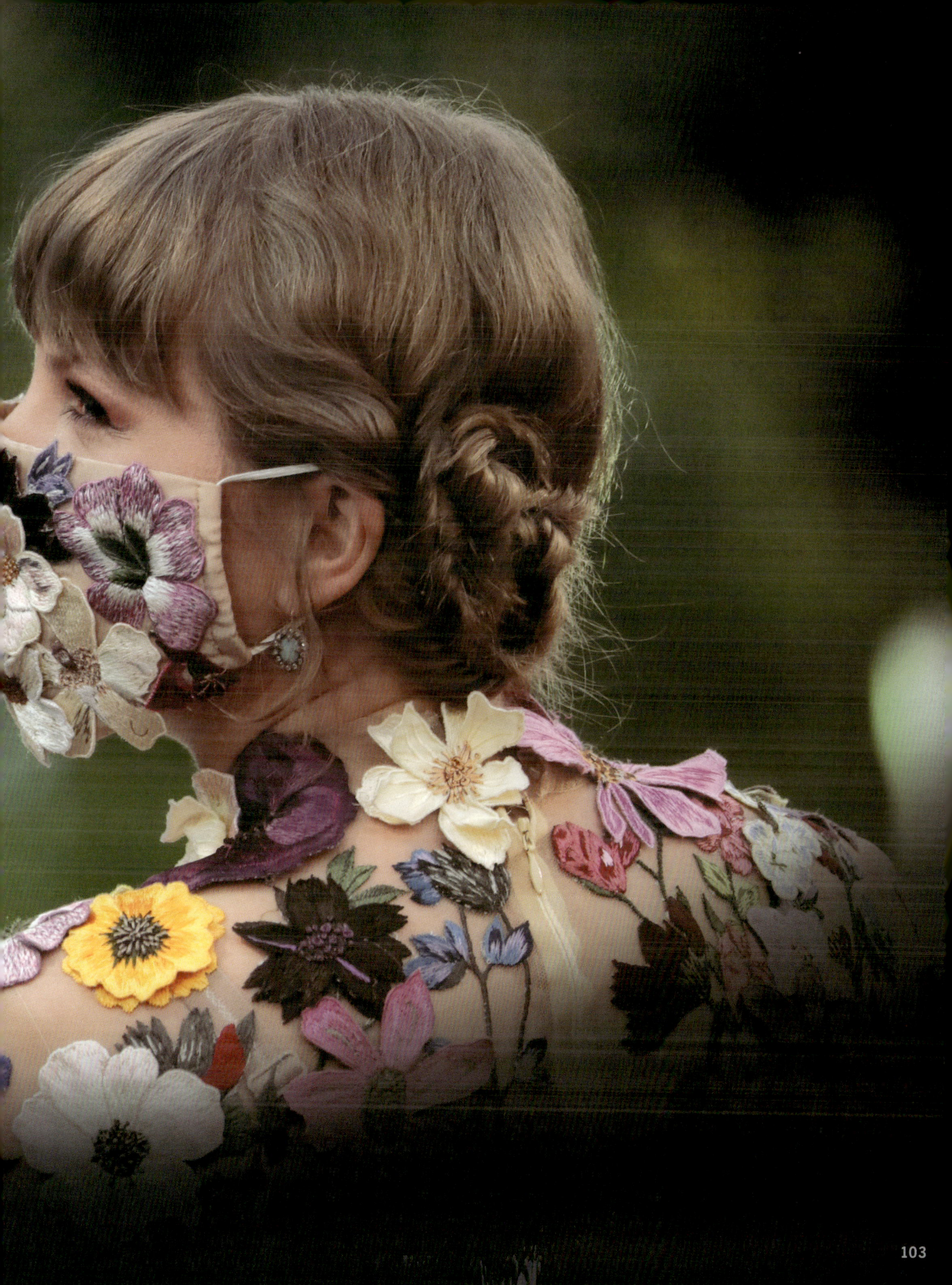

FOLKLORE

Muted Tones. The colour palette for folklore was subdued, featuring neutrals - beige, grey, white and muted earth tones. This was in line with the introspective and melancholy mood of the album – and the times.

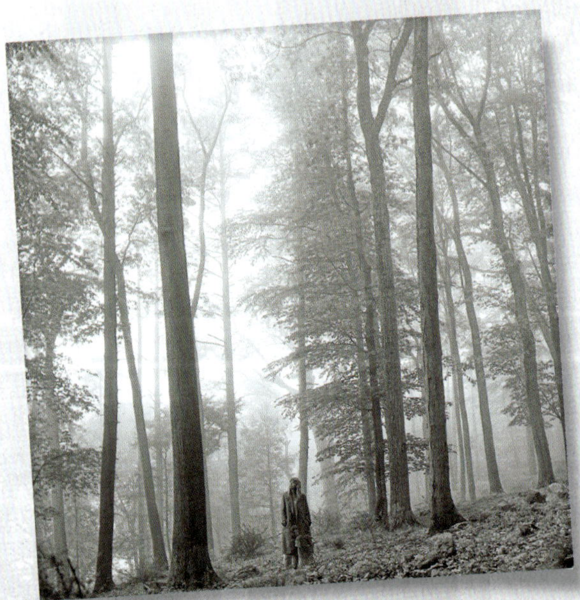

The *folklore* cover shoot, perfectly embodying the album's feminine and rustic vibes

Taylor looking cosy in an earthy tone sweater, posing with the Icon Award during the Virgin Atlantic Attitude Awards in 2020

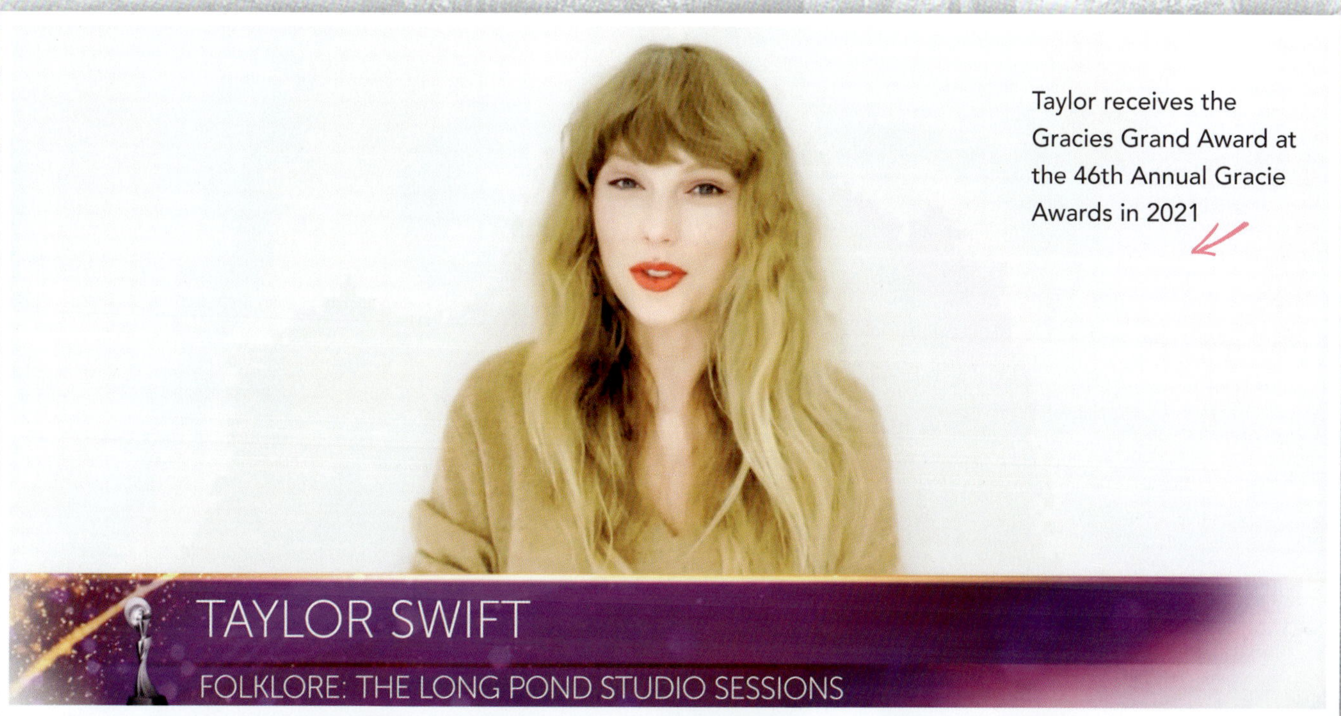

Taylor receives the Gracies Grand Award at the 46th Annual Gracie Awards in 2021

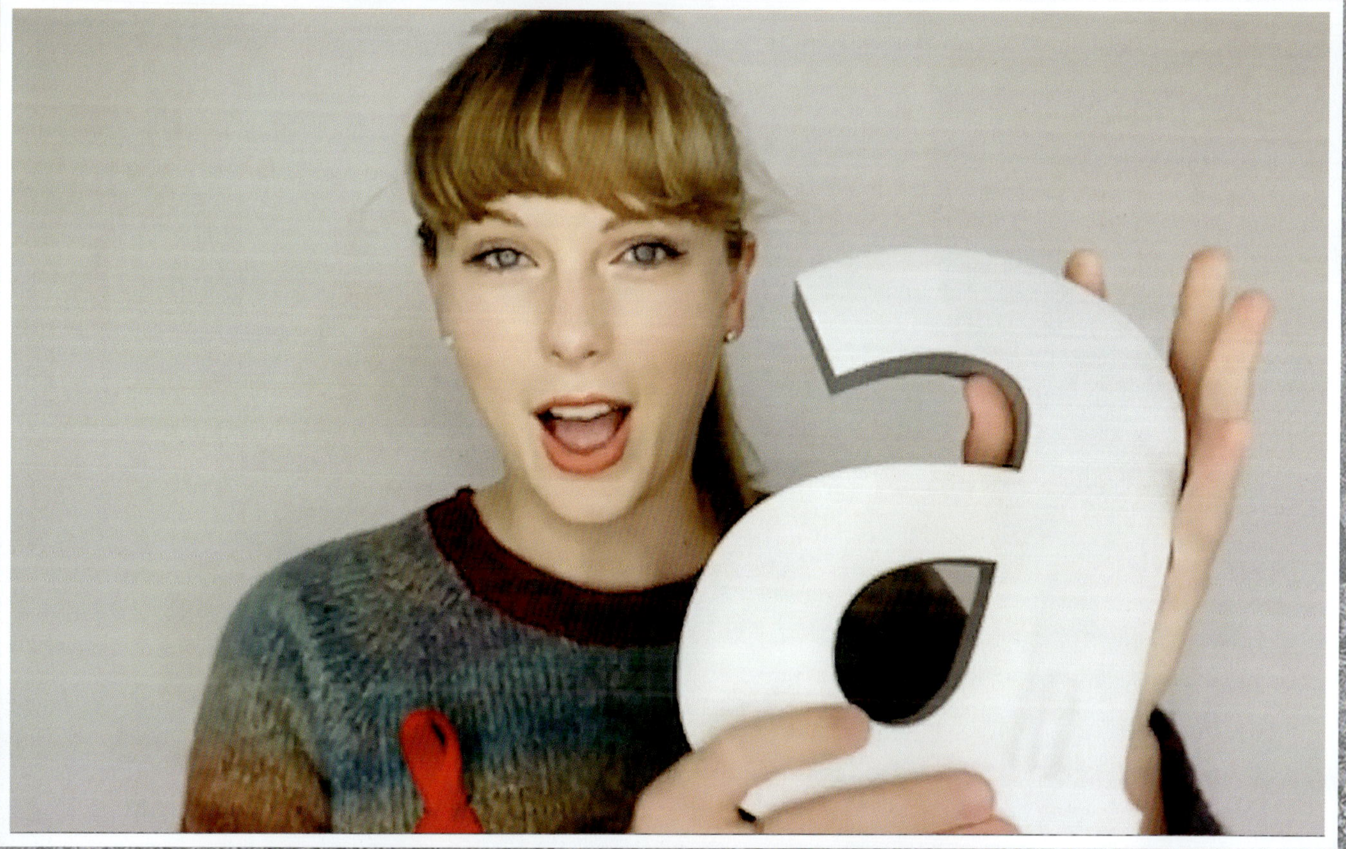

TAYLOR SWIFT

FOLKLORE: THE LONG POND STUDIO SESSIONS

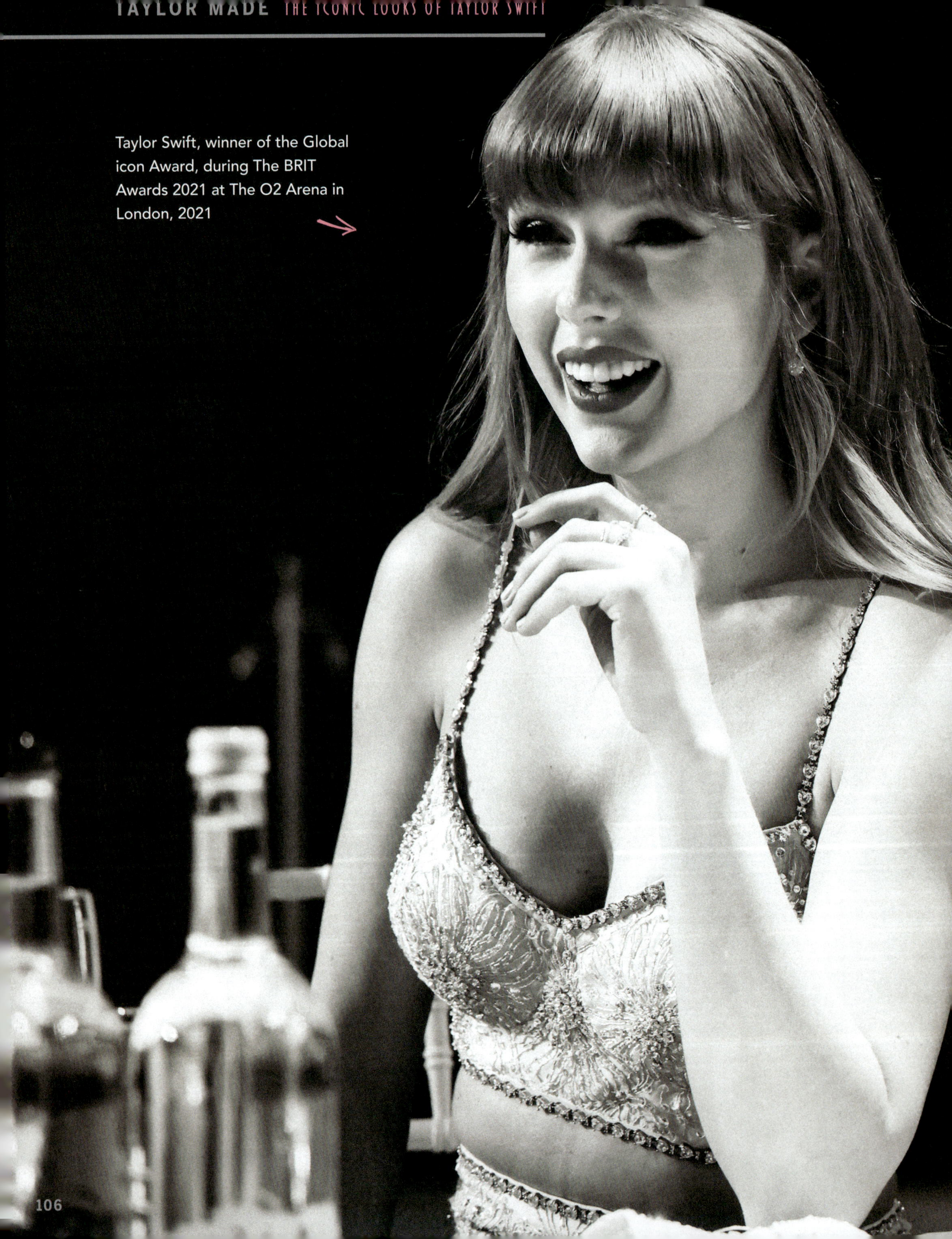

Taylor Swift, winner of the Global icon Award, during The BRIT Awards 2021 at The O2 Arena in London, 2021

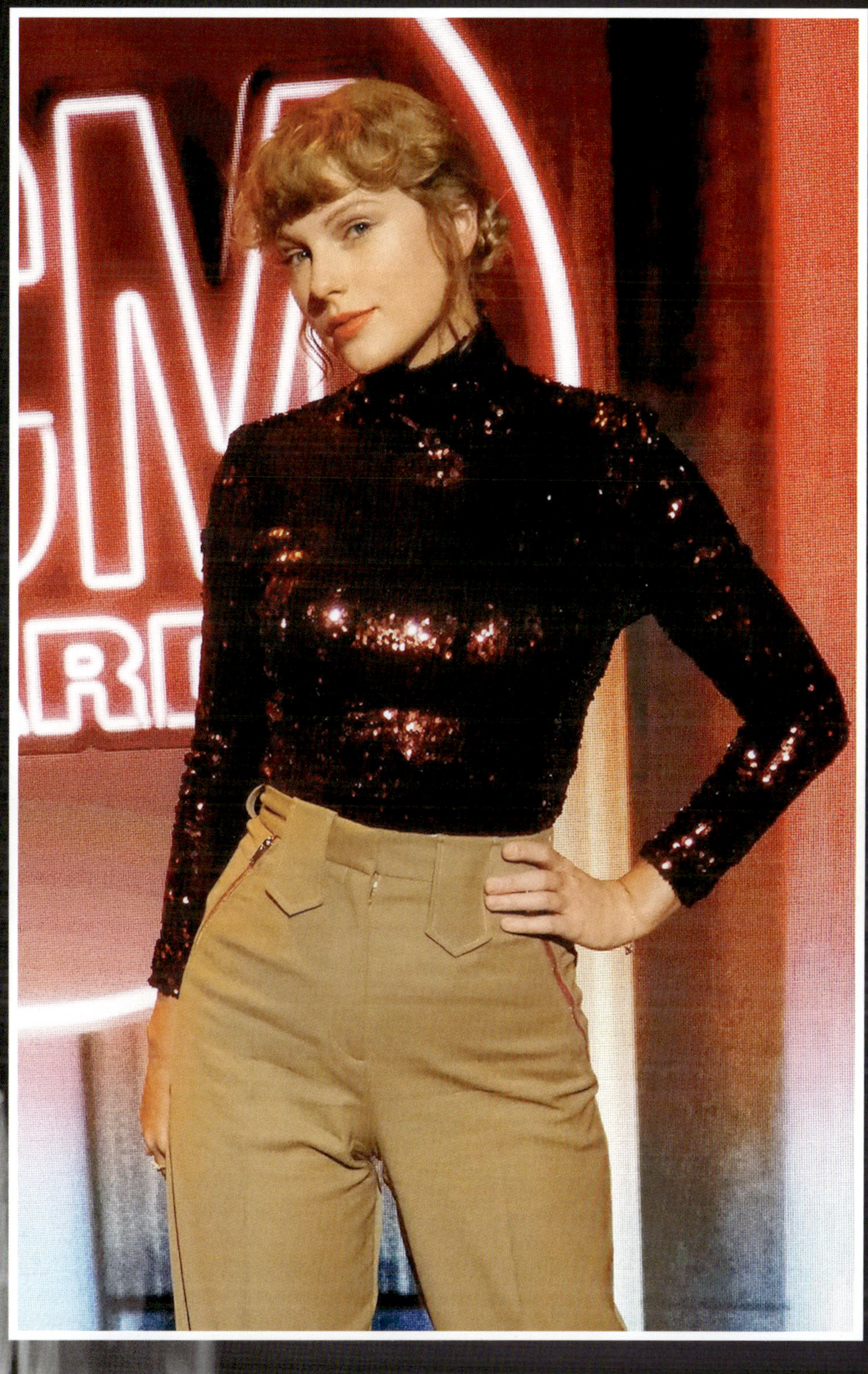

Taylor Swift attends the 55th Academy of Country Music Awards at the Grand Ole Opry in Nashville, Tennessee, 2020

EVERMORE

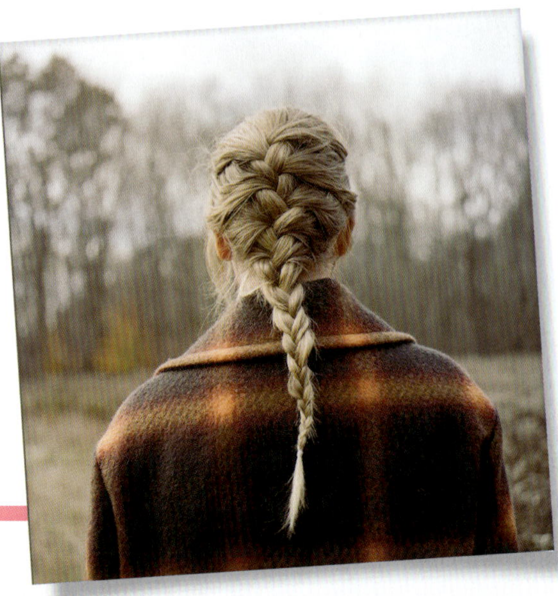

Earthy, Warm Tones. The *evermore* era continued the muted aesthetic of *folklore* but introduced warmer tones like burnt orange, deep greens, and mustard yellows, reflecting the album's autumnal and wintry vibes.

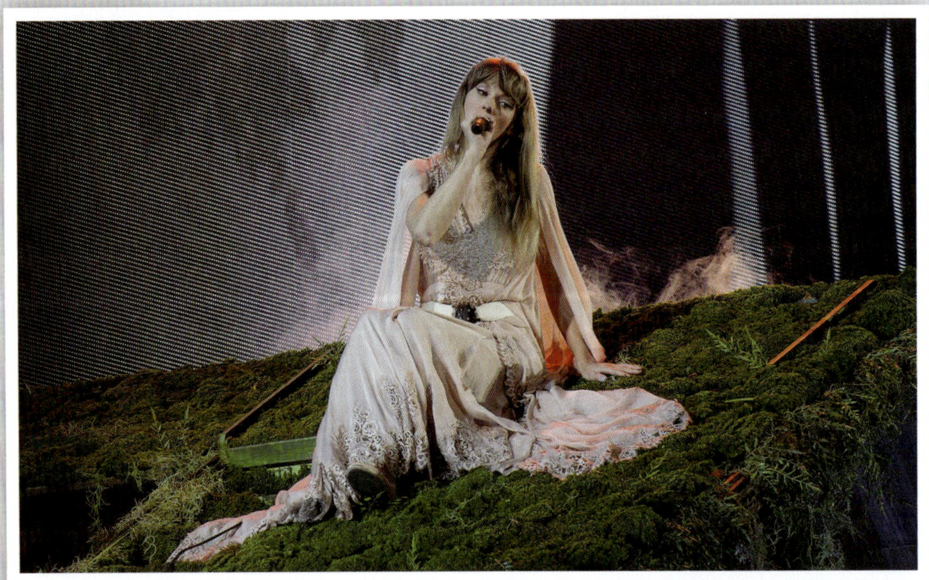

Swift performing "August" from *folklore* at the *Eras* Tour in a nude, floaty gown with beautiful embroidered detailing

Donning a Stella McCartney check-print single-breasted coat that perfectly complements the album's enchanting mood in the *evermore* album cover shoot, 2020

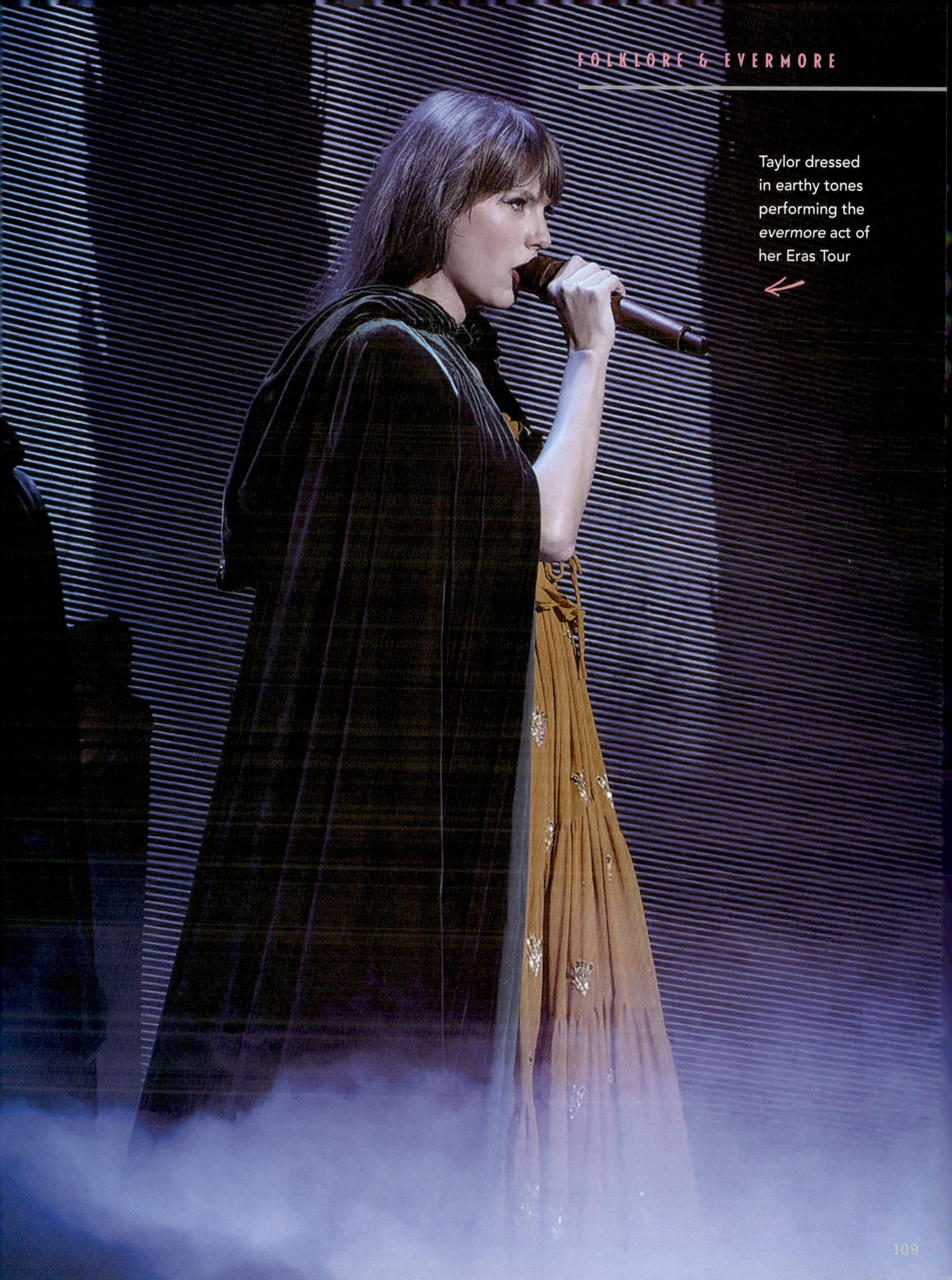

Taylor dressed in earthy tones performing the *evermore* act of her Eras Tour

HAIR AND MAKEUP

Minimal makeup and natural hair. Taylor's makeup was understated, focusing on her natural beauty. She often had loose waves or braids, emphasizing a laid-back, natural appearance. For virtual performances and Zoom interviews, she did her own hair and make-up.

Taylor Swift attends the *All Too Well* premiere at AMC Lincoln Square in New York, 2021

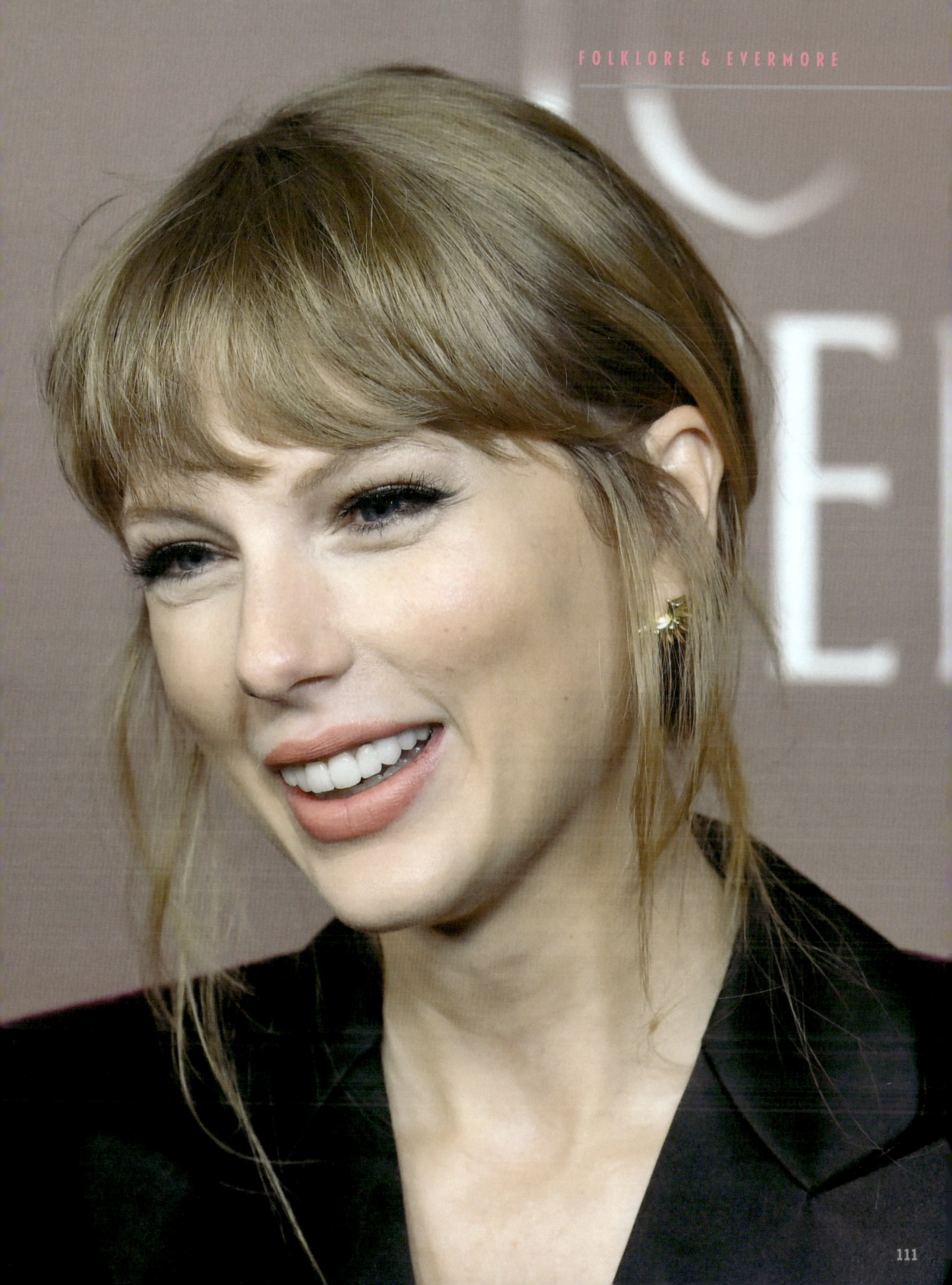

SPARKLY

CHAPTER NINE

MIDNIGHTS

Glamour, mystery, magic and nostalgia blended together to create Taylor's stunning *Midnights* aesthetic. The excitement of late nights, the witching hour, star-studded indigo skies... Swift's 2022 wardrobe captured it all perfectly...

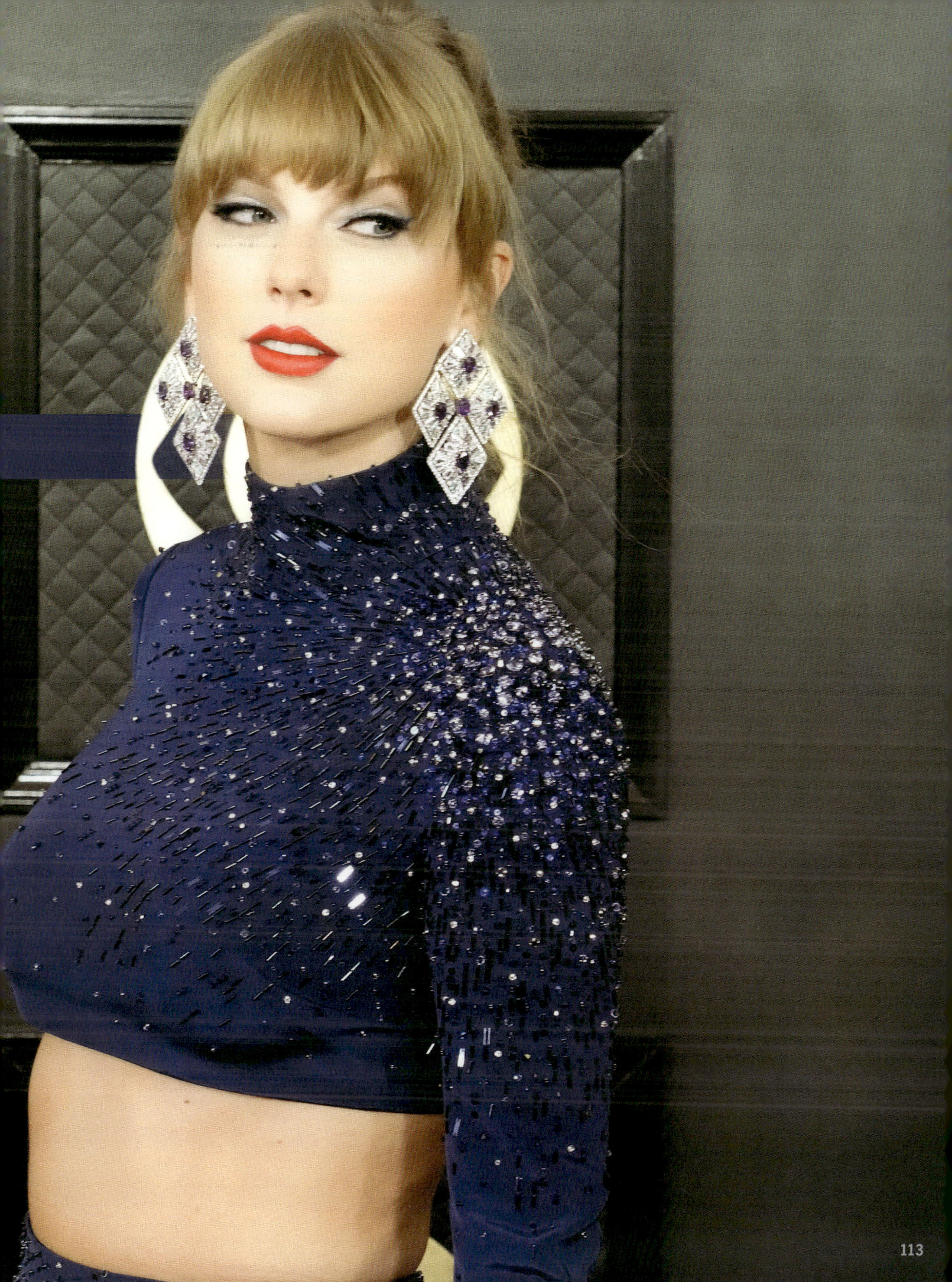

LIGHTING UP THE NIGHT

ndigo, deep blues, purples, inky blacks – the colours of the night sky – were a key part of Taylor's Midnights palette, along with silver, gold and other metallic hues. Outfits often featured sequins, glitter, and shimmering fabrics, evoking the sparkle of stars against a midnight sky. Creams, beiges, and soft greys were paired with darker tones on occasion.

Dazzling at the Nashville Songwriters' Award 2022 in a stunning black sequin jersey dress from Michael Kors' Fall 2022 collection. The dress featured a sleek, sleeveless design with a high neckline and a thigh-high slit, offering a glamorous look of a deep, starry sky

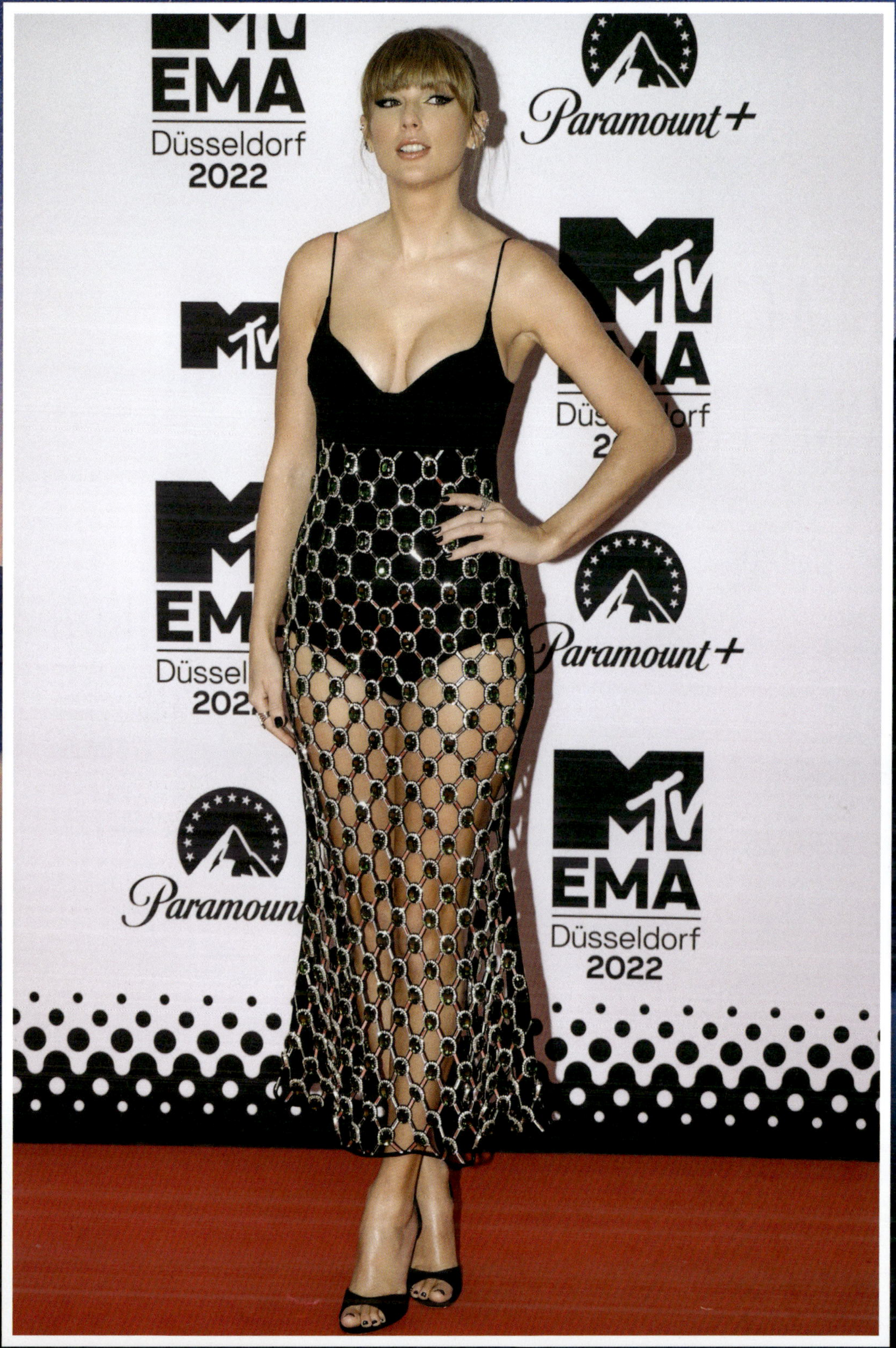

With sleek lines, dramatic cutouts, and intricate, embellished silver detailing, this David Koma dress caught attention at the MTV Europe Music Awards, 2022

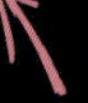

VINTAGE GLAMOUR

We're talking looks that echoed classic Hollywood - flowing gowns, faux fur, and luxurious fabrics such as silk, satin, lace and velvet.

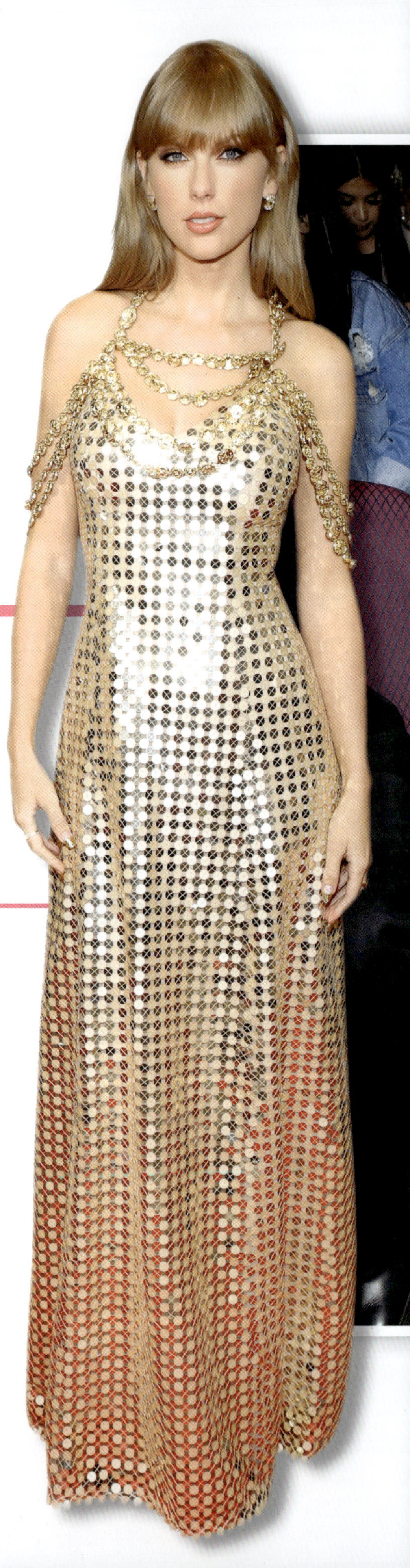

A bespoke, gold Louis Vuitton Gown of dreams at the Toronto Film Festival, 2022

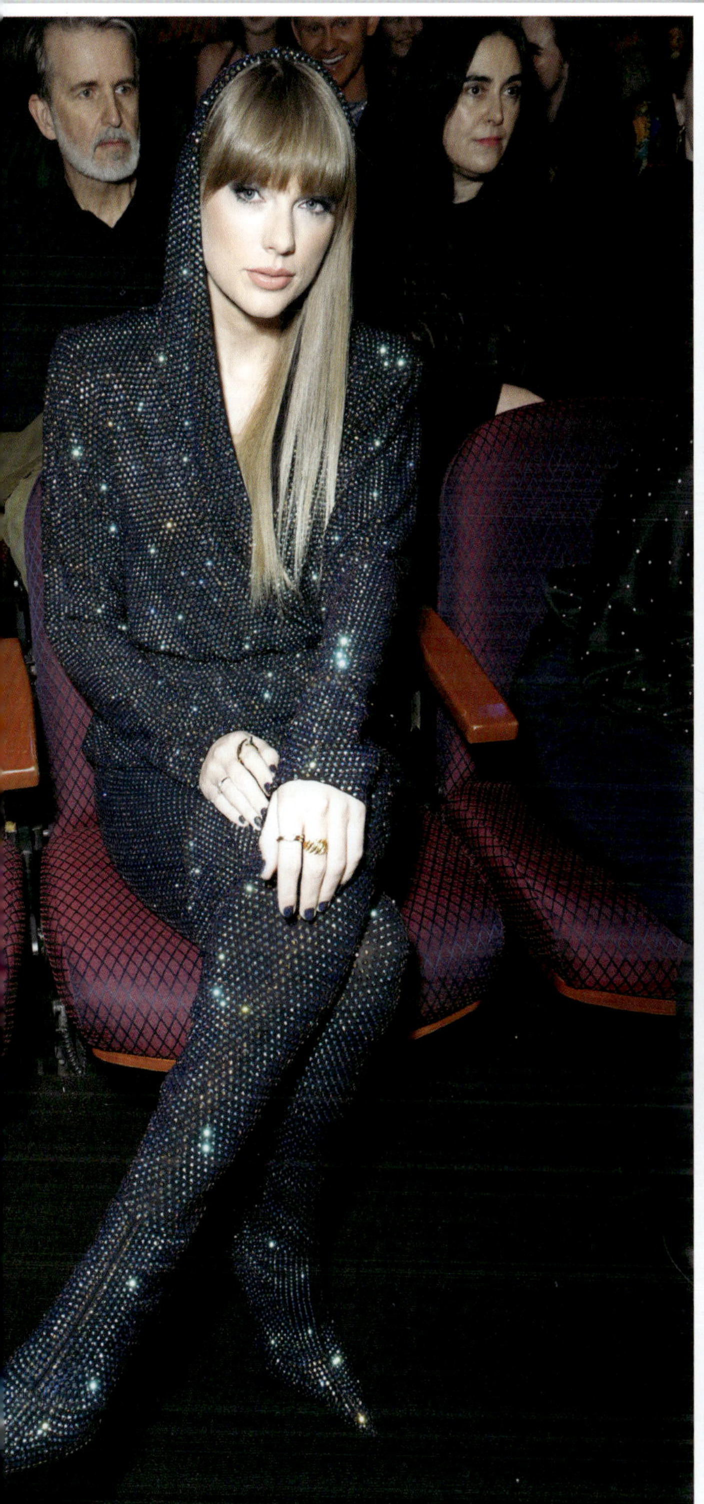

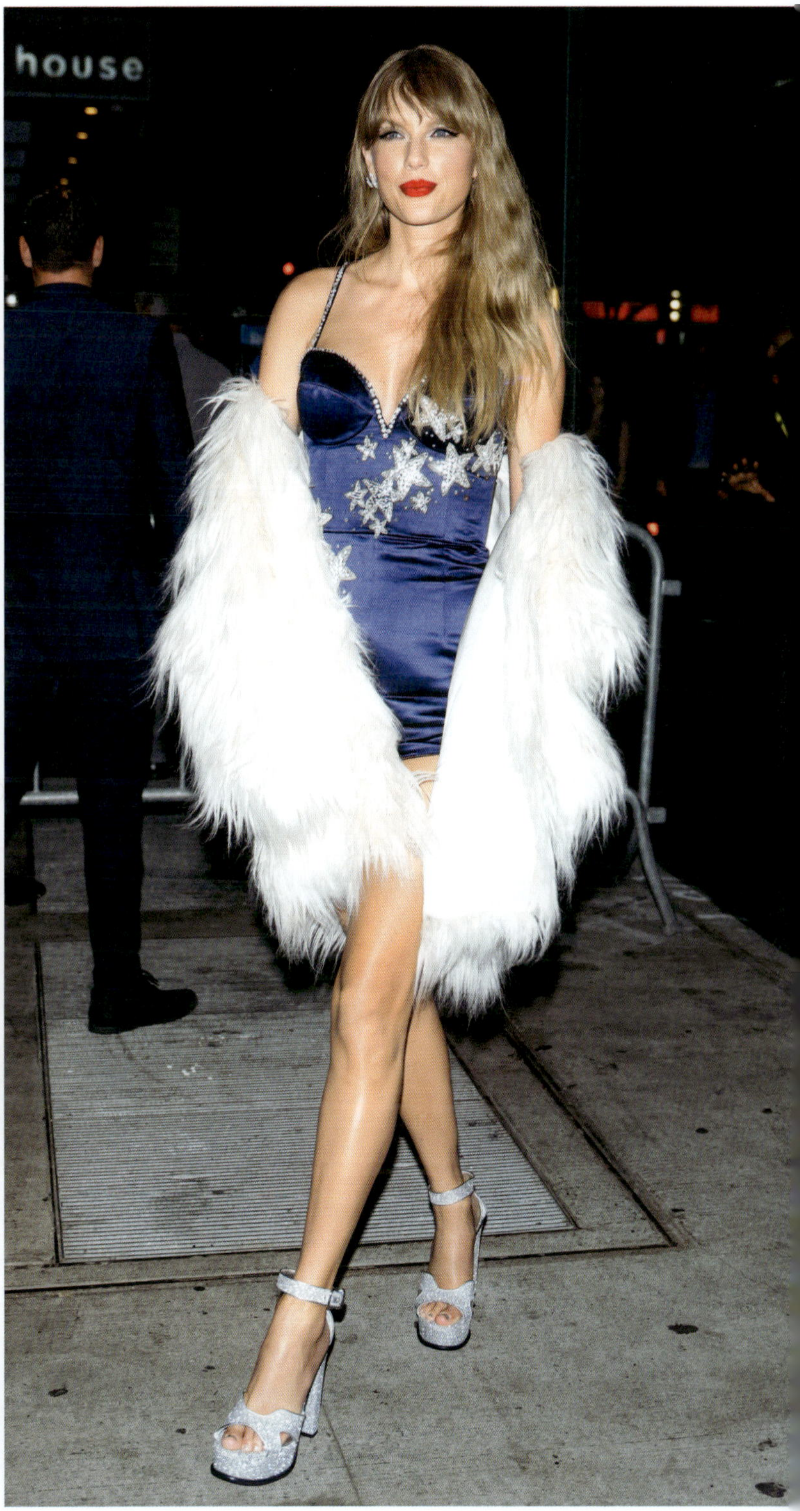

Twinkling at the 2023 iHeartRadio Music Awards in Los Angeles in a crystal-covered Alexandre Vauthier catsuit that sparkles with every move

A deep midnight blue dress from Moschino and glitzy butterfly strap sandals from Alexander McQueen for the MTV VMA After Party in NYC, 2020

HAIR AND MAKEUP

Sleek hairstyles, soft waves, or even bold, voluminous looks were part of the **Midnights aesthetic.** The eyes have it - sharp eyeliner, smoky eyes, and metallic eyeshadows enhance the after-dark, mysterious vibe.

Taylor's silver-toned eyeshadow, bold eyeliner, and voluminous mascara command attention in this makeup look, drawing the spotlight straight to her eyes

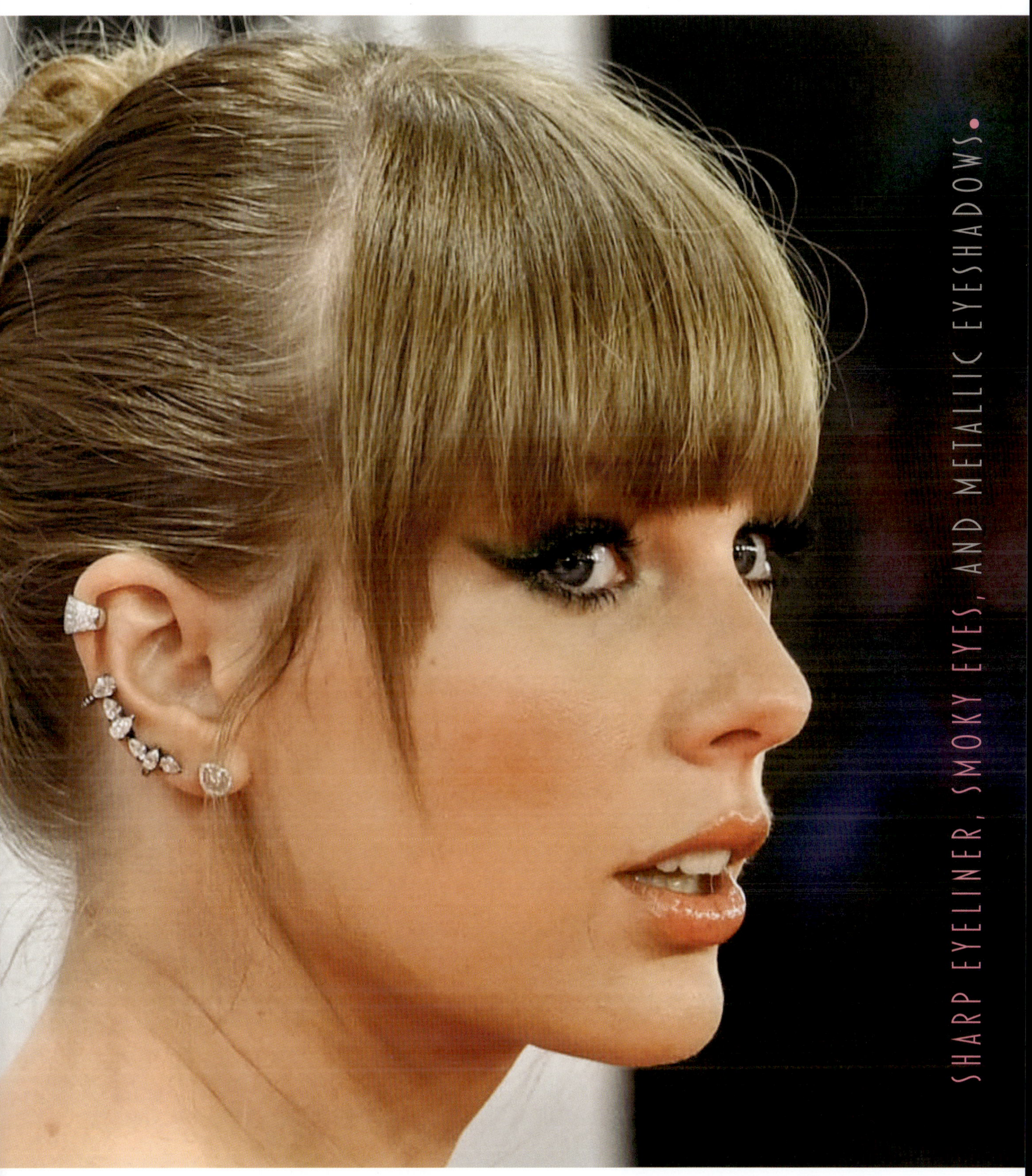

SHARP EYELINER, SMOKY EYES, AND METALLIC EYESHADOWS.

SWIFT'S SARTORIAL SIGNALS!

The times that Taylor has **expertly used fashion** to reflect – or predict – her song-writing...

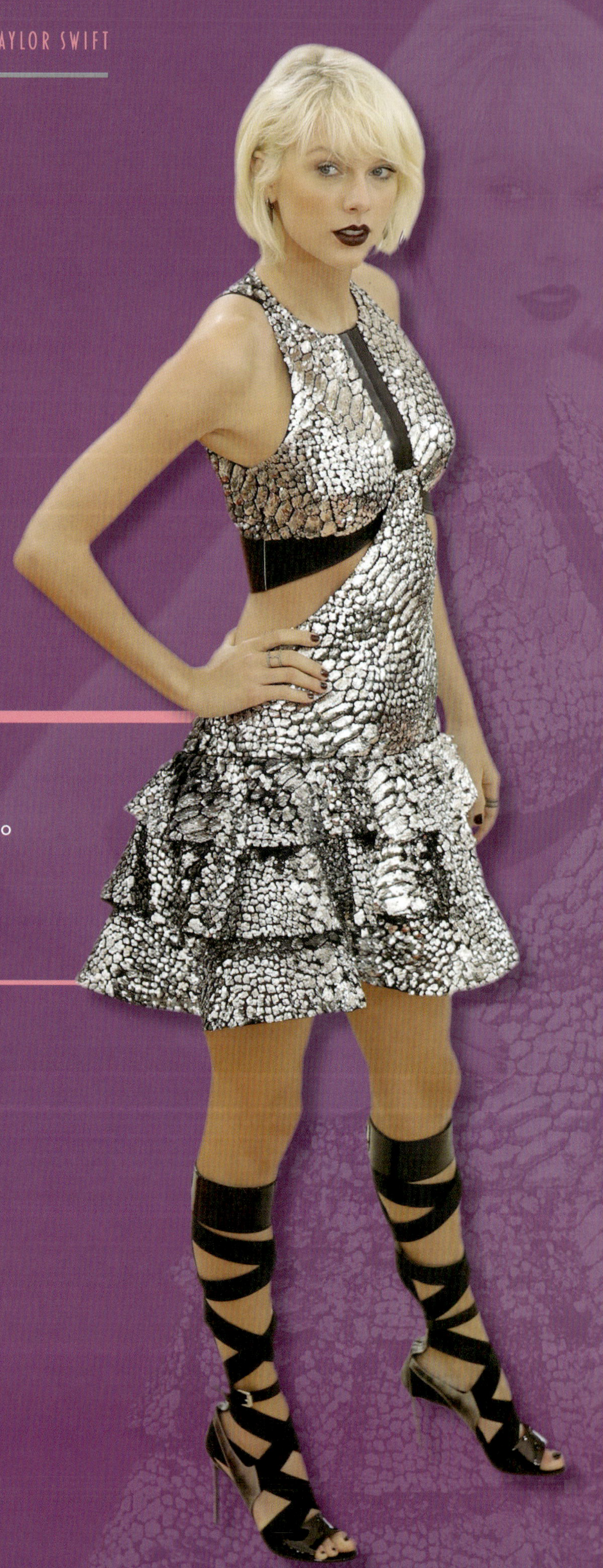

2016 MET GALA

In what would become one of Swift's most-famous red carpet turns, the performer attended the 2016 Met Gala in a sparkling Louis Vuitton mini-dress with gladiator heels and a peroxide-blonde bob, seen for the first time on the cover of US *Vogue* a month earlier. Serious Swifties will know that the events inspiring *Reputation's* subject matter hadn't yet taken place, but it was clear Taylor was going for a darker, more mysterious look which would come to define the visuals for her sixth studio album the following year.

2018 BILLBOARD MUSIC AWARDS

The 2018 Billboard Music Awards marked one of Swift's first public appearances after keeping a low profile while promoting *Reputation*. This light-pink embroidered Versace dress was a departure from the gothic-tinged style she favoured at the time, delighting and briefly mystifying fans. But when *Lover* and its hot-pink visuals were first teased the following year, everything fell into place.

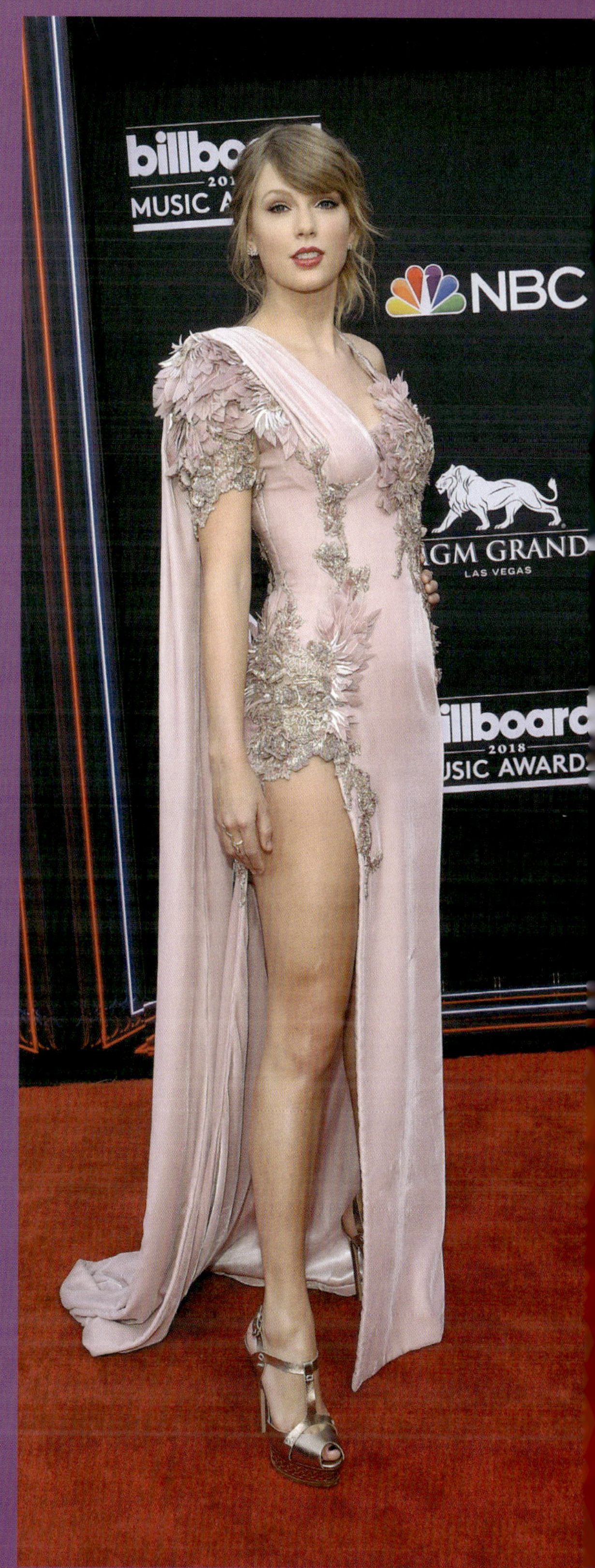

2021

Swift's *Folklore* and *Evermore* albums, released in 2020, featured a down-to-earth approach and incorporated themes of country and indie folk. When she attended the Grammys in 2021, she kept to her naturalistic theme in a floral Oscar de la Renta dress from the brand's autumn/winter 2021/22 collection. It sold out immediately.

2022 MTV VMAS

By now, the word 'Bejewelled' is a core term in the Swiftieverse, but at the 2022 MTV VMAs, people thought she was dazzling just for the sake of it. On the night Swift appeared at the ceremony in this glittering crystal-adorned dress by Oscar de la Renta, she announced the release of her 10th studio album, *Midnights*—a record dedicated to all things after-dark, with explicit mentions of the stars in the night sky.

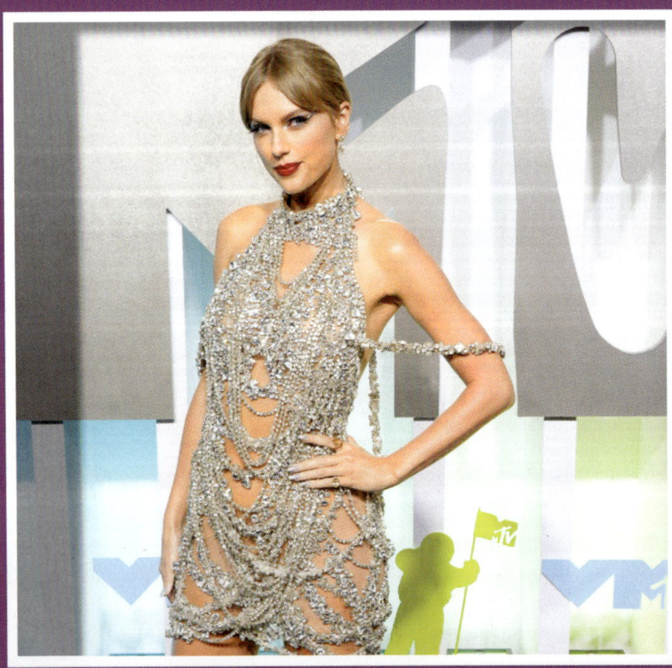

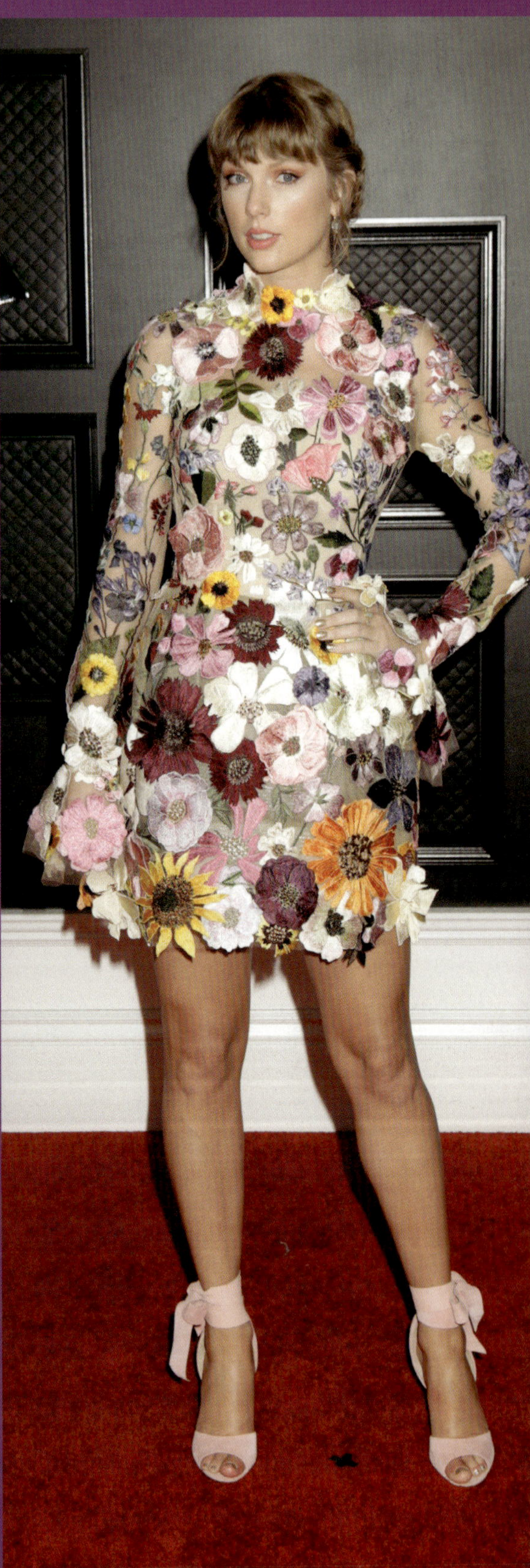

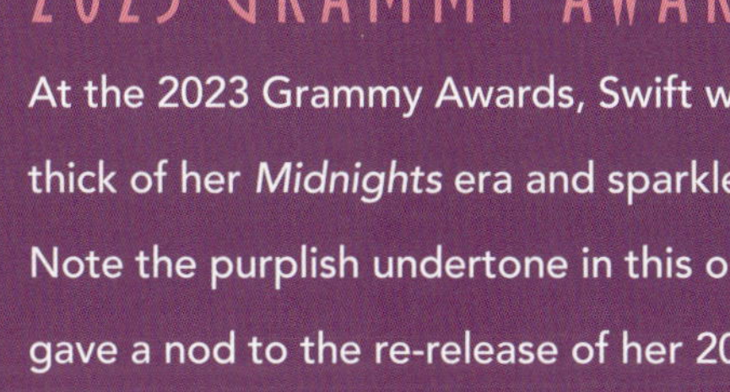

2023 GRAMMY AWARDS

At the 2023 Grammy Awards, Swift was still in the thick of her *Midnights* era and sparkle obsession. Note the purplish undertone in this outfit, which gave a nod to the re-release of her 2010 album *Speak Now* months later. Taylor famously wore a purple dress on the cover.

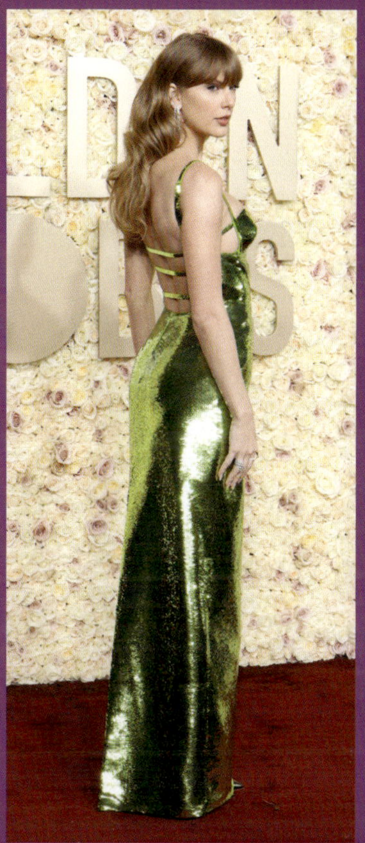

2024 GOLDEN GLOBES'

Taylor's 2024 Golden Globes' sequined green Gucci dress was one of the first looks by the brand's new designer, Sabato De Sarno, to hit the Red Carpet. But keen-eyed fans noted that the dress's bright-green hue was the same colour as the 'snake' emoji on Taylor's album *Reputation*.

2024 GRAMMY AWARDS

The 2024 Grammy Awards marked the first time Swift wore Schiaparelli, choosing a white dress and black gloves from the historic couturier. She wore a stopwatch around her neck (stopped at midnight, no less), as a nod to *Midnights*. But by the end of the night, her classic choice of black-and-white had taken on a different meaning and even ushered in a new era - on stage, Swift announced a new album, *The Tortured Poets Department*, which features a display of black-and-white visuals.

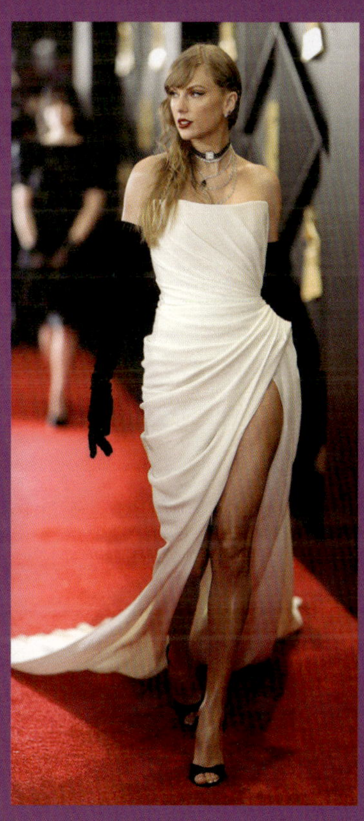

ERAS

Taylor Swift's fashion throughout the Eras Tour in 2023 and 2024 has been a significant part of the show's appeal, with each outfit representing different phases. The *Eras* fashion has been a mix of nostalgia and reinvention, with each outfit carefully crafted to represent the different stages of her career. Fans have loved how she has balanced paying homage to her past while also bringing something new and exciting to each performance. Here are some of the key fashion moments from how Taylor sartorially revisited her Eras on her 2023/24 world tour!

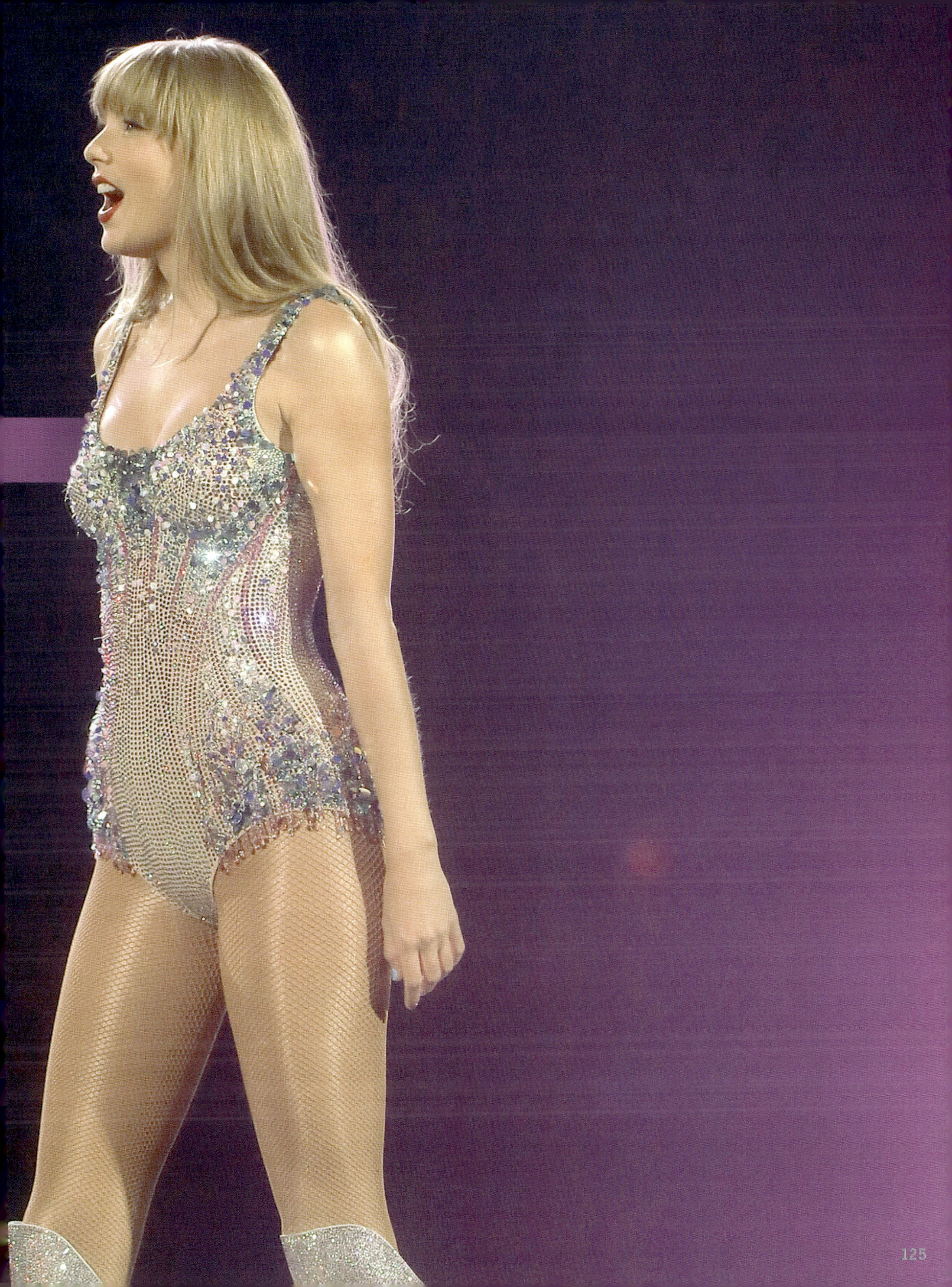

DEBUT ERA/ACOUSTIC SET

Country-inspired looks with a modern twist and more mature style. Roberto Cavalli Custom Gown, Christian Louboutin Custom Heels.

FEARLESS ERA

We're talking gold and glittering dresses a la the original *Fearless* era, but silhouettes were updated to give a more mature look. Custom Sequin Fringe Dress by Roberto Cavalli, Christian Laboutin custom boots.

SPEAK NOW ERA

Fairy Tale inspired gowns – think Cinderella at the Ball. A sparkling princess glow highlighted by the sparkles of the Nicole + Felicia couture gown Taylor wore during the *Speak Now* era of her tour. It is reminiscent of the Valentino gown she wore on the original *Speak Now* tour but grander and blingier.

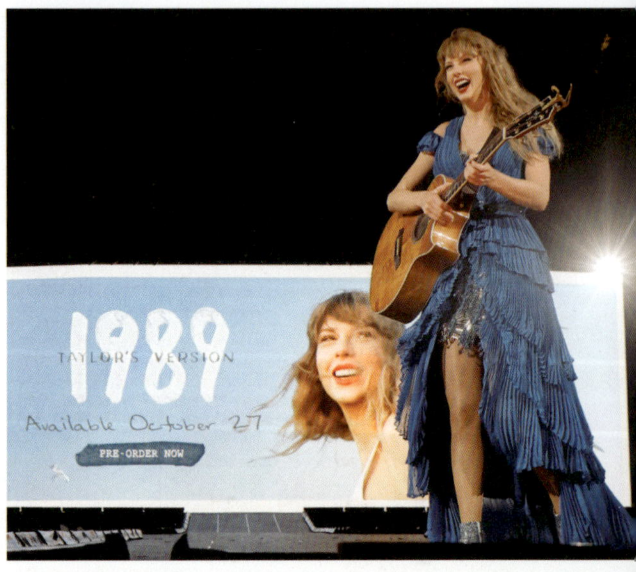

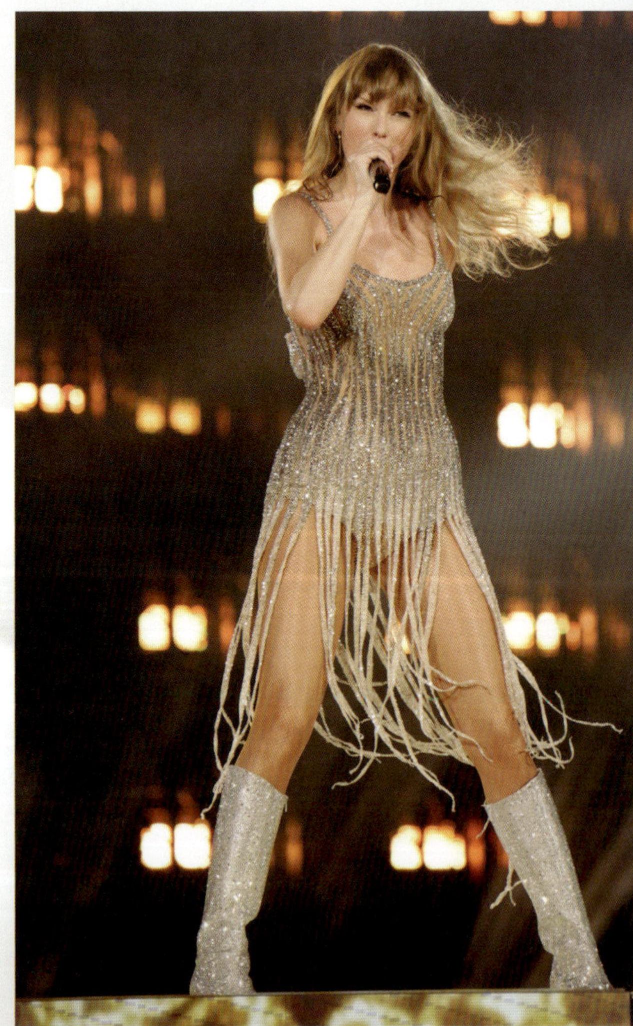

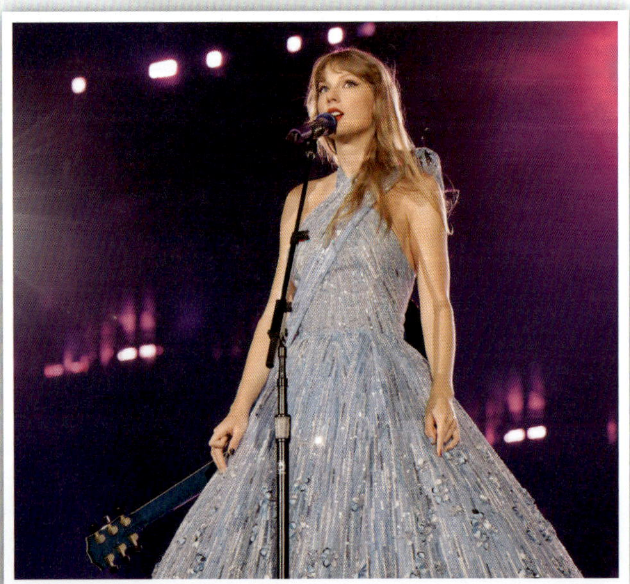

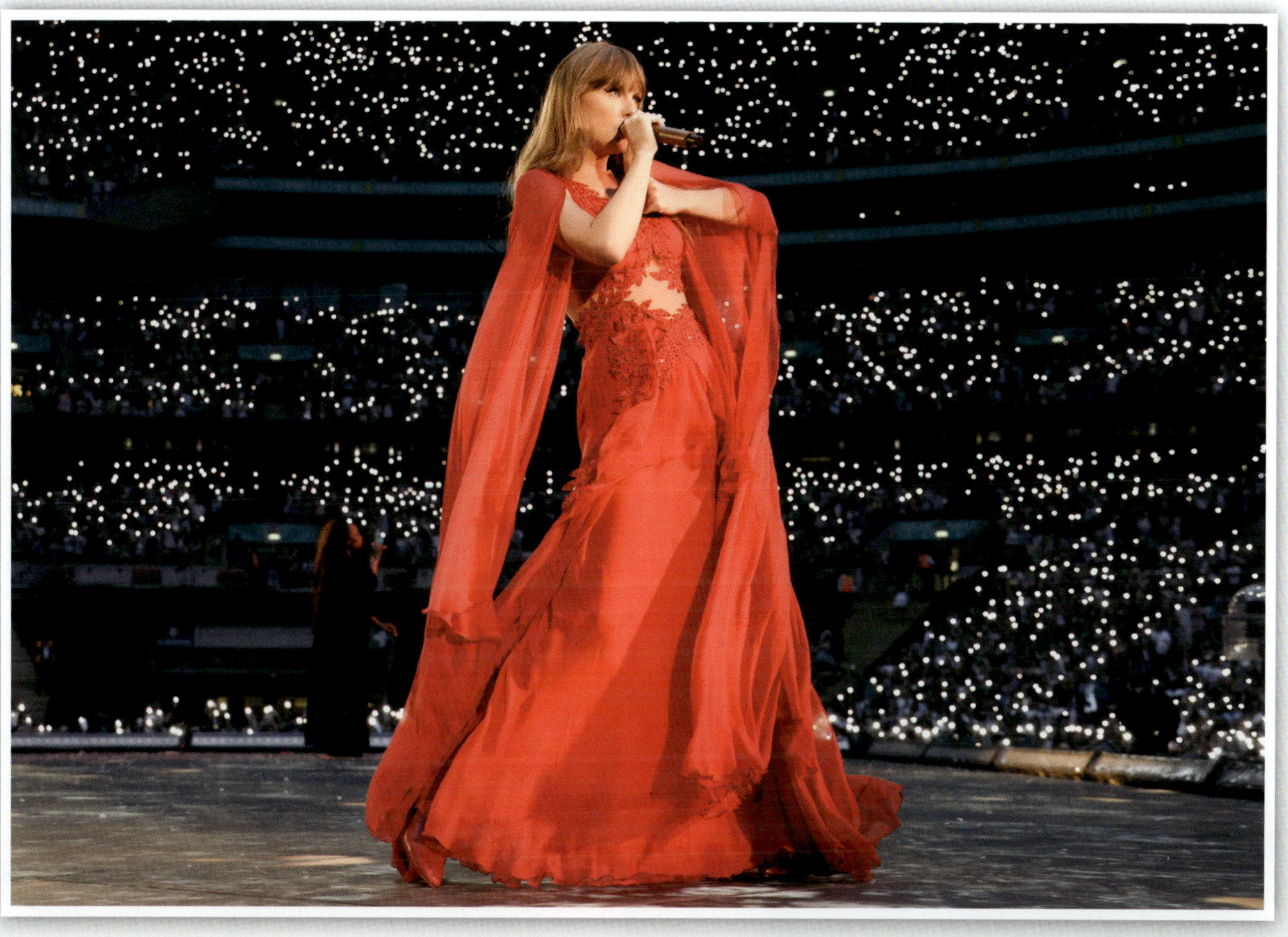

RED ERA ↗

Bold! Vibrant reds with glittering details. Alberta Ferretti Custom Gown.

1989 ERA

Bright, neon colours with a retro 80's vibe. Roberto Cavalli Custom Set in Pink/Green, Christian Louboutin Custom Boots in Blue/Pink. →

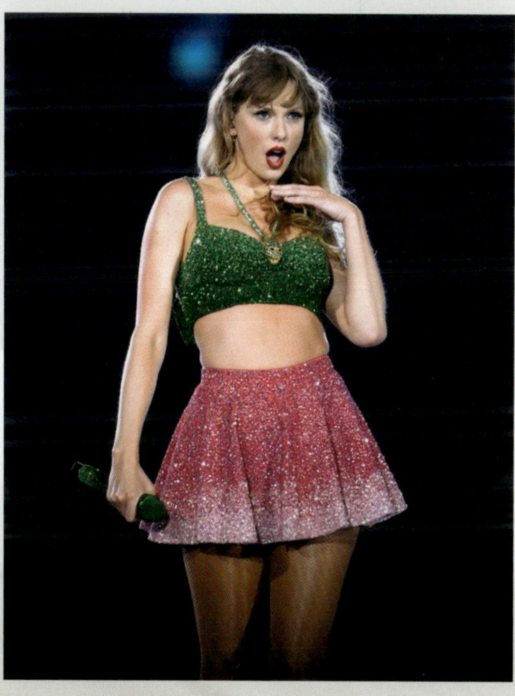

REPUTATION ERA

Dark, edgy pieces, snake motifs. Roberto Cavalli custom catsuit, Christian Louboutin custom boots.

LOVER ERA

Pastel and vibrant colours dominate, often with classic TS shimmering details. Custom Atalier Versace body suit in pastel-hued sparkles, custom studded Louboutins, sparkly custom Versace blazer.

FOLKLORE/EVERMORE ERA

Flowy ethereal dresses. Earthy tones. Bohemian vibes. Custom dress by Etro, custom Christian Laboutin boots.

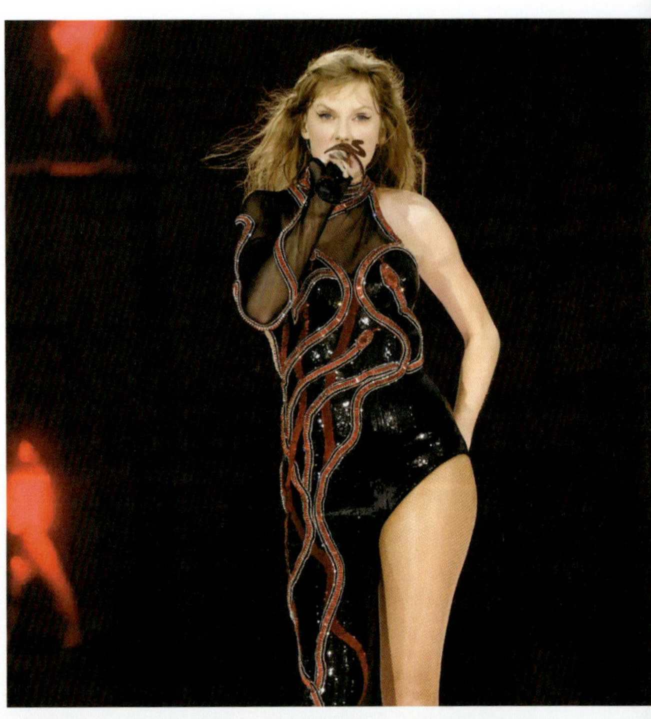

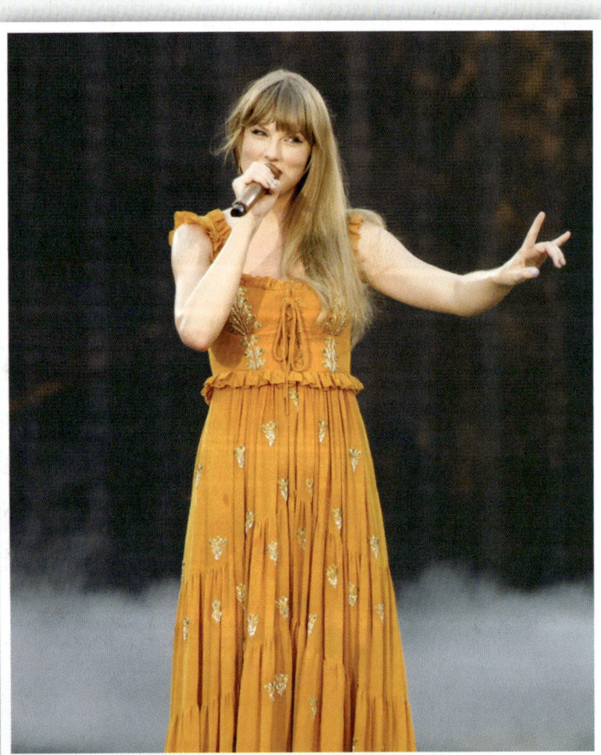

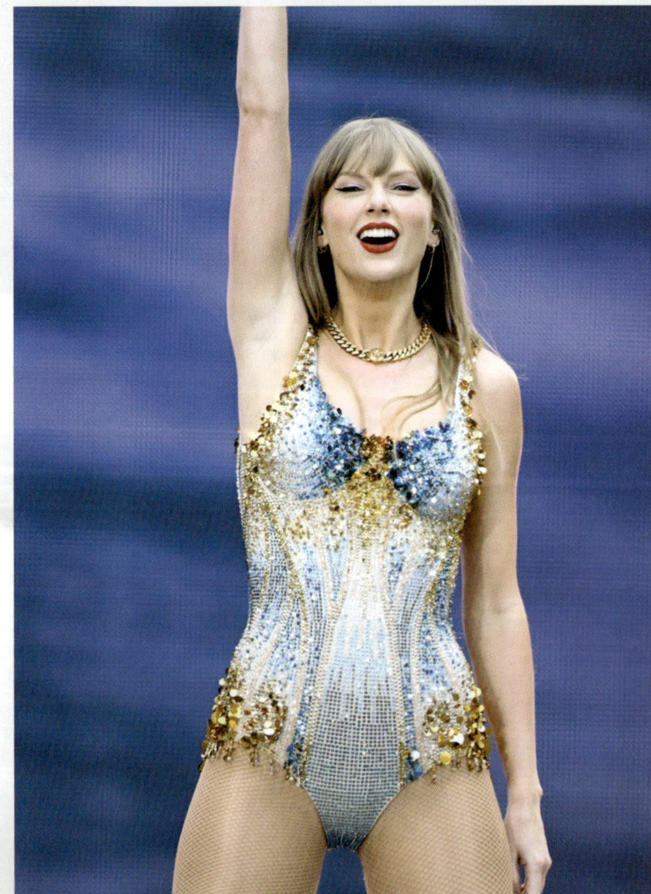

MIDNIGHTS ERA

Shimmering outfits in deep blues and purples, often with celestial motifs, like stars and moons. Zuhair Murad Custom Bodysuit, Christian Louboutin Custom Midnights boots.

THE TORTURED POETS DEPT.

Vivienne Westwood and lingerie-inspired looks. Vivienne Westwood Custom Dress, Joseph Cassell Custom Black Gloves and Christian Louboutin custom boots.

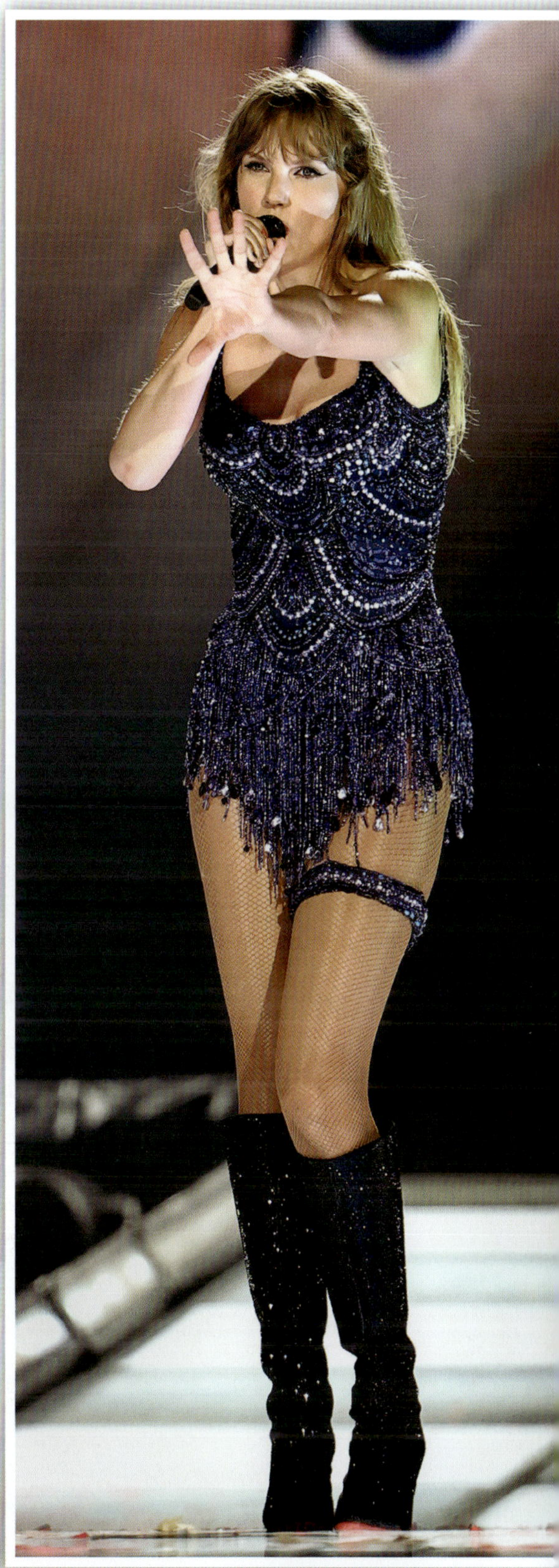

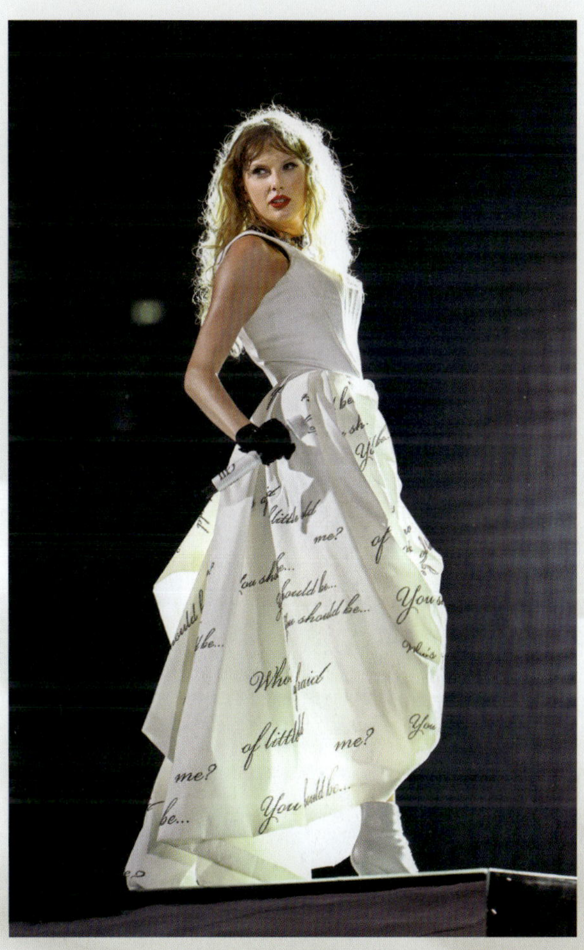

RED CARPET LOOKS

Taylor has a stellar sense of high-fashion style, especially when it comes to the Red Carpet. Here are some of her greatest RC moments...

ERAS TOUR (2024)

Taylor wore a truly fabulous array of ensembles for her smash hit tour but a favourite has to be this stunning lilac gown custom-made by Nicole + Felicia, complete with tiered skirt and criss-cross bodice.

GRAMMY AWARDS (2024)

Taylor stuns in a white Schiaparelli ensemble styled with black opera gloves. She completed the look with open-toed Giuseppe Zanotti heels and diamonds from Lorraine Schwartz.

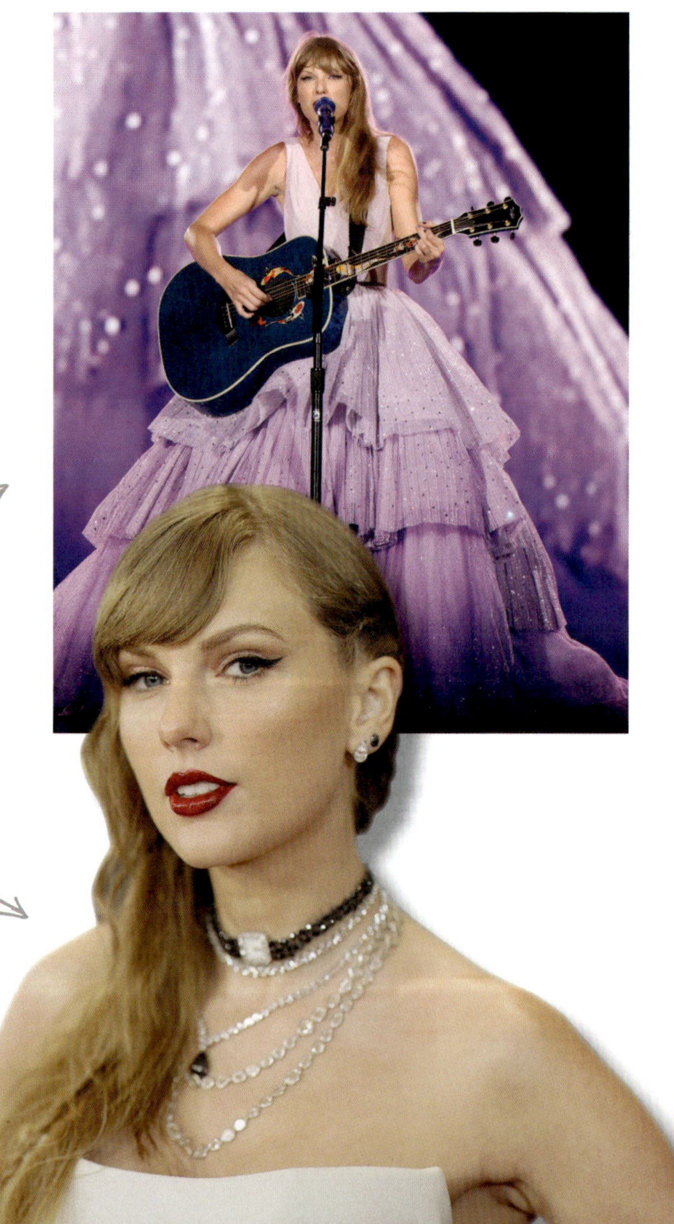

GOLDEN GLOBES (2024)

A sequined green maxi dress courtesy of Gucci, accessorized with matching Christian Louboutin heels and jewellery by De Beers.

TAYLOR'S 34TH BIRTHDAY, (2023)

To celebrate her birthday in NYC, Taylor rocked a black celestial-themed mini dress by the London-based brand Clio Peppiatt. She completed her look with black heels and a chainmail mini purse, both from Aquazzura, and Messika jewellery.

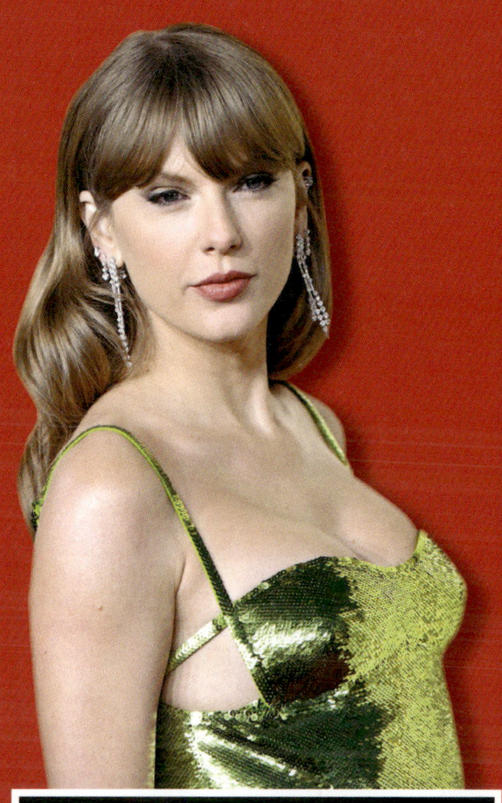

'RENAISSANCE: A FILM BY BEYONCÉ' LONDON PREMIERE (2023)

Taylor wore a sequin column dress by Balmain, complete with a thigh-high split, completing the look with Giuseppe Zanotti heels, Anita Ko jewellery pieces... and disco nails!

GRAMMY AWARDS (2023)

Taylor in a dazzling royal blue two-piece from Roberto Cavalli, featuring a long-sleeve crop top and a coordinating maxi skirt, with the skirt creating a mini-train at her feet. She accessorized the already-stunning look with statement diamond-shaped earrings.

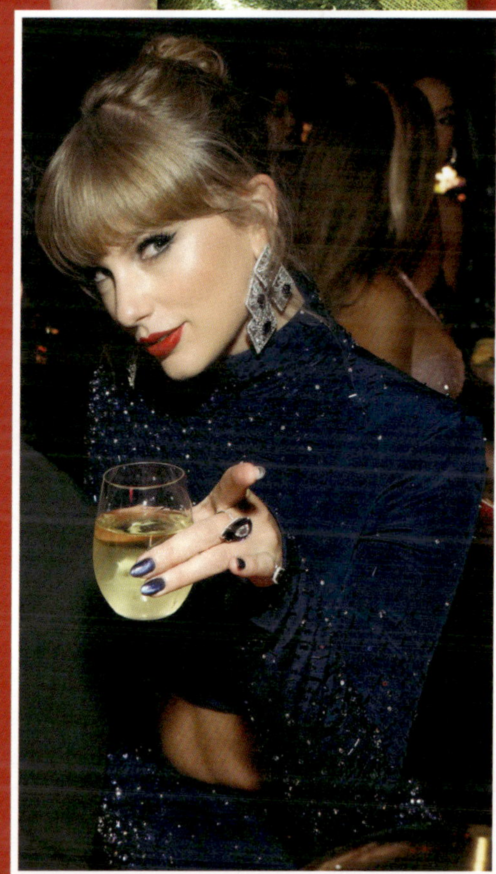

MTV AWARDS (2023)

Tay-Tay rocks a little black dress – with an edge - on the MTV Red carpet. It's a custom-made asymmetrical Versace gown adorned with a high-leg slit plus Jimmy Choo strappy sandals.

AMERICAN MUSIC AWARDS (2022)

For the 2022 American Music Awards, the singer dazzled in a bejewelled, backless gold jumpsuit by The Blonds. She paired the one-piece with strappy, open-toe gold sandals and a variety of shimmering bracelets and rings.

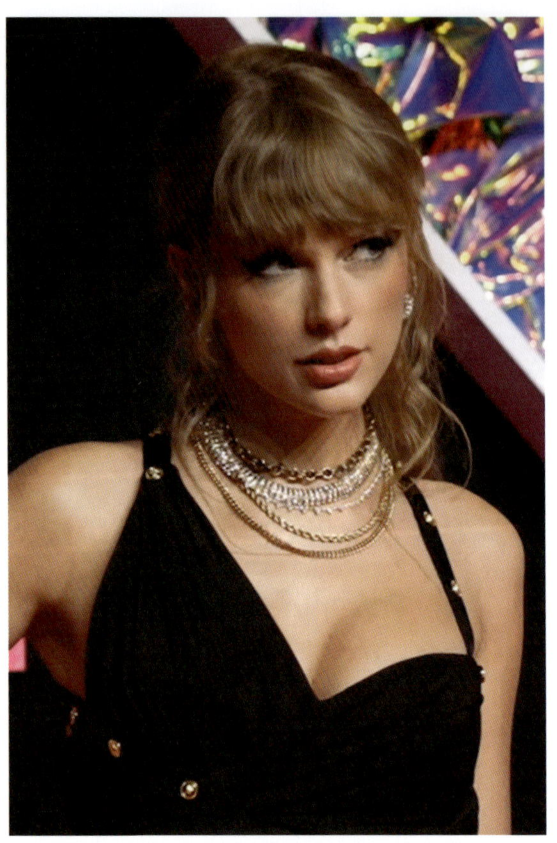

MTV MUSIC AWARDS 2022

Shimmying a David Koma bodysuit dress with an embellished chainmail midi skirt, accessorized with peep-toe black pumps for this RC, TS took home four awards.

NASHVILLE SONGWRITER AWARDS (2022)

For the 2022 Nashville Songwriter Awards—in which she won the Songwriter-Artist of the Decade Award—Taylor opted for a unique silhouette courtesy of Michael Kors. She paired the asymmetrical cut-out sequin dress with strappy bejewelled heels and delicate diamond accessories.

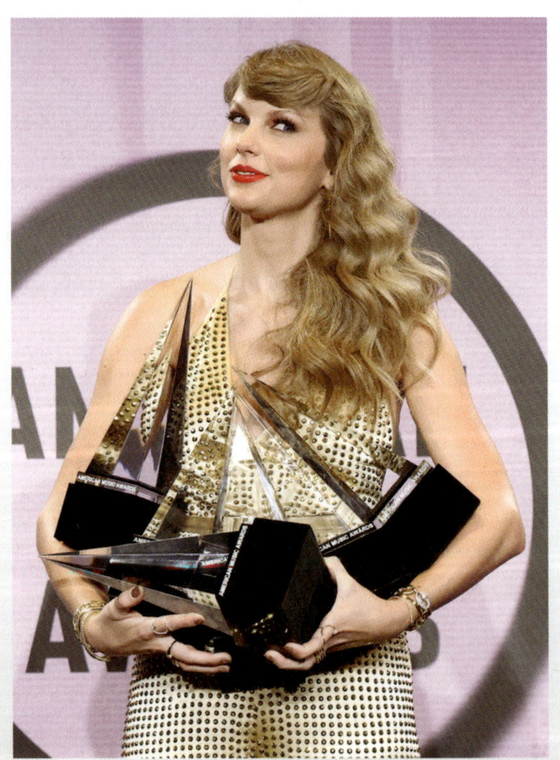

TORONTO INTERNATIONAL FILM FESTIVAL (2022)

Oh wow! Taylor at the 2022 Toronto International Film Festival in a custom Louis Vuitton sequined gown.

MTV VMAS (2022)

Taylor Swift turned heads when she showed up to the 2022 MTV Video Music Awards in a crystal-draped halter Oscar de la Renta mini dress from the brand's resort 2023 collection. As stunning as her dress was, fans swooned over her crystal-embellished, T-strap Christian Louboutin high-heel sandals, too.

REPUBLIC RECORDS MTV VMA AFTER PARTY (2022)

After winning the award for Video of the Year, Best Direction, and Best Long-form Video at the 2022 MTV Video Music Awards, Taylor celebrated in her signature shimmering style with a midnight-blue Moschino romper accented with a burst of sparkling stars. She topped the statement one-piece off with an oversized white fur coat and paired the look with glittery platform heels.

'ALL TOO WELL' NEW YORK PREMIERE (2021)

Taylor dons a tux! For the *All Too Well: The Short Film* New York Premiere, she wore a head-turning plum velvet Etro suit. Perfection!

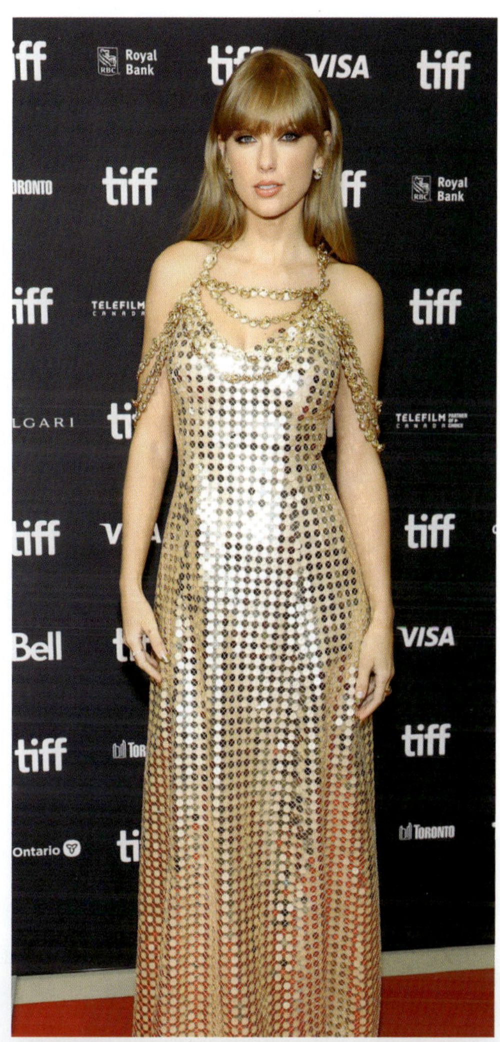

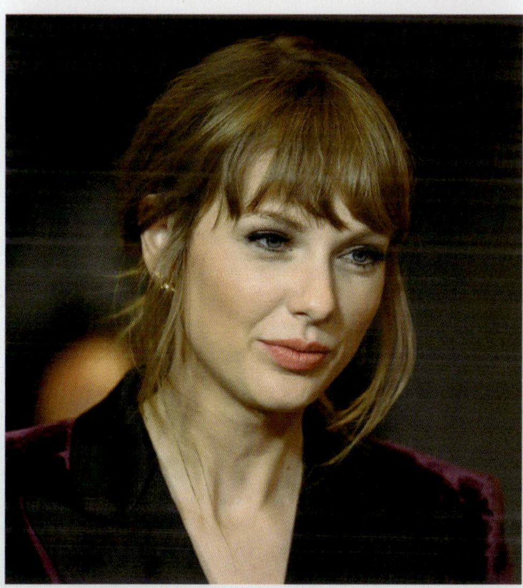

GRAMMY AWARDS (2021)

Taylor broke the internet when she wore this stunning Oscar de la Renta floral mini dress at the 63rd Annual Grammy Awards red carpet. Her album *Evermore* personified.

'MISS AMERICANA' PREMIERE (2020)

The lady loves plaid. Taylor Swift rocks in head-to-toe Carmen March houndstooth.

GOLDEN GLOBE AWARDS (2020)

A retro look for Taylor as she wears a custom Etro navy and gold floral cut-out gown.

'CATS' WORLD PREMIERE (2019)

The movie bombed but not the Taylor, who played Kitty Bombalurina, in this fabulous Oscar de la Renta ruby floral fil coupé satin gown, complete with pockets.

AMERICAN MUSIC AWARDS (2019)

Tay-Tay wows in this Julien Macdonald asymmetrical spaghetti strap dress with thigh-high suede boots. A lucky look for her as she won awards for Best Artist, Best Pop/Rock Album, Best Pop/Rock Female Artist, Best Adult Contemporary Artist, Best Video, and Best Artist of the Decade.

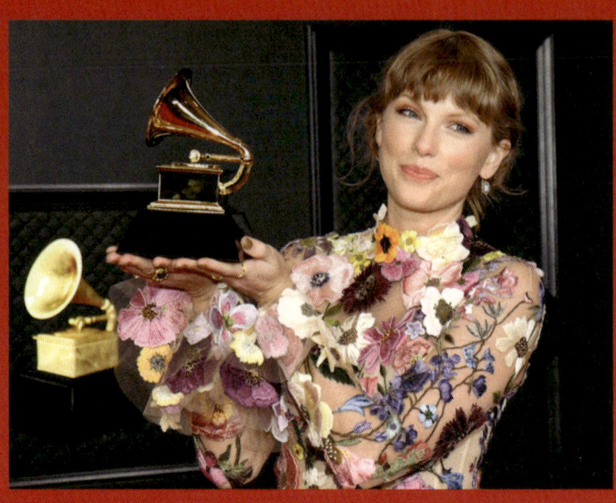

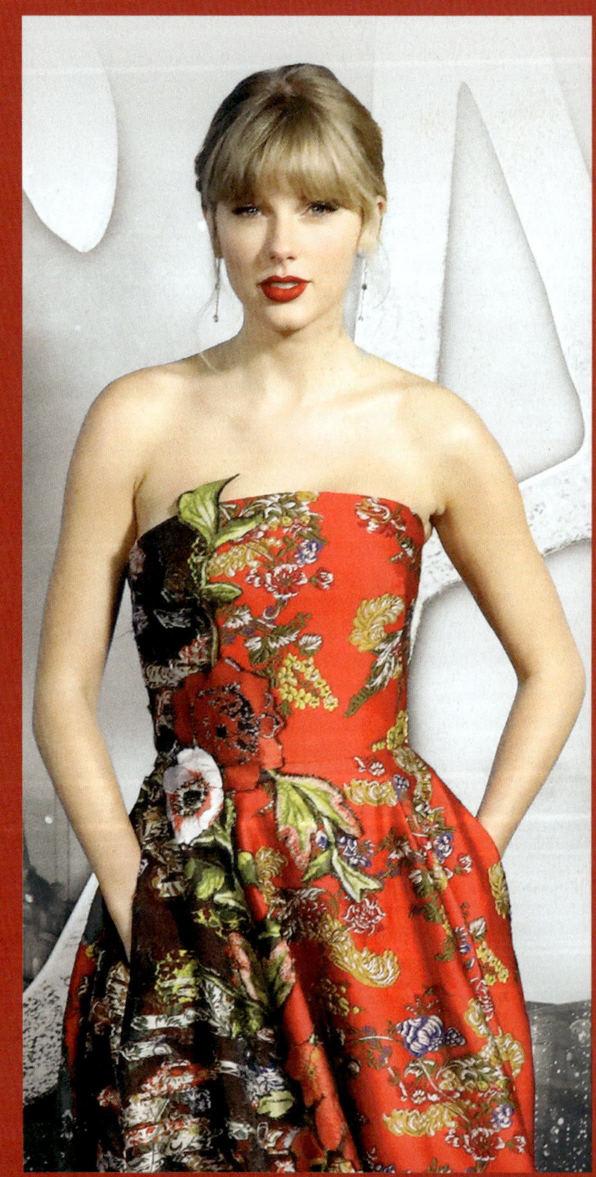

MTV VIDEO MUSIC AWARDS (2019)

Taylor totally rocks in a multicoloured sequined Versace blazer and shimmering over-the-knee black suede boots.

BILLBOARD MUSIC AWARDS (2019)

Lady in lilac ruffles with lacy sleeves by Raisa Vanessa. Check out Taylor's diamond star-shaped climber earring.

'ALL TOO WELL' NEW YORK TIME 100 GALA (2019)

A romantic RC look for TS – a blush and butter yellow tulle J. Mendel gown which she paired with coordinating yellow strappy heels.

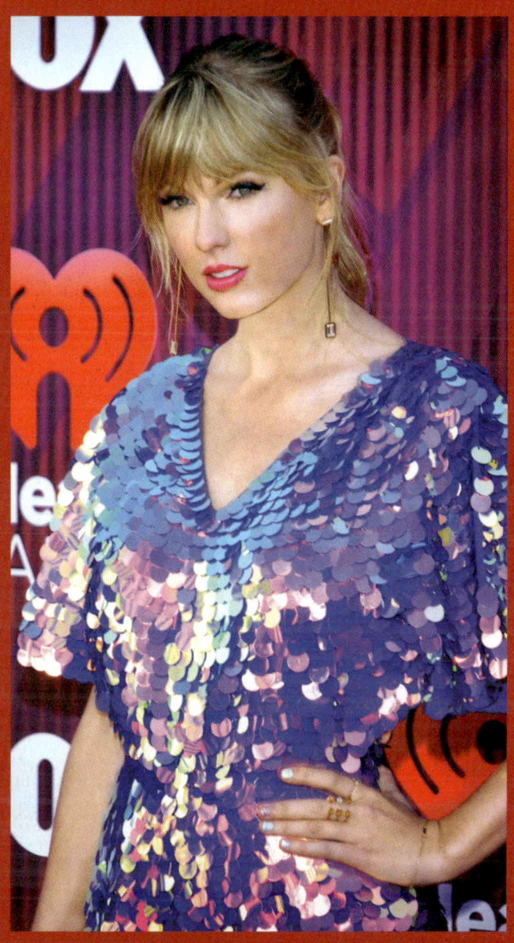

IHEARTRADIO MUSIC AWARDS (2019)

Not all her looks are designer ensembles which cost thousands. For the 2019 iHeartRadio Music Awards, T-Swift showed up in an iridescent Rosa Bloom sequined play suit costing less than £300.

AMERICAN MUSIC AWARDS (2018)

How bright she shines in this light-reflecting Balmain mini dress with matching thigh-high boots.

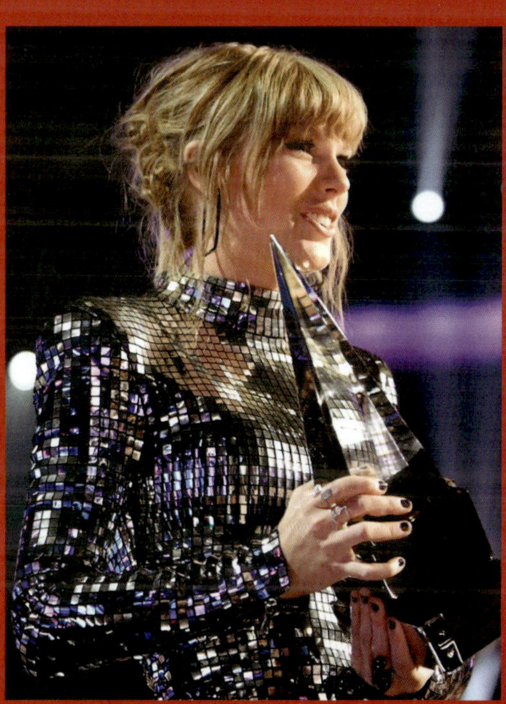

BILLBOARD MUSIC AWARDS (2018)

A retro look for Taylor as she wears a custom Etro navy For Taylor's first red carpet-appearance in years, she chose a Versace gown with a high slit and beautiful embellishments—which took 800 hours to make. She paired the show-stopping gown with heels by Casadei.

GRAMMY AWARDS (2016)

Possibly her most glamorous look ever, an Atelier Versace two-piece gown that was also mega fun.

MTV VIDEO MUSIC AWARDS (2015)

Casual but still uber glam, Taylor poses in this Ashish two-piece shimmer sweatsuit paired with dramatic Christian Louboutin heels.

BILLBOARD MUSIC AWARDS (2015)

Taylor stuns in this sparkly white Balmain cut-out jumpsuit, which she paired with a custom 'Bad Blood' clutch.

IHEARTRADIO MUSIC AWARDS (2015)

Taylor has long been a fan of sparkly, cut-out dresses. Case in point: She wore a glittery Kaufman Franco LBD to the 2015 iHeartRadio Music Awards.

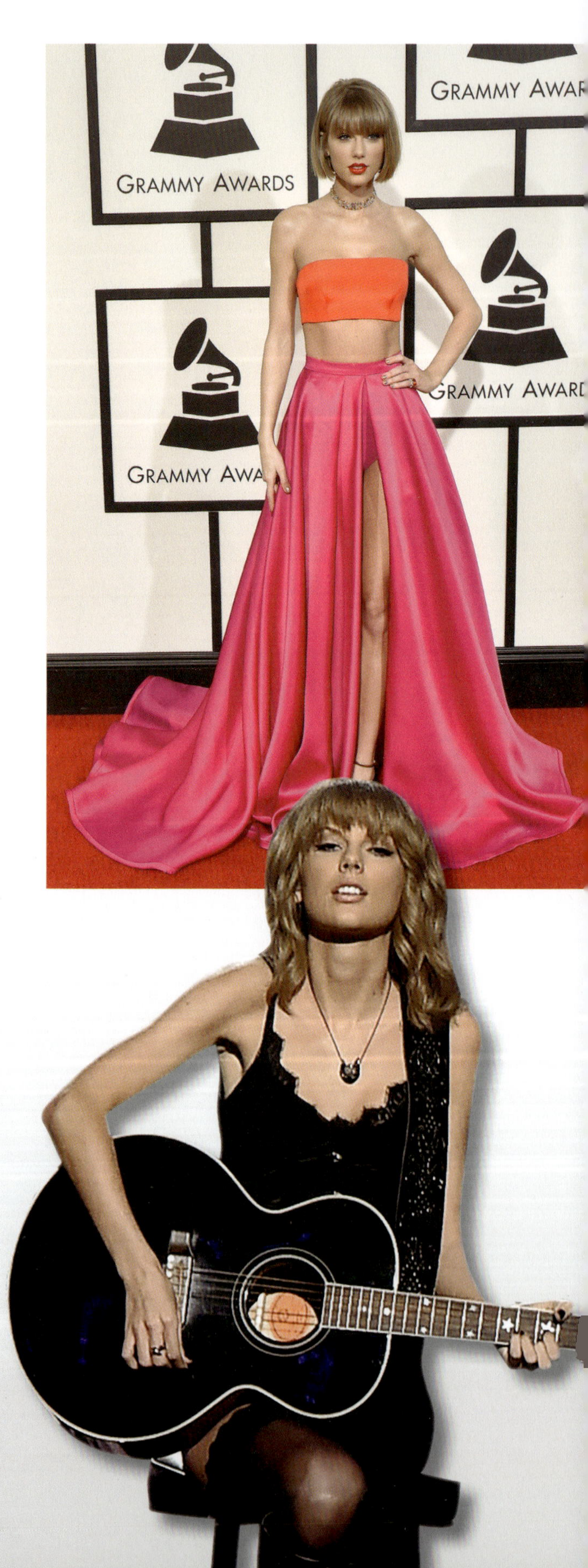

GRAMMY AWARDS (2015)

Sophisticated in an Elie Saab teal ombre gown she wore for the 57th Grammy Awards in 2015, accessorized with contrasting purple Giuseppe Zanotti sandals and shimmering Lorraine Schwartz jewels.

MET GALA (2014)

The theme was 'Beyond Fashion' and TS was beyond gorgeous in a custom beaded satin Oscar de la Renta gown in pink with Louboutin heels and Lorraine Schwartz jewels.

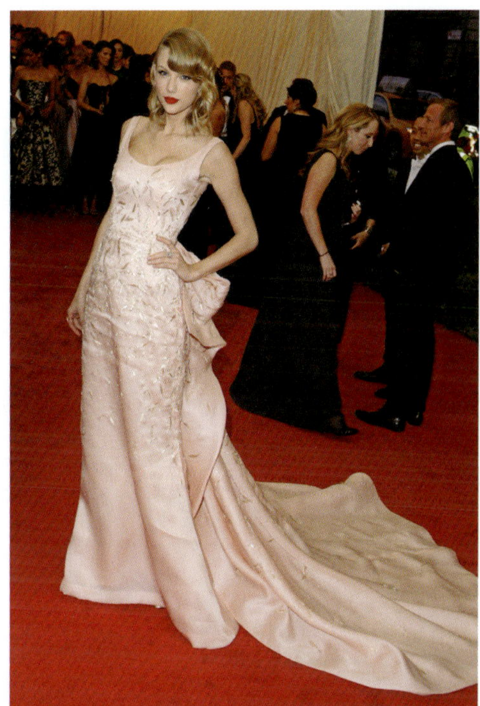

GRAMMY AWARDS (2014)

Taylor positively shimmers in this floor-length, short-sleeved, chainmail Gucci gown.

GRAMMY AWARDS (2010)

Twelve years before the release of her *Midnights* album, Taylor graced the 52nd Annual Grammy Awards red carpet in a sparkling midnight-blue off-the-shoulder Kaufman Franco gown.

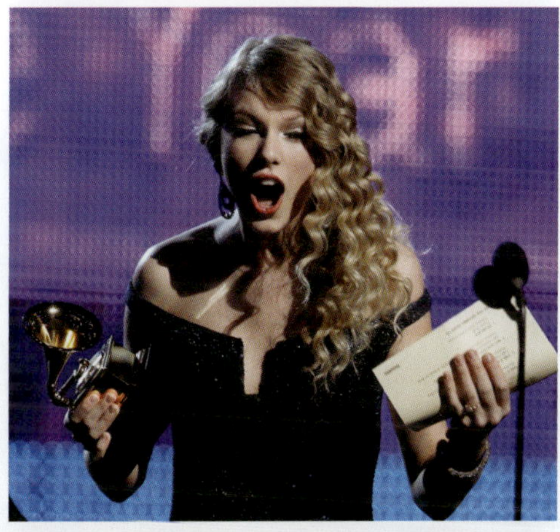

COUNTRY MUSIC ASSOCIATION AWARDS (2009)

In one of her first Red Carpet appearances, Taylor sparkled in a Reem Acra tulle gown with gold sequin detailing. A starry, starry night for the young icon-in-the-making who, at just 19 years old, won the Entertainer of the Year Award, thus becoming the youngest artist to achieve this.

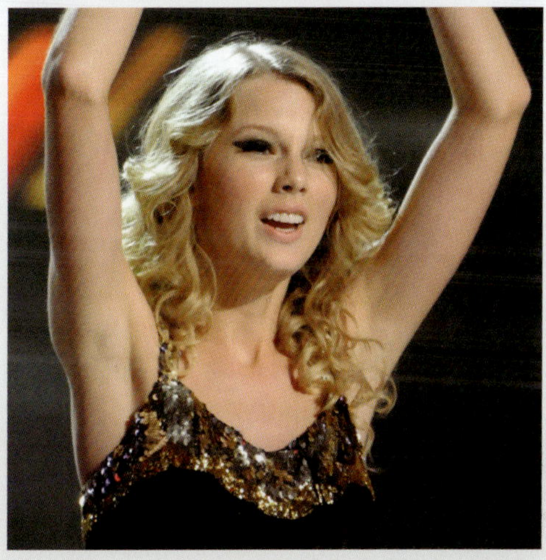

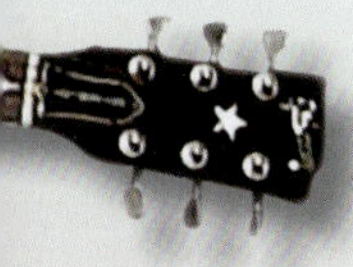

BY DESIGN

Over the years, Taylor has worked with and expressed admiration for several designers, both for her red carpet looks and her on-stage outfits. These designers have helped shape Taylor's iconic fashion sense, reflecting her evolution from country sweetheart to global pop sensation. Here are some of her favourite fashion creators...

OSCAR DE LA RENTA

Taylor has worn Oscar de la Renta for major events, including the 2014 Met Gala, where she donned a stunning pink gown. She admires the timeless and sophisticated designs.

CHRISTIAN LOUBOUTIN

Taylor's go-to shoe designer for many years, Louboutin created over 250 new pairs of shoes and boots for the *Eras* tour alone.

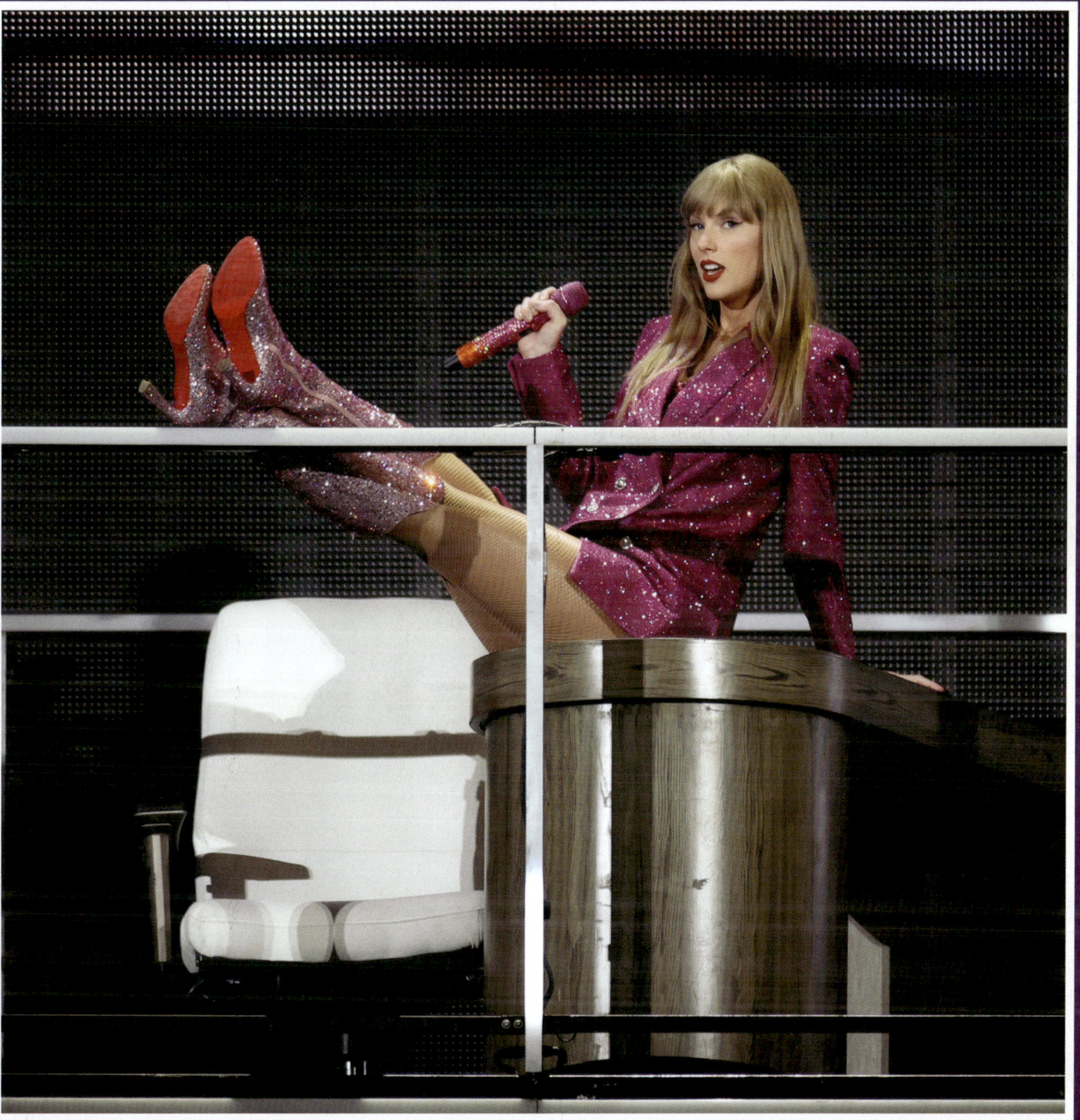

ELIE SAAB

Taylor has often chosen Ellie Saab for her Red Carpet appearances. The designer's feminine and elegant gowns align with her classic style.

VERSACE

Taylor frequently wears Versace, especially during awards shows. The bold and glamorous designs of Versace complement her confident stage presence.

GUCCI

Taylor has been seen in Gucci for various public appearances, appreciating the brand's mix of vintage-inspired and modern styles.

JENNY PACKHAM

Known for her romantic and whimsical designs, Jenny Packham is another designer Taylor favours for her more ethereal and dreamy looks.

STELLA MCCARTNEY

Taylor collaborated with Stella McCartney for her *Lover'* album merchandise. Ms McCartney' designs featured heavily throughout the *Folklore* and *Evermore* eras. Stella's ethical fashion and vibrant designs resonate with Taylor's personal style and values.

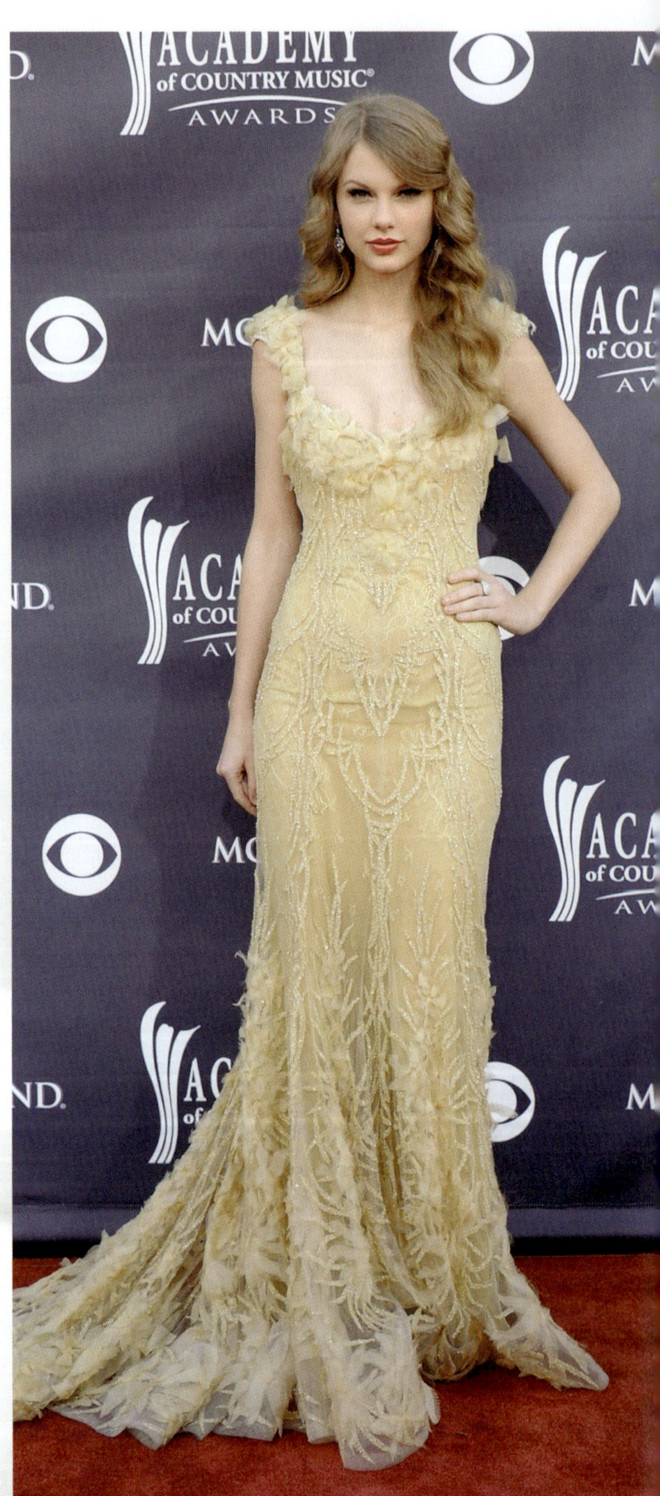

ROBERTO CAVALLI

Fausto Puglisi, creative director of Roberto Cavalli, has been working with Taylor for years. He designed 20 different looks for 2023/24 *Eras* Tour.

REEM ACRA

Taylor has worn Reem Acra's intricately detailed gowns many times – they suit her love for vintage-inspired, glamorous attire.

MARCHESA

Marchesa's luxurious and feminine designs are perfect for Taylor.

J. MENDEL

Elegant and sophisticated J. Mendel is another TS go-to for Red Carpet events.

RALPH LAUREN

Off-duty Taylor appreciates the brand's classic American style.

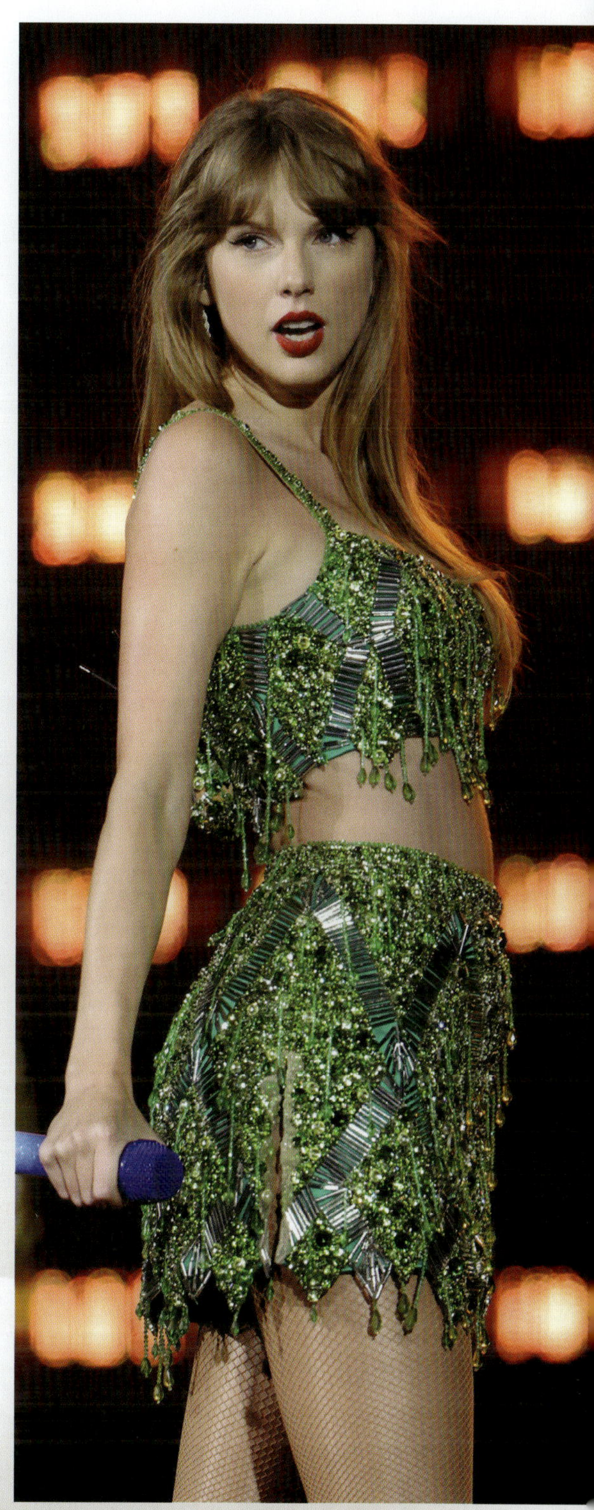

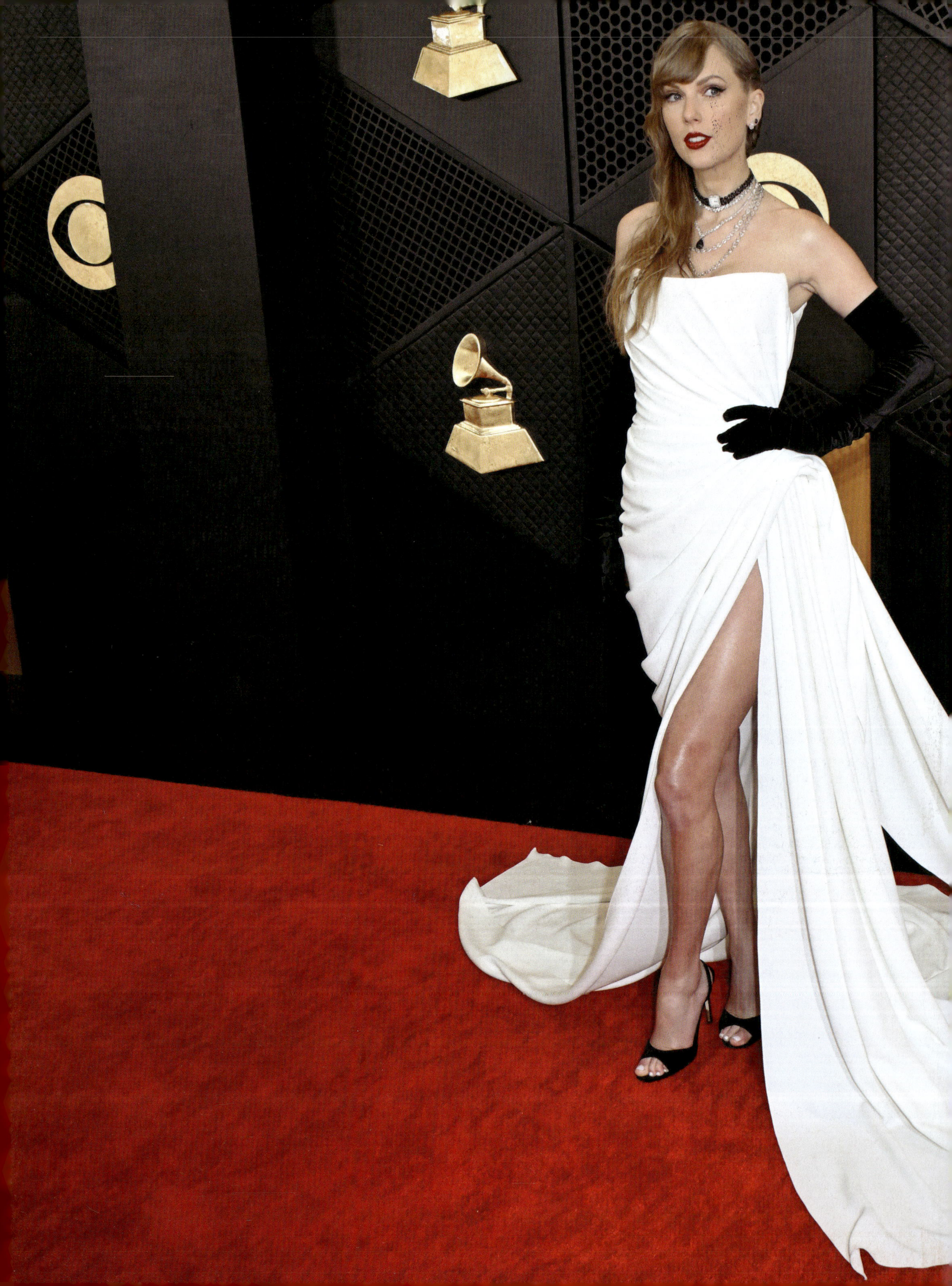